D1482716

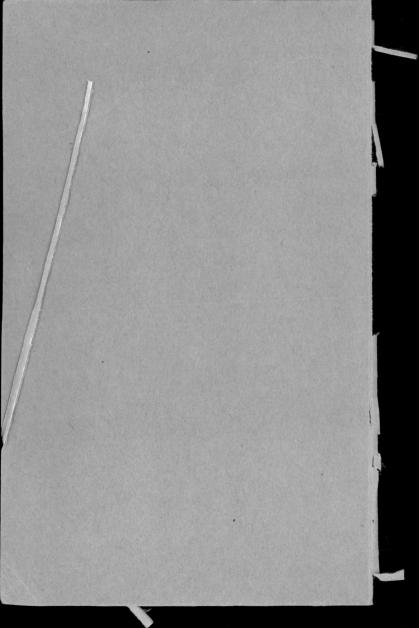

THE MODERN LIBRARY

OF THE WORLD'S BEST BOOKS

THE MASTER BUILDER
PILLARS OF SOCIETY
HEDDA GABLER

By
HENRIK IBSEN

The publishers will be pleased to send, upon request, an illustrated catalogue setting forth the purpose and ideals of The Modern Library, and describing in detail each volume in the series. ¶Every reader of books will find titles he has been looking for, attractively printed, and at an unusually low price

THE MASTER BUILDER
PILLARS OF SOCIETY
HEDDA GABLER

By HENRIK IBSEN

INTRODUCTION BY H. L. MENCKEN

THE MODERN LIBRARY

PUBLISHERS :: :: NEW YORK

MANUFACTURED IN THE UNITED STATES OF AMERICA

FOR THE MODERN LIBRARY, INC., BY H. WOLFF

INTRODUCTION

Ibsen, like Wagner and Manet, has lived down his com-
mentators, and is now ready to be examined and enjoyed
for what he actually was, namely, a first-rate journeyman
dramatist, perhaps the best that ever lived.   Twenty years
ago he was hymned and damned as anything and everything
else: symbolist, seer, prophet, necromancer, maker of rid-
dles, rabble-rouser, cheap shocker, pornographer, spinner of
gossamer nothings.   Fools belabored him and fools defended him; he was near to being suffocated and done for in
the fog of balderdash.   I know of no sure cure for all the
sorrows of the world, social, political or æsthetic, that was
not credited to him, read into him, forced into his baggage.
And I know of no crime against virtue, good order and the
revelation of God that he was not accused of.   The prod-
uct of all this pawing and bawling was the Ibsen legend, that
fabulous picture of a fabulous monster, half Nietzsche and
half Dr. Frank Crane, drenching the world with scandalous
platitudes from a watch-tower in the chilblained North.
The righteous heard of him with creepy shudders; there
was bold talk of denying him the use of the mails; he was
the Gog and the Magog, the Heliogabalus, nay, the downright Kaiser, of that distant and pious era.

No such Ibsen, of course, ever really existed.   The genuine Ibsen was anything but the Anti-Christ thus conjured
up by imprudent partisans and terrified opponents.   On the
contrary, he was a man whose salient quality was precisely
his distrust of, and disdain for, any and all such facile here-
sies; a highly respectable gentleman of the middle class,

v

well-barbered, ease-loving and careful in mind; a very skilful practitioner of a very exacting and lucrative trade; a safe and sane exponent of order, efficiency, honesty and common sense. From end to end of his life there is no record that Ibsen ever wrote a single word or formulated a single idea that might not have been exposed in a newspaper editorial. He believed in all the things that the normal, law-abiding citizen of Christendom believes in, from democracy to romantic love, and from the obligations of duty to the value of virtue, and he always gave them the best of it in his plays. And whenever, mistaking his position, someone charged him with flouting these things or with advocating some notion that stood in opposition to them, he invariably called the plaintiff to book, and denied vehemently that he was guilty, and protested bitterly that it was outrageous to fasten any such wild and naughty stuff upon a reputable man.

Had he been, in truth, the extravagant iconoclast that a misinformed rabbinism tried to make him out, he would have remained, to the end of his career, a mere freak and blank cartridge in the theatre, and of no more influence than such extremists, say, as Max Stirner, Arthur Gobineau and the Marquis de Sade. So long, indeed, as he was generally held to be such an iconoclast, he actually suffered that fate. But when it began to be noticed, first by other dramatists and then by a widening public, that his ideas, after all, were really not extraordinary—that what he said, in the last analysis, was simply what every reasonably intelligent man thought—that his plays, for all their smashing air, were not actually blows at Christian culture—when this began to be understood, then he began to make his way, and all the serious dramatists of Europe began to imitate him. But they saw him, with their keener professional eyes, more clearly than the early and so absurd Ibsenites had seen him. They saw that he was not a brummagen prophet, but a play-maker of astounding skill—one who had a new and better method to teach them. And so, when they set out to follow him, what they imitated was not the imaginary mystifications that foolish fuglemen had read into his dramas, but his direct and adept manner of clothing simple and even self-evident arguments in unusually lucid and brilliant dramatic forms—in brief, his enormously effective technique as a dramatist. He didn't teach them to think extraordinary thoughts; he taught them to put obvious thoughts into sound plays.

All this must be plain to anyone who goes through his so-called social dramas today, despite the confusing memory of all the gabble that went about in the high days of the Ibsen uproar. What ideas does one actually find in them? Such ideas, first and last, as even a Harvard professor might evolve without bursting his brain—for example, that it is unpleasant and degrading for a wife to be treated as a mere mistress and empty-head; that professional patriots and town boomers are frauds; that success in business usually involves doing things that a self-respecting man hesitates to do; that a woman who continues to cohabit with a syphilitic husband may expect to have defective children; that a joint sorrow tends to dampen passion in husband and wife, and so bring them together upon a more secure basis; that a neurotic and lascivious woman is apt to be horrified when she finds that she is pregnant; that a man of 55 or 60 is an ass to fall in love with a flapper of 17; that the world is barbarously cruel to a woman who has violated the Seventh Commandment or a man who has violated the Eighth. If you are discontented with these summaries, then turn to summaries that Ibsen made himself—that is, turn to his notes for his social dramas in his *Nachgelassene Schriften*. Here you will find precisely what he was trying to say. Here you will find, in plain words, the ideas that he started from. They are, without exception, ideas of the utmost simplicity. There is nothing mysterious in them; there is not even anything new in them. Above all, there is no idiotic symbolism in them. They mean just what they say.

As I have said, Ibsen himself was under no delusions about his dramas of ideas. He was a hard-working dramatist and a man of sense: he never allowed the grotesque guesses and fantasies of his advocates to corrupt the clarity of his own purpose. Down to the time he lost his mind—he was then at work on "John Gabriel Borkman"—he never wrote a line that had any significance save the obvious one, and he never forgot for an instant that he was writing, not tracts, but stage-plays. When the sentimental German middle classes mistook "A Doll's House" for a revolutionary document against monogamy, and began grouping him with the preachers of free love, he was as indignant as only a respectable family man can be, and even agreed to write a new ending for the play in order to shut off that nonsense. A year later he wrote "Ghosts" to raise a laugh against the alarmed moralists who had swallowed the free lovers' error. The noise of combat continuing, he decided to make an end of it by burlesquing the Ibsenists, and the result was "The Wild Duck," in which the chief figure is a sort of *reductio ad absurdum* of the modern Drama Leaguer. In "The Master Builder" he took a holiday from social ideas, even the most elemental, and put himself into a play, shedding a salt tear over his lost youth. And in "Hedda Gabler," as if to confute the Ibsen talmudists forever, he fashioned a thumping drama out of the oldest, shoddiest materials of Sardou, Scribe and Feuillet, nay, Meilhac and Halévy, as if to prove, once and for all time, that he was a dramatist first and last, and not a windy evangelist and reformer, and that he could meet any other dramatist, however skilful, on equal terms, and dispose of him neatly and completely.

Ibsen's chief interest, from the beginning to the end of his career as a dramatist, was not with the propagation of ethical ideas, but with the solution of æsthetic problems. He was, in brief, not a preacher, but an artist, and not the moony artist of popular legend, but the alert and competent artist of fact, intent upon the technical difficulties of his business. He gave infinitely more thought to questions of practical dramaturgy—to getting his characters on and off the stage, to building up climaxes, to calculating effects—than he ever gave to the ideational content of his dramas. Almost any idea was good enough, so long as it could be converted into a conflict, and the conflict could be worked out straightforwardly and effectively. Read his letters and you will find him tremendously concerned, from the start, with technical difficulties and expedients—and never mentioning morals, lesson, symbols and that sort of thing at all. So early as the time he wrote "The League of Youth" you will find him discussing the details of dramatic machinery with Dr. Georg Brandes, and laying stress on the fact, with no little vanity, that he has "accomplished the feat of doing without a single monologue, in fact, without a single aside." A bit later he began developing the stage direction; go through his plays and observe how he gradually increased its importance, until in the end it almost overshadowed the dialogue. And if you would get, in brief, the full measure of his contribution to the art of the drama, give hard study to "A Doll's House." Here, for the first time, his new technique was in full working. Here he deposed Scribe and company at one blow, and founded an entirely new order of dramaturgy. Other dramatists, long before him, had concocted dramas of ideas—and good ones. The idea in Augier's "La Mariage d'Olympe" was quite as sound and interesting as that in "A Doll's House;" the idea in Augier's "Les Effrontés" perhaps exceeded it in both ways. But Ibsen got into "A Doll's House" something that Augier and Feuillet and Dumas *fils* and all that crowd of Empire dramatists had never been able to get into their plays, and that was an air of utter and absolute reality, an overwhelming conviction, a complete concealment of the dramatic machinery.

And how did he conceal it? Simply by leaving it out.
Scribe had built up an inordinately complex dramaturgy.
His plays were elaborate and beautiful mechanisms, but still
always mechanisms. He had to sacrifice everything else—
reason, probability, human nature—to make the machine
run. And Augier, Feuillet and Dumas, better men all, followed docilely in his tracks. They were better observers;
they were more keenly interested in the actual life about
them; they managed, despite the artificiality of their technique, to get some genuine human beings into their plays.
But that technique still hung around their necks; they never
quite got rid of it. But Ibsen did. In "A Doll's House"
he threw it overboard for all time. Instead of a complicated
plot, working beautifully toward a foreordained climax, he
presented a few related scenes in the life of a husband and
wife. Instead of a finely wrought fabric of suspense and
emotion nicely balanced, neatly hanging together, he hit
upon an action that was all suspense and all emotion. And instead of carefully calculated explanations,
involving the orthodox couriers and prattling chambermaids,
he let the story tell itself. The result, as William Archer
has said, "was a new order of experience in the theatre."
The audience that came to be pleasantly diverted by the
old, old tricks found its nerves racked by a glimpse through
a terrifying keyhole. This thing was not a stage-play, but
a scandal. It didn't caress and soothe; it arrested and
shocked. It didn't stay discreetly on the stage; it leaped
out over the footlights.

The audience gasped and went out gabbling, and the result was the Ibsen madness, with its twenty years of fold-
erol. But there were dramatists in the house who, with
professional eye, saw more clearly what was afoot, and these
dramatists, once they could shake off the Scribe tradition,
began to imitate Ibsen—Jones and Pinero and later Shaw
in England; Hauptmann and Sudermann in Germany; Gorki
and many another in Russia; Hervieu, Brieux and their like

in France; a swarm of lesser ones in Italy, Scandinavia and Austria. Ibsen, in brief, completely overthrew the well-made play of Scribe, and set up the play that was a direct imitation of reality. He showed that the illusion was not only not helped by the elaborate machinery of Scribe, but that it was actually hindered—that the way to sure and tremendous effects was by the route of simplicity, naturalness, ingenuousness. In "A Doll's House" he abandoned all of the old tricks save two or three; in "Ghosts" he made away with the rest of them, and even managed to do without a plot; by the time he got to "Little Eyolf" there was nothing left of the traditional dramaturgy save the act divisions. It was not, of course, an easy reform to put through. The habits of mind of audiences had to be changed; the lunacies of the Ibsenites had to be lived down, and the moral ire of the anti-Ibsenites; above all, the actors of the time had to be untaught all that they knew about acting, and taught a lot of new things that violated their vanity and hurt their business. But Ibsen's notions had logic behind them, and they had the force of novelty, and there was in them a new and superior opportunity for the dramatist who really had something to say, and so, in the end, they triumphed in the world. Today the methods of Scribe are so archaic that they excite laughter; only the Broadhursts and Kleins of Broadway stoop to them. If an intelligent dramatist were to expose a play built upon the plans of "Verre d'Eau" or "Adrienne Lecouvreur," even the newspaper critics would laugh at him. All that sort of thing now belongs to archeology.

But Ibsen, as I have said, was a dramatist first and last, and not a tin-pot agitator and messiah. He depicted the life of his time and he made use of the ideas of his time; he had no desire to change those ideas, nor even, in the main, to criticise them. "A dramatist's business," he used to say, "is not to answer questions, but merely to ask them." He asked a question in "A Doll's House." He asked another, ironically, in "Ghosts." He asked others in "The

Lady from the Sea," "The Wild Duck" and "Little Eyolf."
In "The Master Builder," rising, so to speak, to a question
of personal privilege, he abandoned his habit and ventured
upon a half-answer. But is there any answer in "Hedda
Gabler?" Surely not. The play is still chewed and belabored by advocates of this answer or that; the very lack
of agreement shows the dramatist's neutrality. "It was not
my desire," he once said, "to deal in this play with so-called
problems. What I wanted to do was to depict human beings, human emotions, and human destinies, upon a ground-
work of certain of the social conditions and principles of the
present day." That is to say, here is your state of society,
here is your woman, here is what she does—what do you
think of it? So, again, in "Pillars of Society." Here is
your society, here are your pillars, here are their rascalities—
what have you to say of it? Joseph Conrad, another great
artist, once put the thing admirably. "My task which I am
trying to achieve," he said, "is, by the power of the written
word, to make you hear, to make you feel—it is, before all,
to make you *see*. That—and no more, and it is everything."

Mencken

Baltimore, Maryland, September, 1917.

CONTENTS

		PAGE
INTRODUCTION		v-xii

THE MASTER BUILDER

ACT I	3
ACT II	38
ACT III	70

PILLARS OF SOCIETY

ACT I	97
ACT II	123
ACT III	155
ACT IV	178

HEDDA GABLER

ACT I	207
ACT II	240
ACT III	269
ACT IV	288

THE MASTER BUILDER
(1892)

PLAY IN THREE ACTS

DRAMATIS PERSONÆ

HALVARD SOLNESS, *Master Builder*.

ALINE SOLNESS, *his wife*.

DOCTOR HERDAL, *physician*.

KNUT BROVIK, *formerly an architect, now in* SOLNESS'S *employment*.

RAGNAR BROVIK, *his son, draughtsman*.

KAIA FOSLI, *his niece, book-keeper*.

MISS HILDA WANGEL.

Some Ladies.

A Crowd in the street.

The action passes in and about SOLNESS'S *house.*

ACT I

A plainly-furnished work-room in the house of HALVARD
SOLNESS. *Folding doors on the left lead out to the hall.
On the right is the door leading to the inner rooms of the
house. At the back is an open door into the draughtsmen's office. In front, on the left, a desk with books,
papers and writing materials. Further back than the
folding-door, a stove. In the right-hand corner, a sofa,
a table, and one or two chairs. On the table a
water-bottle and glass. A smaller table, with a rocking-chair and arm-chair, in front on the right. Lighted
lamps, with shades, on the table in the draughtsmen's
office, on the table in the corner, and on the desk.*

In the draughtsmen's office sit KNUT BROVIK *and his son*
RAGNAR, *occupied with plans and calculations. At the
desk in the outer office stands* KAIA FOSLI, *writing in
the ledger.* KNUT BROVIK *is a spare old man with white
hair and beard. He wears a rather threadbare but
well-brushed black coat, spectacles, and a somewhat
discoloured white neckcloth.* RAGNAR BROVIK *is a well-
dressed, light-haired man in his thirties, with a slight
stoop.* KAIA FOSLI *is a slightly built girl, a little over
twenty, carefully dressed, and delicate-looking. She has
a green shade over her eyes.—All three go on working
for some time in silence.*

*Knut Brovik (rises suddenly, as if in distress, from the
table; breathes heavily and laboriously as he comes forward
into the doorway).* No, I can't bear it much longer!

3

Kaia (going up to him). You are feeling very ill this evening, are you not, uncle?

Brovik. Oh, I seem to get worse every day.

Ragnar (has risen and advances). You ought to go home, father. Try to get a little sleep——

Brovik (impatiently). Go to bed, I suppose? Would you have me stifled outright?

Kaia. Then take a little walk.

Ragnar. Yes, do. I will come with you.

Brovik (with warmth). I will not go till he comes! I am determined to have it out this evening with—(*in a tone of suppressed bitterness*)—with him—with the chief.

Kaia (anxiously). Oh no, uncle—do wait awhile before doing that.

Ragnar. Yes, better wait, father!

Brovik (draws his breath laboriously). Ha—ha—! *I* haven't much time for waiting.

Kaia (listening). Hush! I hear him on the stairs. (*All three go back to their work. A short silence.*)

HALVARD SOLNESS *comes in through the hall door. He is a man no longer young, but healthy and vigorous, with close-cut curly hair, dark moustache and dark thick eyebrows. He wears a greyish-green buttoned jacket with an upstanding collar and broad lapels. On his head he wears a soft grey felt hat, and he has one or two light portfolios under his arm.*

Solness (near the door, points towards the draughtsmen's office, and asks in a whisper:) Are they gone?

Kaia (softly, shaking her head). No. (*She takes the shade off her eyes.* SOLNESS *crosses the room, throws his hat on a chair, places the portfolios on the table by the sofa, and approaches the desk again.* KAIA *goes on writing without intermission, but seems nervous and uneasy.*)

Solness (aloud). What is that you are entering, Miss Fosli?

Kaia (starts). Oh, it is only something that——

Solness. Let me look at it, Miss Fosli. (*Bends over her, pretends to be looking into the ledger, and whispers:*) Kaia!

Kaia (*softly, still writing*). Well?

Solness. Why do you always take that shade off when I come?

Kaia (*as before*). I look so ugly with it on.

Solness (*smiling*). Then you don't like to look ugly, Kaia?

Kaia (*half glancing up at him.*) Not for all the world. Not in your eyes.

Solness (*stroking her hair gently*). Poor, poor little Kaia——

Kaia (*bending her head*). Hush—they can hear you.

[SOLNESS *strolls across the room to the right, turns and pauses at the door of the draughtsmen's office.*

Solness. Has any one been here for me?

Ragnar (*rising*). Yes, the young couple who want a villa built, out at Lövstrand.

Solness (*growling*). Oh, those two! They must wait. I am not quite clear about the plans yet.

Ragnar (*advancing, with some hesitation*). They were very anxious to have the drawings at once.

Solness (*as before*). Yes, of course—so they all are.

Brovik (*looks up*). They say they are longing so to get into a house of their own.

Solness. Yes, yes—we know all that! And so they are content to take whatever is offered them. They get a—a roof over their heads—an address—but nothing to call a home. No thank you! In that case, let them apply to somebody else. Tell them that, the next time they call.

Brovik (*pushes his glasses up on to his forehead and looks in astonishment at him.*) To somebody else? Are you prepared to give up the commission?

Solness (*impatiently*). Yes, yes, yes, devil take it! If that is to be the way of it——. Rather that, than build away at random. (*Vehemently.*) Besides, I know very little about these people as yet.

Brovik. The people are safe enough. Ragnar knows them. He is a friend of the family. Perfectly safe people.

Solness. Oh, safe—safe enough! That is not at all what I mean. Good Lord—don't you understand me either? (*Angrily.*) I won't have anything to do with these strangers. They may apply to whom they please, so far as I am concerned.

Brovik (*rising*). Do you really mean that?

Solness (*sulkily*). Yes I do,—For once in a way. (*He comes forward.*)

> [BROVIK *exchanges a glance with* RAGNAR, *who makes a warning gesture. Then* BROVIK *comes into the front room.*

Brovik. May I have a few words with you?

Solness. Certainly.

Brovik (*to* KAIA). Just go in there for a moment, Kaia.

Kaia (*uneasily*). Oh, but uncle——

Brovik. Do as I say, child. And shut the door after you.

> [KAIA *goes reluctantly into the draughtsmen's office, glances anxiously and imploringly at* SOLNESS, *and shuts the door.*

Brovik (*lowering his voice a little*). I don't want the poor children to know how ill I am.

Solness. Yes, you have been looking very poorly of late.

Brovik. It will soon be all over with me. My strength is ebbing—from day to day.

Solness. Won't you sit down?

Brovik. Thanks—may I?

Solness (*placing the arm-chair more conveniently*). Here —take this chair.—And now?

Brovik (*has seated himself with difficulty*). Well, you see, it's about Ragnar. That is what weighs most upon me. What is to become of him?

Solness. Of course your son will stay with me as long as ever he likes.

Brovik. But that is just what he does not like. He feels that he cannot stay here any longer.

Solness. Why, I should say he was very well off here. But if he wants more money, I should not mind——

Brovik. No, no! It is not that. (*Impatiently.*) But sooner or later he, too, must have a chance of doing something on his own account.

Solness (without looking at him). Do you think that Ragnar has quite talent enough to stand alone?

Brovik. No, that is just the heartbreaking part of it—I have begun to have my doubts about the boy. For you have never said so much as—as one encouraging word about him. And yet I cannot but think there must be something in him—he can't be without talent.

Solness. Well, but he has learnt nothing—nothing thoroughly, I mean. Except, of course, to draw.

Brovik (looks at him with covert hatred, and says hoarsely). You had learned little enough of the business when you were in my employment. But that did not prevent you from setting to work—(*breathing with difficulty*)—and pushing your way up, and taking the wind out of my sails —mine, and so many other people's.

Solness. Yes, you see—circumstances favoured me.

Brovik. You are right there. Everything favoured you. But then how can you have the heart to let me go to my grave—without having seen what Ragnar is fit for? And of course I am anxious to see them married, too—before I go.

Solness (sharply). Is it she who wishes it?

Brovik. Not Kaia so much as Ragnar—he talks about it every day. (*Appealingly.*) You must—you must help him to get some independent work now! I must see something that the lad has done. Do you hear?

Solness (peevishly). Hang it, man, you can't expect me to drag commissions down from the moon for him!

Brovik. He has the chance of a capital commission at this very moment. A big bit of work.

Solness (uneasily, startled). Has he?

Brovik. If you would give your consent.

Solness. What sort of work do you mean?

Brovik (with some hesitation). He can have the building of that villa out at Lövstrand.

Solness. That! Why, I am going to build that myself.

Brovik. Oh, you don't much care about doing it.

Solness (flaring up). Don't care! I? Who dares to say that?

Brovik. You said so yourself just now.

Solness. Oh, never mind what I say.—Would they give Ragnar the building of that villa?

Brovik. Yes. You see, he knows the family. And then —just for the fun of the thing—he has made drawings and estimates and so forth——

Solness. Are they pleased with the drawings? The people who will have to live in the house?

Brovik. Yes. If you would only look through them and approve of them.

Solness. Then they would let Ragnar build their home for them?

Brovik. They were immensely pleased with his idea. They thought it exceedingly original, they said.

Solness. Oho! Original! Not the old-fashioned stuff that *I* am in the habit of turning out!

Brovik. It seemed to them different.

Solness (with suppressed irritation). So it was to see Ragnar that they came here—whilst I was out!

Brovik. They came to call upon you—and at the same time to ask whether you would mind retiring——

Solness (angrily). Retire? I?

Brovik. In case you thought that Ragnar's drawings——

Solness. I? Retire in favour of your son!

Brovik. Retire from the agreement, they meant.

Solness. Oh, it comes to the same thing. (*Laughs angrily.*) So that is it, is it? Halvard Solness is to see about retiring now! To make room for younger men! For the very youngest, perhaps! He must make room! Room! Room!

Brovik. Why, good heavens! there is surely room for more than one single man——

Solness. Oh, there's not so very much room to spare either. But, be that as it may—I will never retire! I will never give way to anybody! Never of my own free will. Never in this world will I do that!

Brovik (rises with difficulty). Then I am to pass out of life without any certainty? Without a gleam of happiness? Without any faith or trust in Ragnar? Without having seen a single piece of work of his doing? Is that to be the way of it?

Solness (turns half aside, and mutters). H'm—don't ask more just now.

Brovik. I must have an answer to this one question. Am I to pass out of life in such utter poverty?

Solness (seems to struggle with himself; finally he says, in a low but firm voice:) You must pass out of life as best you can.

Brovik. Then be it so. (*He goes up the room.*)

Solness (following him, half in desperation). Don't you understand that I cannot help it? I am what I am, and I cannot change my nature!

Brovik. No, no; I suppose you can't. (*Reels and supports himself against the sofa-table.*) May I have a glass of water?

Solness. By all means. (*Fills a glass and hands it to him.*)

Brovik. Thanks. (*Drinks and puts the glass down again.*)

[SOLNESS *goes up and opens the door of the draughtsmen's office.*

Solness. Ragnar—you must come and take your father home. (RAGNAR *rises quickly. He and* KAIA *come into the work-room.*)

Ragnar. What is the matter, father?

Brovik. Give me your arm. Now let us go.

Ragnar. Very well. You had better put your things on, too, Kaia.

Solness. Miss Fosli must stay— just for a moment. There is a letter I want written.

Brovik (*looks at* SOLNESS). Good night. Sleep well— if you can.

Solness. Good night.

> [BROVIK *and* RAGNAR *go out by the hall-door.* KAIA *goes to the desk.* SOLNESS *stands with bent head, to the right, by the arm-chair.*

Kaia (*dubiously*). Is there any letter——?

Solness (*curtly*). No, of course not. (*Looks sternly at her.*) Kaia!

Kaia (*anxiously, in a low voice*). Yes!

Solness (*points imperatively to a spot on the floor*). Come here! At once!

Kaia (*hesitatingly*). Yes.

Solness (*as before*). Nearer!

Kaia (*obeying*). What do you want with me?

Solness (*looks at her for a while*). Is it you I have to thank for all this?

Kaia. No, no, don't think that!

Solness. But confess now—you want to get married!

Kaia (*softly*). Ragnar and I have been engaged for four or five years, and so——

Solness. And so you think it time there were an end to it. Is not that so?

Kaia. Ragnar and Uncle say I must. So I suppose I shall have to give in.

Solness (*more gently*). Kaia, don't you really care a little bit for Ragnar, too?

Kaia. I cared very much for Ragnar once—before I came here to you.

Solness. But you don't now? Not in the least?

Kaia (passionately, clasping her hands and holding them out towards him). Oh, you know very well there is only one person I care for now! One, and one only, in all the world! I shall never care for any one else.

Solness. Yes, you say that. And yet you go away from me—leave me alone here with everything on my hands.

Kaia. But could I not stay with you, even if Ragnar——?

Solness (repudiating the idea). No, no, that is quite impossible. If Ragnar leaves me and starts work on his own account, then of course he will need you himself.

Kaia (wringing her hands). Oh, I feel as if I could not be separated from you! It's quite, quite impossible!

Solness. Then be sure you get those foolish notions out of Ragnar's head. Marry him as much as you please— *(alters his tone.)*—I mean—don't let him throw up his good situation with me. For then I can keep you too, my dear Kaia.

Kaia. Oh yes, how lovely that would be, if it could only be managed!

Solness (clasps her head with his two hands and whispers). For I cannot get on without you, you see. I must have you with me every single day.

Kaia (in nervous exaltation). My God! My God!

Solness (kisses her hair.) Kaia—Kaia!

Kaia (sinks down before him). Oh, how good you are to me! How unspeakably good you are!

Solness (vehemently). Get up! For goodness' sake get up! I think I hear some one! *(He helps her to rise. She staggers over to the desk.)*

MRS. SOLNESS *enters by the door on the right. She looks thin and wasted with grief, but shows traces of bygone beauty. Blonde ringlets. Dressed with good taste, wholly in black. Speaks somewhat slowly and in a plaintive voice.*

Mrs. Solness (in the doorway). Halvard!

Solness (turns). Oh, are you there, my dear——?

Mrs. Solness (with a glance at KAIA*).* I am afraid I am disturbing you.

Solness. Not in the least. Miss Fosli has only a short letter to write.

Mrs. Solness. Yes, so I see.

Solness. What do you want with me, Aline?

Mrs. Solness. I merely wanted to tell you that Dr. Herdal is in the drawing-room. Won't you come and see him, Halvard?

Solness (looks suspiciously at her). H'm—is the doctor so very anxious to talk to me?

Mrs. Solness. Well, not exactly anxious. He really came to see me; but he would like to say how-do-you-do to you at the same time.

Solness (laughs to himself). Yes, I daresay. Well, you must ask him to wait a little.

Mrs. Solness. Then you will come in presently?

Solness. Perhaps I will. Presently, presently, dear. In a little while.

Mrs. Solness (glancing again at KAIA*).* Well, now, don't forget, Halvard.

[*Withdraws and closes the door behind her.*

Kaia (softly). Or dear, oh dear—I am sure Mrs. Solness thinks ill of me in some way!

Solness. Oh, not in the least. Not more than usual at any rate. But all the same, you had better go now, Kaia.

Kaia. Yes, yes, now I must go.

Solness (severely). And mind you get that matter settled for me. Do you hear?

Kaia. Oh, if it only depended on me——

Solness. I will have it settled, I say! And to-morrow too—not a day later!

Kaia (*terrified*). If there's nothing else for it, I am quite willing to break off the engagement.

Solness (*angrily*). Break it off. Are you mad? Would you think of breaking it off?

Kaia (*distracted*). Yes, if necessary. For I must—I must stay here with you! I can't leave you! That is utterly—utterly impossible!

Solness (*with a sudden outburst*). But deuce take it— how about Ragnar then! It's Ragnar that I——

Kaia (*looks at him with terrified eyes*). It is chiefly on Ragnar's account, that—that you——

Solness (*collecting himself.*) No, no, of course not! You don't understand me either. (*Gently and softly.*) Of course it is you I want to keep—you above everything, Kaia. But for that very reason, you must prevent Ragnar, too, from throwing up his situation. There, there,—now go home.

Kaia. Yes, yes—good-night, then.

Solness. Good-night. (*As she is going.*) Oh, stop a moment! Are Ragnar's drawings in there?

Kaia. I did not see him take them with him.

Solness. Then just go and find them for me. I might perhaps glance over them, after all.

Kaia (*happy*). Oh yes, please do!

Solness. For your sake, Kaia dear. Now, let me have them at once, please. (KAIA *hurries into the draughtsmen's office, searches anxiously in the table-drawer, finds a portfolio and brings it with her.*)

Kaia. Here are all the drawings.

Solness. Good. Put them down there on the table.

Kaia (*putting down the portfolio*). Good-night, then. (*Beseechingly.*) And please, please think kindly of me.

Solness. Oh, that I always do. Good-night, my dear little Kaia. (*Glances to the right.*) Go, go now!

MRS. SOLNESS *and* DR. HERDAL *enter by the door on the right. He is a stoutish, elderly men, with a round, good-humoured face, clean shaven, with thin, light hair, and gold spectacles.*

Mrs. Solness (*still in the doorway*). Halvard, I cannot keep the doctor any longer.

Solness. Well then, come in here.

Mrs. Solness (*to* KAIA, *who is turning down the desk-lamp*). Have you finished the letter already, Miss Fosli?

Kaia (*in confusion*). The letter——?

Solness. Yes, it was quite a short one.

Mrs. Solness. It must have been very short.

Solness. You may go now, Miss Fosli. And please come in good time to-morrow morning.

Kaia. I will be sure to. Good-night, Mrs. Solness. (*She goes out by the hall door.*)

Mrs. Solness. She must be quite an acquisition to you, Halvard, this Miss Fosli.

Solness. Yes, indeed. She is useful in all sorts of ways.

Mrs. Solness. So it seems.

Dr. Herdal. Is she good at book-keeping too?

Solness. Well—of course she has had a good deal of practice during these two years. And then she is so nice and willing to do whatever one asks of her.

Mrs. Solness. Yes, that must be very delightful——

Solness. It is. Especially when one is not too much accustomed to that sort of thing.

Mrs. Solness (*in a tone of gentle remonstrance*). Can you say that, Halvard?

Solness. Oh, no, no, my dear Aline; I beg your pardon.

Mrs. Solness. There's no occasion.—Well then, doctor, you will come back later on, and have a cup of tea with us?

Dr. Herdal. I have only that one patient to see, and then I'll come back.

Mrs. Solness. Thank you. (*She goes out by the door on the right.*)

Solness. Are you in a hurry, doctor?

Dr. Herdal. No, not at all.

Solness. May I have a little chat with you?

Dr. Herdal. With the greatest of pleasure.

Solness. Then let us sit down. (*He motions the doctor to take the rocking-chair, and sits down himself in the arm-chair. Looks searchingly at him*). Tell me—did you notice anything odd about Aline?

Dr. Herdal. Do you mean just now, when she was here?

Solness. Yes, in her manner to me. Did you notice anything?

Dr. Herdal (*smiling*). Well, I admit—one couldn't well avoid noticing that your wife—h'm——

Solness. Well?

Dr. Herdal. —that your wife is not particularly fond of this Miss Fosli.

Solness. Is that all? I have noticed that myself.

Dr. Herdal. And I must say I am scarcely surprised at it.

Solness. At what?

Dr. Herdal. That she should not exactly approve of your seeing so much of another woman, all day and every day.

Solness. No, no, I suppose you are right there—and Aline too. But it's impossible to make any change.

Dr. Herdal. Could you not engage a clerk?

Solness. The first man that came to hand? No, thank you—that would never do for me.

Dr. Herdal. But now, if your wife——? Suppose, with her delicate health, all this tries her too much?

Solness. Even then—I might almost say—it can make no difference. I must keep Kaia Fosli. No one else could fill her place.

Dr. Herdal. No one else?

Solness (*curtly*). No, no one.

Dr. Herdal (*drawing his chair closer*). Now listen to me, my dear Mr. Solness. May I ask you a question, quite between ourselves?

Solness. By all means.

Dr. Herdal. Women, you see—in certain matters, they have a deucedly keen intuition——

Solness. They have, indeed. There is not the least doubt of that. But——?

Dr. Herdal. Well, tell me now—if your wife can't endure this Kaia Fosli——?

Solness. Well, what then?

Dr. Herdal. —may she not have just—just the least little bit of reason for this instinctive dislike?

Solness (looks at him and rises). Oho!

Dr. Herdal. Now don't be offended—but hasn't she?

Solness (with curt decision). No.

Dr. Herdal. No reason of any sort?

Solness. No other reason than her own suspicious nature.

Dr. Herdal. I know you have known a good many women in your time.

Solness. Yes, I have.

Dr. Herdal. And have been a good deal taken with some of them, too.

Solness. Oh yes, I don't deny it.

Dr. Herdal. But as regards Miss Fosli, then? There is nothing of that sort in the case?

Solness. No; nothing at all—on my side.

Dr. Herdal. But on her side?

Solness. I don't think you have any right to ask that question, doctor.

Dr. Herdal. Well, you know, we were discussing your wife's intuition.

Solness. So we were. And for that matter—(*lowers his voice*)—Aline's intuition, as you call it—in a certain sense it has not been so far astray.

Dr. Herdal. Aha! there we have it!

Solness (sits down). Doctor Herdal—I am going to tell you a strange story—if you care to listen to it.

Dr. Herdal. I like listening to strange stories.

Solness. Very well then. I daresay you recollect that

I took Knut Brovik and his son into my employment—after the old man's business had gone to the dogs.

Dr. Herdal. Yes, so I have understood.

Solness. You see, they really are clever fellows, these two. Each of them has talent in his own way. But then the son took it into his head to get engaged; and the next thing, of course, was that he wanted to get married—and begin to build on his own account. That is the way with all these young people.

Dr. Herdal (*laughing*). Yes, they have a bad habit of wanting to marry.

Solness. Just so. But of course that did not suit my plans; for I needed Ragnar myself—and the old man too. He is exceedingly good at calculating bearing-strains and cubic contents—and all that sort of devilry, you know.

Dr. Herdal. Oh yes, no doubt that's indispensable.

Solness. Yes, it is. But Ragnar was absolutely bent on setting to work for himself. He would hear of nothing else.

Dr. Herdal. But he has stayed with you all the same.

Solness. Yes, I'll tell you how that came about. One day this girl, Kaia Fosli, came to see them on some errand or other. She had never been here before. And when I saw how utterly infatuated they were with each other, the thought occurred to me: if I could only get her into the office here, then perhaps Ragnar too would stay where he is.

Dr. Herdal. That was not at all a bad idea.

Solness. Yes, but at the time I did not breathe a word of what was in my mind. I merely stood and looked at her —and kept on wishing intently that I could have her here. Then I talked to her a little, in a friendly way—about one thing and another. And then she went away.

Dr. Herdal. Well?

Solness. Well, then, next day, pretty late in the evening, when old Brovik and Ragnar had gone home, she came here again, and behaved as if I had made an arrangement with her.

Dr. Herdal. An arrangement? What about?

Solness. About the very thing my mind had been fixed on. But I hadn't said one single word about it.

Dr. Herdal. That was most extraordinary.

Solness. Yes, was it not? And now she wanted to know what she was to do here—whether she could begin the very next morning, and so forth.

Dr. Herdal. Don't you think she did it in order to be with her sweetheart?

Solness. That was what occurred to me at first. But no, that was not it. She seemed to drift quite away from him—when once she had come here to me.

Dr. Herdal. She drifted over to you, then?

Solness. Yes, entirely. If I happen to look at her when her back is turned, I can tell that she feels it. She quivers and trembles the moment I come near her. What do you think of that?

Dr. Herdal. H'm—that's not very hard to explain.

Solness. Well, but what about the other thing? That she believed I had said to her what I had only wished and willed—silently—inwardly—to myself? What do you say to that? Can you explain that, Dr. Herdal?

Dr. Herdal. No, I won't undertake to do that.

Solness. I felt sure you would not; and so I have never cared to talk about it till now. But it's a cursed nuisance to me in the long run, you understand. Here I have to go on day after day pretending——. And it's a shame to treat her so, too, poor girl. (*Vehemently.*) But I cannot do anything else. For if she runs away from me—then Ragnar will be off too.

Dr. Herdal. And you have not told your wife the rights of the story?

Solness. No.

Dr. Herdal. Then why on earth don't you?

Solness (*looks fixedly at him, and says in a low voice:*)

Because I seem to find a sort of—of salutary self-torture in allowing Aline to do me an injustice.

Dr. Herdal (shakes his head). I don't in the least understand what you mean.

Solness. Well, you see—it is like paying off a little bit of a huge, immeasurable debt——

Dr. Herdal. To your wife?

Solness. Yes; and that always helps to relieve one's mind a little. One can breathe more freely for a while, you understand.

Dr. Herdal. No, goodness knows, I don't understand at all——

Solness (breaking off, rises again). Well, well, well—then we won't talk any more about it. (*He saunters across the room, returns, and stops beside the table. Looks at the doctor with a sly smile.*) I suppose you think you have drawn me out nicely now, doctor?

Dr. Herdal (with some irritation). Drawn you out? Again I have not the faintest notion what you mean, Mr. Solness.

Solness. Oh come, out with it; I have seen it quite clearly, you know.

Dr. Herdal. What have you seen?

Solness (in a low voice, slowly). That you have been quietly keeping an eye upon me.

Dr. Herdal. That *I* have! And why in all the world should I do that?

Solness. Because you think that I—— (*Passionately.*) Well, devil take it—you think the same of me as Aline does.

Dr. Herdal. And what does she think about you?

Solness (having recovered his self-control). She has begun to think that I am—that I am—ill.

Dr. Herdal. Ill! You! She has never hinted such a thing to me. Why, what can she think is the matter with you?

Solness (leans over the back of the chair and whispers).

Aline has made up her mind that I am mad. That is what she thinks.

Dr. Herdal (*rising*). Why, my dear good fellow——!

Solness. Yes, on my soul she does! I tell you it is so. And she has got you to think the same! Oh, I can assure you, doctor, I see it in your face as clearly as possible. You don't take me in so easily, I can tell you.

Dr. Herdal (*looks at him in amazement*). Never, Mr. Solness—never has such a thought entered my mind.

Solness (*with an incredulous smile*). Really? Has it not?

Dr. Herdal. No, never! Nor your wife's mind either, I am convinced. I could almost swear to that.

Solness. Well, I wouldn't advise you to. For, in a certain sense, you see, perhaps—perhaps she is not so far wrong in thinking something of the kind.

Dr. Herdal. Come now, I really must say——

Solness (*interrupting, with a sweep of his hand*). Well, well, my dear doctor—don't let us discuss this any further. We had better agree to differ. (*Changes to a tone of quiet amusement.*) But look here now, doctor—h'm——

Dr. Herdal. Well?

Solness. Since you don't believe that I am—ill—and crazy, and mad, and so forth——

Dr. Herdal. What then?

Solness. Then I daresay you fancy that I am an extremely happy man.

Dr. Herdal. Is that mere fancy?

Solness (*laughs*). No, no—of course not! Heaven forbid! Only think—to be Solness the master builder! Halvard Solness! What could be more delightful?

Dr. Herdal. Yes, I must say it seems to me you have had the luck on your side to an astounding degree.

Solness (*suppresses a gloomy smile*). So I have, I can't complain on that score.

Dr. Herdal. First of all that grim old robbers' castle

was burnt down for you. And that was certainly a great piece of luck.

Solness (*seriously*). It was the home of Aline's family. Remember that.

Dr. Herdal. Yes, it must have been a great grief to her.

Solness. She has not got over it to this day—not in all these twelve or thirteen years.

Dr. Herdal. Ah, but what followed must have been the worst blow for her.

Solness. The one thing with the other.

Dr. Herdal. But you—yourself—you rose upon the ruins. You began as a poor boy from a country village—and now you are at the head of your profession. Ah, yes, Mr. Solness, you have undoubtedly had the luck on your side.

Solness (*looking at him with embarrassment*). Yes, but that is just what makes me so horribly afraid.

Dr. Herdal. Afraid? Because you have the luck on your side!

Solness. It terrifies me—terrifies me every hour of the day. For sooner or later the luck must turn, you see.

Dr. Herdal. Oh nonsense! What should make the luck turn?

Solness (*with firm assurance*). The younger generation.

Dr. Herdal. Pooh! The younger generation! You are not laid on the shelf yet, I should hope. Oh no—your position here is probably firmer now than it has ever been.

Solness. The luck will turn. I know it—I feel the day approaching. Some one or other will take it into his head to say: Give me a chance! And then all the rest will come clamouring after him, and shake their fists at me and shout: Make room—make room—make room! Yes, just you see, doctor—presently the younger generation will come knock- at my door——

Dr. Herdal (*laughing*). Well, and what if they do?

Solness. What if they do? Then there's an end of Hal-vard Solness. (*There is a knock at the door on the left.*)

Solness (starts). What's that? Did you not hear something?

Dr. Herdal. Some one is knocking at the door.

Solness (loudly). Come in.

HILDA WANGEL *enters by the hall door. She is of middle height, supple, and delicately built. Somewhat sunburnt. Dressed in a tourist costume, with skirt caught up for walking, a sailor's collar open at the throat, and a small sailor hat on her head. Knapsack on back, plaid in strap, and alpenstock.*

Hilda (goes straight up to SOLNESS, *her eyes sparkling with happiness).* Good evening!

Solness (looks doubtfully at her). Good evening——

Hilda (laughs). I almost believe you don't recognise me!

Solness. No—I must admit that—just for the moment——

Dr. Herdal (approaching). But I recognise you, my dear young lady——

Hilda (pleased). Oh, is it you that——

Dr. Herdal. Of course it is. (*To* SOLNESS.) We met at one of the mountain stations this summer. (*To* HILDA.) What became of the other ladies?

Hilda. Oh, they went westward.

Dr. Herdal. They didn't much like all the fun we used to have in the evenings.

Hilda. No, I believe they didn't.

Dr. Herdal (holds up his finger at her). And I am afraid it can't be denied that you flirted a little with us.

Hilda. Well that was better fun than to sit there knitting stockings with all those old women.

Dr. Herdal (laughs). There I entirely agree with you.

Solness. Have you come to town this evening?

Hilda. Yes, I have just arrived.

Dr. Herdal. Quite alone, Miss Wangel?

Hilda. Oh yes!

Solness. Wangel? Is your name Wangel?

Hilda (*looks in amused surprise at him*). Yes, of course it is.

Solness. Then you must be a daughter of the district doctor up at Lysanger?

Hilda (*as before*). Yes, who else's daughter should I be?

Solness. Oh, then I suppose we met up there, that summer when I was building a tower on the old church.

Hilda (*more seriously*). Yes, of course it was then we met.

Solness. Well, that is a long time ago.

Hilda (*looks hard at him*). It is exactly ten years.

Solness. You must have been a mere child then, I should think.

Hilda (*carelessly*). Well, I was twelve or thirteen.

Dr. Herdal. Is this the first time you have ever been up to town, Miss Wangel?

Hilda. Yes, it is indeed.

Solness. And don't you know any one here?

Hilda. Nobody but you. And of course, your wife.

Solness. So you know her, too?

Hilda. Only a little. We spent a few days together at the sanatorium.

Solness. Ah, up there?

Hilda. She said I might come and pay her a visit if ever I came up to town. (*Smiles.*) Not that that was necessary.

Solness. Odd that she should never have mentioned it.

[HILDA *puts her stick down by the stove, takes off the knapsack and lays it and the plaid on the sofa.* DR. HERDAL *offers to help her.* SOLNESS *stands and gazes at her.*

Hilda (*going towards him*). Well, now I must ask you to let me stay the night here.

Solness. I am sure there will be no difficulty about that.

Hilda. For I have no other clothes than those I stand

in, except a change of linen in my knapsack. And that has to go to the wash, for it's very dirty.

Solness. Oh yes, that can be managed. Now I'll just let my wife know——

Dr. Herdal. Meanwhile I will go and see my patient.

Solness. Yes, do; and come again later on.

Dr. Herdal (playfully, with a glance at HILDA). Oh, that I will, you may be very certain! (*Laughs.*) So your prediction has come true, Mr. Solness!

Solness. How so?

Dr. Herdal. The younger generation did come knocking at your door.

Solness (cheerfully). Yes, but in a very different way from what I meant.

Dr. Herdal. Very different, yes. That's undeniable.

[*He goes out by the hall door.* SOLNESS *opens the door on the right and speaks into the side room.*

Solness. Aline! Will you come in here, please. Here is a friend of yours—Miss Wangel.

Mrs. Solness (appears in the doorway). Who do you say it is? (*Sees* HILDA.) Oh, is it you, Miss Wangel? (*Goes up to her and offers her hand.*) So you have come to town after all.

Solness. Miss Wangel has this moment arrived; and she would like to stay the night here.

Mrs. Solness. Here with us? Oh yes, certainly.

Solness. Till she can get her things a little in order, you know.

Mrs. Solness. I will do the best I can for you. It's no more than my duty. I suppose your trunk is coming on later?

Hilda. I have no trunk.

Mrs. Solness. Well, it will be all right, I daresay. In the meantime, you must excuse my leaving you here with my husband, until I can get a room made a little comfortable for you.

Solness. Can we not give her one of the nurseries? They are all ready as it is.

Mrs. Solness. Oh yes. There we have room and to spare. (*To* HILDA.) Sit down now, and rest a little. (*She goes out to the right.*)

> [HILDA, *with her hands behind her back, strolls about the room and looks at various objects.* SOLNESS *stands in front, beside the table, also with his hands behind his back, and follows her with his eyes.*

Hilda (*stops and looks at him*). Have you several nurseries?

Solness. There are three nurseries in the house.

Hilda. That's a lot. Then I suppose you have a great many children?

Solness. No. We have no child. But now you can be the child here, for the time being.

Hilda. For to-night, yes. I shall not cry. I mean to sleep as sound as a stone.

Solness. Yes, you must be very tired, I should think.

Hilda. Oh no! But all the same—— It's so delicious to lie and dream.

Solness. Do you dream much of nights?

Hilda. Oh yes! Almost always.

Solness. What do you dream about most?

Hilda. I shan't tell you to-night. Another time, perhaps.

> [*She again strolls about the room, stops at the desk and turns over the books and papers a little.*

Solness (*approaching*). Are you searching for anything?

Hilda. No, I am merely looking at all these things. (*Turns.*) Perhaps I mustn't?

Solness. Oh, by all means.

Hilda. Is it you that write in this great ledger?

Solness. No, it's my book-keeper.

Hilda. Is it a woman?

Solness (smiles). Yes.

Hilda. One you employ here, in your office?

Solness. Yes.

Hilda. Is she married?

Solness. No, she is single.

Hilda. Oh, indeed!

Solness. But I believe she is soon going to be married.

Hilda. That's a good thing for her.

Solness. But not such a good thing for me. For then I shall have nobody to help me.

Hilda. Can't you get hold of some one else who will do just as well?

Solness. Perhaps you would stay here and write in the ledger?

Hilda (measures him with a glance). Yes, I daresay! No, thank you—nothing of that sort for me.

> [*She again strolls across the room, and sits down in the rocking-chair.* SOLNESS *too goes to the table.*

Hilda (continuing). For there must surely be plenty of other things to be done here. (*Looks smiling at him.*) Don't you think so, too?

Solness. Of course. First of all, I suppose, you want to make a round of the shops, and get yourself up in the height of fashion.

Hilda (amused). No, I think I shall let that alone!

Solness. Indeed.

Hilda. For you must know I have run through all my money.

Solness (laughs). Neither trunk nor money, then.

Hilda. Neither one nor the other. But never mind—it doesn't matter now.

Solness. Come now, I like you for that.

Hilda. Only for that?

Solness. For that among other things. (*Sits in the armchair.*) Is your father alive still?

Hilda. Yes, father's alive.

Solness. Perhaps you are thinking of studying here?

Hilda. No, that hadn't occurred to me.

Solness. But I suppose you will be staying for some time?

Hilda. That must depend upon circumstances.

> [*She sits awhile rocking herself and looking at him, half seriously, half with a suppressed smile. Then she takes off her hat and puts it on the table in front of her.*

Hilda. Mr. Solness!

Solness. Well?

Hilda. Have you a very bad memory?

Solness. A bad memory? No, not that I am aware of.

Hilda. Then have you nothing to say to me about what happened up there?

Solness (*in momentary surprise*). Up at Lysanger? (*Indifferently.*) Why, it was nothing much to talk about, it seems to me.

Hilda (*looks reproachfully at him*). How can you sit there and say such things?

Solness. Well, then, you talk to me about it.

Hilda. When the tower was finished, we had grand doings in the town.

Solness. Yes, I shall not easily forget that day.

Hilda (*smiles*). Will you not? That comes well from you.

Solness. Comes well?

Hilda. There was music in the churchyard—and many, many hundreds of people. We school-girls were dressed in white; and we all carried flags.

Solness. Ah yes, those flags—I can tell you I remember them!

Hilda. Then you climbed right up the scaffolding, straight to the very top; and you had a great wreath with you; and you hung that wreath right away up on the weather-vane.

Solness (*curtly interrupting*). I always did that in those days. It was an old custom.

Hilda. It was so wonderfully thrilling to stand below and look up at you. Fancy, if he should fall over! He—the master builder himself!

Solness (as if to divert her from the subject). Yes, yes, yes, that might very well have happened, too. For one of those white-frocked little devils,—she went on in such a way, and screamed up at me so——

Hilda (sparkling with pleasure). "Hurrah for Master Builder Solness!" Yes!

Solness. —and waved and flourished with her flag, so that I—so that it almost made me giddy to look at it.

Hilda (in a lower voice, seriously). That little devil—that was *I*.

Solness (fixes his eyes steadily upon her). I am sure of that now. It must have been you.

Hilda (lively again). Oh, it was so gloriously thrilling! I could not have believed there was a builder in the whole world that could build such a tremendously high tower. And then, that you yourself should stand at the very top of it, as large as life! And that you should not be the least bit dizzy! It was that above everything that made one—made one dizzy to think of.

Solness. How could you be so certain that I was not——?

Hilda (scouting the idea). No indeed! Oh no! I knew that instinctively. For if you had been, you could never have stood up there and sung.

Solness (looks at her in astonishment). Sung? Did *I* sing?

Hilda. Yes, I should think you did.

Solness (shakes his head). I have never sung a note in my life.

Hilda. Yes indeed, you sang then. It sounded like harps in the air.

Solness (thoughtfully). This is very strange—all this.

Hilda (is silent awhile, looks at him and says in a low

voice:) But then,—it was after that—and the real thing happened.

Solness. The real thing?

Hilda (sparkling with vivacity). Yes, I surely don't need to remind you of that?

Solness. Oh yes, do remind me a little of that, too.

Hilda. Don't you remember that a great dinner was given in your honour at the Club?

Solness. Yes, to be sure. It must have been the same afternoon, for I left the place next morning.

Hilda. And from the Club you were invited to come round to our house to supper.

Solness. Quite right, Miss Wangel. It is wonderful how all these trifles have impressed themselves on your mind.

Hilda. Trifles! I like that! Perhaps it was a trifle, too, that I was alone in the room when you came in?

Solness. Were you alone?

Hilda (without answering him). You didn't call me a little devil then?

Solness. No, I suppose I did not.

Hilda. You said I was lovely in my white dress, and that I looked like a little princess.

Solness. I have no doubt you did, Miss Wangel.—And besides—I was feeling so buoyant and free that day——

Hilda. And then you said that when I grew up I should be your princess.

Solness (laughing a little). Dear, dear—did I say that too?

Hilda. Yes, you did. And when I asked how long I should have to wait, you said that you would come again in ten years—like a troll and carry me off—to Spain or some such place. And you promised you would buy me a kingdom there.

Solness (as before). Yes, after a good dinner one doesn't haggle about the halfpence. But did I really say all that?

Hilda (*laughs to herself*). Yes. And you told me. too what the kingdom was to be called.

Solness. Well, what was it?

Hilda. It was to be called the kingdom of Orangia,* you said.

Solness. Well, that was an appetising name.

Hilda. No, I didn't like it a bit; for it seemed as though you wanted to make game of me.

Solness. I am sure that cannot have been my intention.

Hilda. No, I should hope not—considering what you did next——

Solness. What in the world did I do next?

Hilda. Well, that's the finishing touch, if you have forgotten that too. I should have thought no one could help remembering such a thing as that.

Solness. Yes, yes, just give me a hint, and then perhaps ——Well——

Hilda (*looks fixedly at him*). You came and kissed me, Mr. Solness.

Solness (*open-mouthed, rising from his chair*). *I* did!

Hilda. Yes, indeed you did. You took me in both your arms, and bent my head back, and kissed me—many times.

Solness. Now really, my dear Miss Wangel——!

Hilda (*rises*). You surely cannot mean to deny it?

Solness. Yes, I do. I deny it altogether!

Hilda (*looks scornfully at him*). Oh, indeed!

> [*She turns and goes slowly close up to the stove, where she remains standing motionless, her face averted from him, her hands behind her back. Short pause.*

Solness (*goes cautiously up behind her*). Miss Wangel——!

Hilda (*is silent and does not move*).

Solness. Don't stand there like a statue. You must have

---

* In the original "Appelsinia," "appelsin" meaning "orange."

dreamt all this. (*Lays his hand on her arm.*) Now just listen——

Hilda (*makes an impatient movement with her arm*).

Solness (*as a thought flashes upon him*). Or——! Wait a moment! There is something under all this, you may depend!

Hilda (*does not move*).

Solness (*in a low voice, but with emphasis*). I must have thought all that. I must have wished it—have willed it— have longed to do it. And then——. May not that be the explanation?

Hilda (*is still silent*).

Solness (*impatiently*). Oh very well, deuce take it all— then I did it, I suppose.

Hilda (*turns her head a little, but without looking at him*). Then you admit it now?

Solness. Yes—whatever you like.

Hilda. You came and put your arms around me?

Solness. Oh yes!

Hilda. And bent my head back?

Solness. Very far back.

Hilda. And kissed me?

Solness. Yes, I did.

Hilda. Many times?

Solness. As many as ever you like.

Hilda (*turns quickly towards him and has once more the sparkling expression of gladness in her eyes*). Well, you see, I got it out of you at last!

Solness (*with a slight smile*). Yes—just think of my forgetting such a thing as that.

Hilda (*again a little sulky, retreats from him*). Oh, you have kissed so many people in your time, I suppose.

Solness. No, you mustn't think that of me. (HILDA *seats herself in the arm-chair.* SOLNESS *stands and leans against the rocking-chair. Looks observantly at her.*) Miss Wangel!

Hilda. Yes!

Solness. How was it now? What came of all this—between us two?

Hilda. Why, nothing more came of it. You know that quite well. For then the other guests came in, and then—bah!

Solness. Quite so! The others came in. To think of my forgetting that too!

Hilda. Oh, you haven't really forgotten anything: you are only a little ashamed of it all. I am sure one doesn't forget things of that kind.

Solness. No, one would suppose not.

Hilda (*lively again, looks at him*). Perhaps you have even forgotten what day it was?

Solness. What day——?

Hilda. Yes, on what day did you hang the wreath on the tower? Well? Tell me at once!

Solness. H'm—I confess I have forgotten the particular day. I only knew it was ten years ago. Some time in the autumn.

Hilda (*nods her head slowly several times*). It was ten years ago—on the 19th of September.

Solness. Yes, it must have been about that time. Fancy your remembering that too! (*Stops.*) But wait a moment——! Yes—it's the 19th of September to-day.

Hilda. Yes, it is; and the ten years are gone. And you didn't come—as you promised me.

Solness. Promised you? Threatened, I suppose you mean?

Hilda. I don't think there was any sort of threat in that.

Solness. Well then, a little bit of fun.

Hilda. Was that all you wanted? To make fun of me?

Solness. Well, or to have a little joke with you. Upon my soul, I don't recollect. But it must have been something of that kind; for you were a mere child then.

Hilda. Oh, perhaps I wasn't quite such a child either. Not such a mere chit as you imagine.

Solness (*looks searchingly at her*). Did you really and seriously expect me to come again?

Hilda (*conceals a half-teasing smile*). Yes, indeed; I did expect that of you.

Solness. That I should come back to your home, and take you away with me?

Hilda. Just like a troll—yes.

Solness. And make a princess of you?

Hilda. That's what you promised.

Solness. And give you a kingdom as well?

Hilda (*looks up at the ceiling*). Why not? Of course it need not have been an actual, every-day sort of kingdom.

Solness. But something else just as good?

Hilda. Yes, at least as good. (*Looks at him a moment.*) I thought, if you could build the highest church-towers in the world, you could surely manage to raise a kingdom of one sort or another as well.

Solness (*shakes his head*). I can't quite make you out, Miss Wangel.

Hilda. Can you not? To me it seems all so simple.

Solness. No, I can't make up my mind whether you mean all you say, or are simply having a joke with me.

Hilda (*smiles*). Making fun of you, perhaps? I, too?

Solness. Yes, exactly. Making fun—of both of us. (*Looks at her.*) Is it long since you found out that I was married?

Hilda. I have known it all along. Why do you ask me that?

Solness (*lightly*). Oh, well, it just occurred to me. (*Looks earnestly at her, and says in a low voice.*) What have you come for?

Hilda. I want my kingdom. The time is up.

Solness (*laughs involuntarily*). What a girl you are!

Hilda (*gaily*). Out with my kingdom, Mr. Solness! (*Raps with her fingers.*) The kingdom on the table!

Solness (*pushing the rocking-chair nearer and sitting down*). Now, seriously speaking—what have you come for? What do you really want to do here?

Hilda. Oh, first of all, I want to go around and look at all the things that you have built.

Solness. That will give you plenty of exercise.

Hilda. Yes, I know you have built a tremendous lot.

Solness. I have indeed—especially of late years.

Hilda. Many church-towers among the rest? Immensely high ones?

Solness. No. I build no more church-towers now. Nor churches either.

Hilda. What do you build then?

Solness. Homes for human beings.

Hilda (*reflectively*). Couldn't you build a little—a little bit of a church-tower over these homes as well?

Solness (*starting*). What do you mean by that?

Hilda. I mean—something that points—points up into the free air. With the vane at a dizzy height.

Solness (*pondering a little*). Strange that you should say that—for that is just what I am most anxious to do.

Hilda (*impatiently*). Why don't you do it, then?

Solness (*shakes his head*). No, the people will not have it.

Hilda. Fancy their not wanting it!

Solness (*more lightly*). But now I am building a new home for myself—just opposite here.

Hilda. For yourself?

Solness. Yes. It is almost finished. And on that there is a tower.

Hilda. A high tower?

Solness. Yes.

Hilda. Very high?

Solness. No doubt people will say it is too high—too high for a dwelling-house.

Hilda. I'll go out and look at that tower the first thing to-morrow morning.

Solness (*sits resting his cheek on his hand, and gazes at her*). Tell me, Miss Wangel—what is your name? Your Christian name, I mean?

Hilda. Why, Hilda, of course.

Solness (*as before*). Hilda? Indeed?

Hilda. Don't you remember that? You called me Hilda yourself—that day when you misbehaved.

Solness. Did I really?

Hilda. But then you said "little Hilda"; and I didn't like that.

Solness. Oh, you didn't like that, Miss Hilda?

Hilda. No, not at such a time as that. But—"Princess Hilda"—that will sound very well, I think.

Solness. Very well indeed. Princess Hilda of—of—, what was to be the name of the kingdom?

Hilda. Pooh! I won't have anything to do with that stupid kingdom. I have set my heart upon quite a different one!

Solness (*has leaned back in the chair, still gazing at her*). Isn't it strange——? The more I think of it now, the more it seems to me as though I had gone about all these years torturing myself with—h'm——

Hilda. With what?

Solness. With the effort to recover something—some experience, which I seemed to have forgotten. But I never had the least inkling of what it could be.

Hilda. You should have tied a knot in your pockethandkerchief, Mr. Solness.

Solness. In that case, I should simply have had to go racking my brains to discover what the knot could mean.

Hilda. Oh, yes, I suppose there are trolls of that kind in the world, too.

Solness (*rises slowly*). What a good thing it is that you have come to me now.

Hilda (*looks deeply into his eyes*). Is it a good thing?

Solness. For I have been so lonely here. I have been

gazing so helplessly at it all. (*In a lower voice.*) I must tell you—I have begun to be so afraid—so terribly afraid of the younger generation.

Hilda (*with a little snort of contempt*). Pooh—is the younger generation a thing to be afraid of?

Solness. It is indeed. And that is why I have locked and barred myself in. (*Mysteriously.*) I tell you the younger generation will one day come and thunder at my door! They will break in upon me!

Hilda. Then I should say you ought to go out and open the door to the younger generation.

Solness. Open the door?

Hilda. Yes. Let them come in to you on friendly terms, as it were.

Solness. No, no, no! The younger generation—it means retribution, you see. It comes, as if under a new banner, heralding the turn of fortune.

Hilda (*rises, looks at him, and says with a quivering twitch of her lips*). Can I be of any use to you, Mr. Solness?

Solness. Yes, you can indeed! For you, too, come—under a new banner, it seems to me. Youth marshalled against youth——!

DR. HERDAL *comes in by the hall-door.*

Dr. Herdal. What—you and Miss Wangel here still?

Solness. Yes. We have had no end of things to talk about.

Hilda. Both old and new.

Dr. Herdal. Have you really?

Hilda. Oh, it has been the greatest fun. For Mr. Solness —he has such a miraculous memory. All the least little details he remembers instantly.

MRS. SOLNESS *enters by the door on the right.*

Mrs. Solness. Well, Miss Wangel, your room is quite ready for you now.

Hilda. Oh, how kind you are to me!

Solness (*to* MRS. SOLNESS). The nursery?

Mrs. Solness. Yes, the middle one. But first let us go in to supper.

Solness (*nods to* HILDA). Hilda shall sleep in the nursery, she shall.

Mrs. Solness (*looks at him*). Hilda?

Solness. Yes, Miss Wangel's name is Hilda. I knew her when she was a child.

Mrs. Solness. Did you really, Halvard? Well, shall we go? Supper is on the table.

> [*She takes* DR. HERDAL'S *arm and goes out with him to the right.* HILDA *has meanwhile been collecting her travelling things.*

Hilda (*softly and rapidly to* SOLNESS). Is it true, what you said? Can I be of use to you?

Solness (*takes the things from her*). You are the very being I have needed most.

Hilda (*looks at him with happy, wondering eyes and clasps her hands*). But then, great heavens——!

Solness (*eagerly*). What——?

Hilda. Then I have my kingdom!

Solness (*involuntarily*). Hilda——!

Hilda (*again with the quivering twitch of her lips*). Almost—I was going to say.

> [*She goes out to the right,* SOLNESS *follows her.*]

ACT II

A prettily furnished small drawing-room in SOLNESS'S *house.
In the back, a glass door leading out to the veranah and
garden. The right-hand corner is cut off transversely by
a large bay-window, in which are flower-stands. The
left-hand corner is similarly cut off by a transverse wall,
in which is a small door papered like the wall. On each
side, an ordinary door. In front, on the right, a console
table with a large mirror over it. Well-filled stands of
plants and flowers. In front, on the left, a sofa with a
table and chairs. Further back, a bookcase. Well forward in the room, before the bay window, a small table
and some chairs. It is early in the day.*

SOLNESS *sits by the little table with* RAGNAR BROVIK'S *portfolio open in front of him. He is turning the drawings
over and closely examining some of them.* MRS. SOL-
NESS *moves about noiselessly with a small watering-pot,
attending to her flowers. She is dressed in black as
before. Her hat, cloak and parasol lie on a chair near
the mirror. Unobserved by her,* SOLNESS *now and again
follows her with his eyes. Neither of them speaks.*

KAIA FOSLI *enters quietly by the door on the left.*

Solness (*turns his head, and says in an off-hand tone of
indifference*). Well, is that you?

Kaia. I merely wished to let you know that I have come.

Solness. Yes, yes, that's all right. Hasn't Ragnar come
too?

Kaia. No, not yet. He had to wait a little while to see
the doctor. But he is coming presently to hear—

38

Solness. How is the old man to-day?

Kaia. Not well. He begs you to excuse him; he is obliged to keep his bed to-day.

Solness. Why, of course; by all means let him rest. But now, get to work.

Kaia. Yes. (*Pauses at the door.*) Do you wish to speak to Ragnar when he comes?

Solness. No—I don't know that I have anything particular to say to him.

[KAIA *goes out again to the left.* SOLNESS *remains seated, turning over the drawings.*

Mrs. Solness (*over beside the plants*). I wonder if he isn't going to die now, as well?

Solness (*looks up to her*). As well as who?

Mrs. Solness (*without answering*). Yes, yes—depend upon it, Halvard, old Brovik is going to die too. You'll see that he will.

Solness. My dear Aline, ought you not to go out for a little walk?

Mrs. Solness. Yes, I suppose I ought to.

[*She continues to attend to the flowers.*

Solness (*bending over the drawings*). Is she still asleep?

Mrs. Solness (*looking at him*). Is it Miss Wangel you are sitting there thinking about?

Solness (*indifferently*). I just happened to recollect her.

Mrs. Solness. Miss Wangel was up long ago.

Solness. Oh, was she?

Mrs. Solness. When I went in to see her, she was busy putting her things in order.

[*She goes in front of the mirror and slowly begins to put on her hat.*

Solness (*after a short pause*). So we have found a use for one of our nurseries after all, Aline.

Mrs. Solness. Yes, we have.

Solness. That seems to me better than to have them all standing empty.

Mrs. Solness. That emptiness is dreadful; you are right there.

Solness (closes the portfolio, rises and approaches her). You will find that we shall get on far better after this, Aline. Things will be more comfortable. Life will be easier—especially for you.

Mrs. Solness (looks at him). After this?

Solness. Yes, believe me, Aline——

Mrs. Solness. Do you mean—because she has come here?

Solness (checking himself). I mean, of course—when once we have moved into the new house.

Mrs. Solness (takes her cloak). Ah, do you think so, Halvard? Will it be better then?

Solness. I can't think otherwise. And surely you think so too?

Mrs. Solness. I think nothing at all about the new house.

Solness (cast down). It's hard for me to hear you say that; for you know it is mainly for your sake that I have built it.

[*He offers to help her on with her cloak.*

Mrs. Solness (evades him). The fact is, you do far too much for my sake.

Solness (with a certain vehemence). No, no, you really mustn't say that, Aline! I cannot bear to hear you say such things!

Mrs. Solness. Very well, then I won't say it, Halvard.

Solness. But I stick to what *I* said. You'll see that things will be easier for you in the new place.

Mrs. Solness. O heavens—easier for me——!

Solness (eagerly). Yes, indeed they will! You may be quite sure of that! For you see—there will be so very, very much there that will remind you of your own home——

Mrs. Solness. The home that used to be father's and mother's—and that was burnt to the ground——

Solness (in a low voice). Yes, yes, my poor Aline. That was a terrible blow for you.

Mrs. Solness (*breaking out in lamentation*). You may build as much as ever you like, Halvard—you can never build up again a real home for me!

Solness (*crosses the room*). Well, in heaven's name, let us talk no more about it then.

Mrs. Solness. Oh yes, Halvard, I understand you very well. You are so anxious to spare me—and to find excuses for me too—as much as ever you can.

Solness (*with astonishment in his eyes*). You! Is it you —yourself, that you are talking about, Aline?

Mrs. Solness. Yes, who else should it be but myself?

Solness (*involuntarily to himself*). That too!

Mrs. Solness. As for the old house, I wouldn't mind so much about that. When once misfortune was in the air— why——

Solness. Ah, you are right there. Misfortune will have its way—as the saying goes.

Mrs. Solness. But it's what came of the fire—the dreadful thing that followed——! That is the thing! That, that, that!

Solness (*vehemently*). Don't think about that, Aline!

Mrs. Solness. Ah, that is exactly what I cannot help thinking about. And now, at last, I must speak about it, too; for I don't seem able to bear it any longer. And then never to be able to forgive myself——

Solness. (*exclaiming*). Yourself——!

Mrs. Solness. Yes, for I had duties on both sides—both towards you and towards the little ones. I ought to have hardened myself—not to have let the horror take such hold upon me—nor the grief for the burning of my old home. (*Wrings her hands.*) Oh, Halvard, if I had only had the strength!

Solness (*softly, much moved, comes closer*). Aline—you must promise me never to think these thoughts any more.— Promise me that, dear!

Mrs. Solness. Oh, promise, promise! One can promise anything.

Solness (*clenches his hands and crosses the room*). Oh, but this is hopeless, hopeless! Never a ray of sunlight! Not so much as a gleam of brightness to light up our home!

Mrs. Solness. This is no home, Halvard.

Solness. Oh no, you may well say that. (*Gloomily*). And God knows whether you are not right in saying that it will be no better for us in the new house, either.

Mrs. Solness. It will never be any better. Just as empty —just as desolate—there as here.

Solness (*vehemently*). Why in all the world have we built it then? Can you tell me that?

Mrs. Solness. No; you must answer that question for yourself.

Solness (*glances suspiciously at her*). What do you mean by that, Aline?

Mrs. Solness. What do I mean?

Solness. Yes, in the devil's name! You said it so strangely—as if you had hidden some meaning in it.

Mrs. Solness. No, indeed, I assure you——

Solness (*comes closer*). Oh, come now—I know what I know. I have both my eyes and my ears about me, Aline— you may depend upon that!

Mrs. Solness. Why what are you talking about? What is it?

Solness (*places himself in front of her*). Do you mean to say you don't find a kind of lurking, hidden meaning in the most innocent word I happen to say?

Mrs. Solness. I, do you say? I do that?

Solness (*laughs*). Ho-ho-ho! It's natural enough, Aline! When you have a sick man on your hands——

Mrs. Solness (*anxiously*). Sick? Are you ill, Halvard?

Solness (*violently*). A half-mad man then! A crazy man! Call me what you will.

Mrs. Solness (feels blindly for a chair and sits down). Halvard—for God's sake——

Solness. But you are wrong, both you and the doctor. I am not in the state you imagine.

> [*He walks up and down the room.* MRS. SOLNESS *follows him anxiously with her eyes. Finally he goes up to her.*

Solness (calmly). In reality there is nothing whatever the matter with me.

Mrs. Solness. No, there isn't, is there? But then what is it that troubles you so?

Solness. Why this, that I often feel ready to sink under this terrible burden of debt——

Mrs. Solness. Debt, do you say? But you owe no one anything, Halvard!

Solness (softly, with emotion). I owe a boundless debt to you—to you—to you, Aline.

Mrs. Solness (rises slowly). What is behind all this? You may just as well tell me at once.

Solness. But there is nothing behind it; I have never done you any wrong—not wittingly and wilfully, at any rate. And yet—and yet it seems as though a crushing debt rested upon me and weighed me down.

Mrs. Solness. A debt to me?

Solness. Chiefly to you.

Mrs. Solness. Then you are—ill after all, Halvard.

Solness (gloomily). I suppose I must be—or not far from it. (*Looks towards the door to the right, which is opened at this moment.*) Ah! now it grows lighter.

HILDA WANGEL *comes in. She has made some alteration in her dress, and let down her skirt.*

Hilda. Good morning, Mr. Solness!

Solness (nods). Slept well?

Hilda. Quite deliciously! Like a child in a cradle. Oh —I lay and stretched myself like—like a princess!

Solness (smiles a little). You were thoroughly comfort-able then?

Hilda. I should think so.

Solness. And no doubt you dreamed, too.

Hilda. Yes, I did. But that was horrid.

Solness. Was it?

Hilda. Yes, for I dreamed I was falling over a frightfully high, sheer precipice. Do you never have that kind of dream?

Solness. Oh yes—now and then——

Hilda. It's tremendously thrilling—when you fall and fall——

Solness. It seems to make one's blood run cold.

Hilda. Do you draw your legs up under you while you are falling?

Solness. Yes, as high as ever I can.

Hilda. So do I.

Mrs. Solness (takes her parasol). I must go into town now, Halvard. (*To* Hilda.) And I'll try to get one or two things that you may require.

Hilda (making a motion to throw her arms round her neck). Oh, you dear, sweet Mrs. Solness! You are really much too kind to me! Frightfully kind——

Mrs. Solness (deprecatingly, freeing herself). Oh, not at all. It's only my duty, so I am very glad to do it.

Hilda (offended, pouts). But really, I think I am quite fit to be seen in the streets—now that I've put my dress to rights. Or do you think I am not?

Mrs. Solness. To tell you the truth, I think people would stare at you a little.

Hilda (contemptuously). Pooh! Is that all? That only amuses me.

Solness (with suppressed ill-humour). Yes, but people might take it into their heads that you were mad too, you see.

Hilda. Mad? Are there so many mad people here in town, then?

Solness (*points to his own forehead*). Here you see one at all events.

Hilda. You——Mr. Solness!

Mrs. Solness. Oh, don't talk like that, my dear Halvard!

Solness. Have you not noticed that yet?

Hilda. No, I certainly have not. (*Reflects and laughs a little.*) And yet—perhaps in one single thing.

Solness. Ah, do you hear that, Aline?

Mrs. Solness. What is that one single thing, Miss Wangel?

Hilda. No, I won't say.

Solness. Oh yes, do!

Hilda. No thank you—I am not so mad as that.

Mrs. Solness. When you and Miss Wangel are alone, I daresay she will tell you, Halvard.

Solness. Ah—you think she will?

Mrs. Solness. Oh yes, certainly. For you have known her so well in the past. Ever since she was a child—you tell me.

[*She goes out by the door on the left.*

Hilda (*after a little while*). Does your wife dislike me very much?

Solness. Did you think you noticed anything of the kind?

Hilda. Did you not notice it yourself?

Solness (*evasively*). Aline has become exceedingly shy with strangers of late years.

Hilda. Has she really?

Solness. But if only you could get to know her thoroughly——! Ah! she is so good—so kind—so excellent a creature——

Hilda (*impatiently*). But if she is all that—what made her say that about her duty?

Solness. Her duty?

Hilda. She said that she would go out and buy something for me, because it was her duty. Oh I can't bear that ugly, horrid word!

Solness. Why not?

Hilda. It sounds so cold, and sharp, and stinging. Duty —duty—duty. Don't you think so, too? Doesn't it seem to sting you?

Solness. H'm—haven't thought much about it.

Hilda. Yes, it does. And if she is so good—as you say she is—why should she talk in that way?

Solness. But, good Lord, what would you have had her say, then?

Hilda. She might have said she would do it because she had taken a tremendous fancy to me. She might have said something like that—something really warm and cordial, you understand.

Solness (*looks at her*). Is that how you would like to have it?

Hilda. Yes, precisely. (*She wanders about the room, stops at the bookcase and looks at the books.*) What a lot of books you have.

Solness. Yes, I have got together a good many.

Hilda. Do you read them all, too?

Solness. I used to try to. Do you read much?

Hilda. No, never! I have given it up. For it all seems so irrelevant.

Solness. That is just my feeling.

[HILDA *wanders about a little, stops at the small table, opens the portfolio and turns over the contents.*

Hilda. Are all these drawings yours?

Solness. No, they are drawn by a young man whom I employ to help me.

Hilda. Some one you have taught?

Solness. Oh yes, no doubt he has learnt something from me, too.

Hilda (*sits down*). Then I suppose he is very clever. (*Looks at a drawing.*) Isn't he?

Solness. Oh, he might be worse. For my purpose——

Hilda. Oh yes—I'm sure he is frightfully clever.

Solness. Do you think you can see that in the drawings?

Hilda. Pooh—these scrawlings! But if he has been learning from you——

Solness. Oh, so far as that goes—there are plenty of people that have learnt from me, and have come to little enough for all that.

Hilda (*looks at him and shakes her head*). No, I can't for the life of me understand how you can be so stupid.

Solness. Stupid? Do you think I am so very stupid?

Hilda. Yes, I do indeed. If you are content to go about here teaching all these people——

Solness (*with a slight start*). Well, and why not?

Hilda (*rises, half serious, half laughing*). No indeed, Mr. Solness! What can be the good of that? No one but you should be allowed to build. You should stand quite alone —do it all yourself. Now you know it.

Solness (*involuntarily*). Hilda——!

Hilda. Well!

Solness. How in the world did that come into your head?

Hilda. Do you think I am so very far wrong then?

Solness. No, that's not what I mean. But now I'll tell you something.

Hilda. Well?

Solness. I keep on—incessantly—in silence and alone— brooding on that very thought.

Hilda. Yes, that seems to me perfectly natural.

Solness (*looks somewhat searchingly at her*). Perhaps you have noticed it already?

Hilda. No, indeed I haven't.

Solness. But just now—when you said you thought I was—off my balance? In one thing, you said——

Hilda. Oh, I was thinking of something quite different.

Solness. What was it?

Hilda. I am not going to tell you.

Solness (*crosses the room*). Well, well—as you please.

(*Stops at the bow-window.*) Come here, and I will show you something.

Hilda (*approaching*). What is it?

Solness. Do you see—over there in the garden——?

Hilda. Yes?

Solness (*points*). Right above the great quarry——?

Hilda. That new house, you mean?

Solness. The one that is being built, yes. Almost finished.

Hilda. It seems to have a very high tower.

Solness. The scaffolding is still up.

Hilda. Is that your new house?

Solness. Yes.

Hilda. The house you are soon going to move into?

Solness. Yes.

Hilda (*looks at him*). Are there nurseries in that house, too?

Solness. Three, as there are here.

Hilda. And no child,

Solness. And there never will be one.

Hilda (*with a half-smile*). Well, isn't it just as I said—?

Solness. That——?

Hilda. That you are a little—a little mad after all.

Solness. Was that what you were thinking of?

Hilda. Yes, of all the empty nurseries I slept in.

Solness (*lowers his voice*). We have had children—Aline and I.

Hilda (*looks eagerly at him*). Have you——?

Solness. Two little boys. They were of the same age.

Hilda. Twins, then.

Solness. Yes, twins. It's eleven or twelve years ago now.

Hilda (*cautiously*). And so both of them——? You have lost both the twins, then?

Solness (*with quiet emotion*). We kept them only about three weeks. Or scarcely so much. (*Bursts forth.*) Oh, Hilda, I can't tell you what a good thing it is for me that

you have come! For now at last I have some one I can talk to!

Hilda. Can you not talk to—her, too?

Solness. Not about this. Not as I want to talk and must talk. (*Gloomily.*) And not about so many other things, either.

Hilda (*in a subdued voice*). Was that all you meant when you said you needed me?

Solness. That was mainly what I meant—at all events, yesterday. For to-day I am not so sure—(*Breaking off.*) Come here and let us sit down, Hilda. Sit there on the sofa —so that you can look into the garden. (HILDA *seats herself in the corner of the sofa.* SOLNESS *brings a chair closer.*) Should you like to hear about it?

Hilda. Yes, I shall love to sit and listen to you.

Solness (*sits down*). Then I will tell you all about it.

Hilda. Now I can see both the garden and you, Mr. Solness. So now, tell away! Begin!

Solness (*points towards the bow-window*). Out there on the rising ground—where you see the new house——

Hilda. Yes?

Solness. Aline and I lived there in the first years of our married life. There was an old house up there that had belonged to her mother; and we inherited it, and the whole of the great garden with it.

Hilda. Was there a tower on that house, too?

Solness. No, nothing of the kind. From the outside it looked like a great, dark, ugly wooden box; but all the same, it was snug and comfortable enough inside.

Hilda. Then did you pull down the ramshackle old place?

Solness. No, it burnt down.

Hilda. The whole of it?

Solness. Yes.

Hilda. Was that a great misfortune for you?

Solness. That depends on how you look at it. As a builder, the fire was the making of me——

Hilda. Well, but——?

Solness. It was just after the birth of the two little boys——

Hilda. The poor little twins, yes.

Solness. They came healthy and bonny into the world. And they were growing too—you could see the difference from day to day.

Hilda. Little children do grow quickly at first.

Solness. It was the prettiest sight in the world to see Aline lying with the two of them in her arms.—But then came the night of the fire——

Hilda (*excitedly*). What happened? Do tell me! Was any one burnt?

Solness. No, not that. Every one got safe and sound out of the house——

Hilda. Well, and what then——?

Solness. The fright had shaken Aline terribly. The alarm—the escape—the break-neck hurry—and then the ice-cold night air—for they had to be carried out just as they lay—both she and the little ones.

Hilda. Was it too much for them?

Solness. Oh no, they stood it well enough. But Aline fell into a fever, and it affected her milk. She would insist on nursing them herself; because it was her duty, she said. And both our little boys, they—(*clenching his hands.*)— they—oh!

Hilda. They did not get over that?

Solness. No, that they did not get over. That was how we lost them.

Hilda. It must have been terribly hard for you.

Solness. Hard enough for me; but ten times harder for Aline. (*Clenching his hands in suppressed fury.*) Oh, that such things should be allowed to happen here in the world! (*Shortly and firmly.*) From the day I lost them, I had no heart for building churches.

Hilda. Did you not like the church-tower in our town?

Solness. I didn't like it. I know how free and happy I felt when that tower was finished.

Hilda. *I* know that, too.

Solness. And now I shall never—never build anything of that sort again! Neither churches nor church-towers.

Hilda (*nods slowly*). Nothing but houses for people to live in.

Solness. Homes for human beings, Hilda.

Hilda. But homes with high towers and pinnacles upon them.

Solness. If possible. (*Adopts a lighter tone.*) But, as I said before, that fire was the making of me—as a builder, I mean.

Hilda. Why don't you call yourself an architect, like the others?

Solness. I have not been systematically enough taught for that. Most of what I know I have found out for myself.

Hilda. But you succeeded all the same.

Solness. Yes, thanks to the fire. I laid out almost the whole of the garden in villa lots; and there I was able to build after my own heart. So I came to the front with a rush.

Hilda (*looks keenly at him*). You must surely be a very happy man, as matters stand with you.

Solness (*gloomily*). Happy? Do you say that, too—like all the rest of them?

Hilda. Yes, I should say you must be. If you could only cease thinking about the two little children——

Solness (*slowly*). The two little children—they are not so easy to forget, Hilda.

Hilda (*somewhat uncertainly*). Do you still feel their loss so much—after all these years?

Solness (*looks fixedly at her, without replying*). A happy man you said——

Hilda. Well, now, are you not happy—in other respects?

Solness (continues to look at her). When I told you all
this about the fire—h'm——

Hilda. Well?

Solness. Was there not one special thought that you—
that you seized upon?

Hilda (reflects in vain) No. What thought should that
be?

Solness (with subdued emphasis). It was simply and
solely by that fire that I was enabled to build homes for
human beings. Cosy, comfortable, bright homes, where
father and mother and the whole troop of children can live
in safety and gladness, feeling what a happy thing it is to
be alive in the world—and most of all to belong to each
other—in great things and in small.

Hilda (ardently). Well, and is it not a great happiness
for you to be able to build such beautiful homes?

Solness. The price, Hilda! The terrible price I had to
pay for the opportunity!

Hilda. But can you never get over that?

Solness. No. That I might build homes for others, I
had to forego—to forego for all time—the home that might
have been my own. I mean a home for a troop of children
—and for father and mother, too.

Hilda (cautiously). But need you have done that? For
all time, you say?

Solness (nods slowly). That was the price of this happiness that people talk about. (*Breathes heavily.*) This happiness—h'm—this happiness was not to be bought any
cheaper, Hilda.

Hilda (as before). But may it not come right even yet?

Solness. Never in this world—never. That is another
consequence of the fire—and of Aline's illness afterwards.

Hilda (looks at him with an indefinable expression). And
yet you build all these nurseries?

Solness (seriously). Have you never noticed, Hilda, how

the impossible—how it seems to beckon and cry aloud to one?

Hilda (*reflecting*). The impossible? (*With animation.*) Yes, indeed! Is that how you feel too?

Solness. Yes, I do.

Hilda. There must be—a little of the troll in you too.

Solness. Why of the troll?

Hilda. What would you call it, then?

Solness (*rises*). Well, well, perhaps you are right. (*Vehemently*). But how can I help turning into a troll, when this is how it always goes with me in everything—in everything!

Hilda. How do you mean?

Solness (*speaking low, with inward emotion*). Mark what I say to you, Hilda. All that I have succeeded in doing, building, creating—all the beauty, security, cheerful comfort—ay, and magnificence too—(*Clenches his hands.*) Oh, is it not terrible even to think of——!

Hilda. What is so terrible?

Solness. That all this I have to make up for, to pay for —not in money, but in human happiness. And not with my own happiness only, but with other people's too. Yes, yes, do you see that, Hilda? That is the price which my position as an artist has cost me—and others. And every single day I have to look on while the price is paid for me anew. Over again, and over again—and over again for ever!

Hilda (*rises and looks steadily at him*). Now I can see that you are thinking of—of her.

Solness. Yes, mainly of Aline. For Aline—she, too, had her vocation in life, just as much as I had mine. (*His voice quivers.*) But her vocation has had to be stunted, and crushed, and shattered—in order that mine might force its way to—to a sort of great victory. For you must know that Aline—she, too, had a talent for building.

Hilda. She! For building?

Solness (*shakes his head*). Not houses and towers, and spires—not such things as I work away at——

Hilda. Well, but what then?

Solness (*softly, with emotion*). For building up the souls of little children, Hilda. For building up children's souls in perfect balance, and in noble and beautiful forms. For enabling them to soar up into erect and full-grown human souls. That was Aline's talent. And there it all lies now—unused and unusable for ever—of no earthly service to any one—just like the ruins left by a fire.

Hilda. Yes, but even if this were so——?

Solness. It is so! It is so! I know it!

Hilda. Well, but in any case it is not your fault.

Solness (*fixes his eyes on her, and nods slowly*). Ah, that is the great, terrible question. That is the doubt that is gnawing me—night and day.

Hilda. That?

Solness. Yes. Suppose the fault was mine—in a certain sense.

Hilda. Your fault! The fire!

Solness. All of it; the whole thing. And yet, perhaps—I may not have had anything to do with it.

Hilda (*looks at him with a troubled expression*). Oh, Mr. Solness—if you can talk like that, I am afraid you must be —ill, after all.

Solness. H'm—I don't think I shall ever be of quite sound mind on that point.

RAGNAR BROVIK *cautiously opens the little door in the left-hand corner.* HILDA *comes forward.*

Ragnar (*when he sees* HILDA). Oh. I beg pardon, Mr. Solness—(*He makes a movement to withdraw.*)

Solness. No, no, don't go. Let us get it over.

Ragnar. Oh, yes—if only we could.

Solness. I hear your father is no better?

Ragnar. Father is fast growing weaker—and therefore I beg and implore you to write a few kind words for me on one of the plans! Something for father to read before he—

Solness (*vehemently*). I won't hear anything more about those drawings of yours!

Ragnar. Have you looked at them?

Solness. Yes—I have.

Ragnar. And they are good for nothing? And *I* am good for nothing, too?

Solness (*evasively*). Stay here with me, Ragnar. You shall have everything your own way. And then you can marry Kaia, and live at your ease—and happily too, who knows? Only don't think of building on your own account.

Ragnar. Well, well, then I must go home and tell father what you say—I promised I would.—Is this what I am to tell father—before he dies?

Solness (*with a groan*). Oh tell him—tell him what you will, for me. Best to say nothing at all to him! (*With a sudden outburst*). I cannot do anything else, Ragnar!

Ragnar. May I have the drawings to take with me?

Solness. Yes, take them—take them by all means! They are lying there on the table.

Ragnar (*goes to the table*). Thanks.

Hilda (*puts her hand on the portfolio*). No, no; leave them here.

Solness. Why?

Hilda. Because I want to look at them, too.

Solness. But you have been—— (*To* RAGNAR). Well, leave them here, then.

Ragnar. Very well.

Solness. And go home at once to your father.

Ragnar. Yes. I suppose I must.

Solness (*as if in desperation*). Ragnar—you must not ask me to do what is beyond my power! Do you hear, Ragnar? You must not!

Ragnar. No, no. I beg your pardon——

[*He bows, and goes out by the corner door.* HILDA

goes over and sits down on a chair near the mirror.

Hilda (*looks angrily at* SOLNESS). That was a very ugly thing to do.

Solness. Do you think so, too?

Hilda. Yes, it was horribly ugly—and hard and bad and cruel as well.

Solness. Oh, you don't understand my position.

Hilda. No matter——. I say you ought not to be like that.

Solness. You said yourself, only just now, that no one but *I* ought to be allowed to build.

Hilda. *I* may say such things—but you must not.

Solness. I most of all, surely, who have paid so dear for my position.

Hilda. Oh yes—with what you call domestic comfort—and that sort of thing.

Solness. And with my peace of soul into the bargain.

Hilda (*rising*). Peace of soul! (*With feeling.*) Yes, yes, you are right in that! Poor Mr. Solness—you fancy that—

Solness (*with a quiet, chuckling laugh*). Just sit down again, Hilda, and I'll tell you something funny.

Hilda (*sits down; with intent interest*). Well?

Solness. It sounds such a ludicrous little thing; for, you see, the whole story turns upon nothing but a crack in a chimney.

Hilda. No more than that?

Solness. No, not to begin with.

[*He moves a chair nearer to* HILDA *and sits down.*

Hilda (*impatiently, taps on her knee*). Well, now for the crack in the chimney!

Solness. I had noticed the split in the flue long, long before the fire. Every time I went up into the attic, I looked to see if it was still there.

Hilda. And it was?

Solness. Yes; for no one else knew about it.

Hilda. And you said nothing?

Solness. Nothing.

Hilda. And did not think of repairing the flue either?

Solness. Oh yes, I thought about it—but never got any further. Every time I intended to set to work, it seemed just as if a hand held me back. Not to-day, I thought—to-morrow; and nothing ever came of it.

Hilda. But why did you keep putting it off like that?

Solness. Because I was revolving something in my mind. (*Slowly, and in a low voice.*) Through that little black crack in the chimney, I might, perhaps, force my way upwards—as a builder.

Hilda (*looking straight in front of her*). That must have been thrilling.

Solness. Almost irresistible—quite irresistible. For at that time it apeared to me a perfectly simple and straightforward matter. I would have had it happen in the wintertime—a little before midday. I was to be out driving Aline in the sleigh. The servants at home would have made huge fires in the stoves.

Hilda. For, of course, it was to be bitterly cold that day?

Solness. Rather biting, yes—and they would want Aline to find it thoroughly snug and warm when she came home.

Hilda. I suppose she is very chilly by nature?

Solness. She is. And as we drove home, we were to see the smoke.

Hilda. Only the smoke?

Solness. The smoke first. But when we came up to the garden gate, the whole of the old timber-box was to be a rolling mass of flames.—That is how I wanted it to be, you see.

Hilda. Oh why, why could it not have happened so!

Solness. You may well say that, Hilda.

Hilda. Well, but now listen, Mr. Solness. Are you perfectly certain that the fire was caused by that little crack in the chimney?

Solness. No, on the contrary—I am perfectly certain that the crack in the chimney had nothing whatever to do with the fire.

Hilda. What?

Solness. It has been clearly ascertained that the fire broke out in a clothes-cupboard—in a totally different part of the house.

Hilda. Then what is all this nonsense you are talking about the crack in the chimney?

Solness. May I go on talking to you a little, Hilda?

Hilda. Yes, if you'll only talk sensibly——

Solness. I will try. (*He moves his chair nearer.*)

Hilda. Out with it, then, Mr. Solness.

Solness (*confidentially*). Don't you agree with me, Hilda, that there exist special, chosen people who have been endowed with the power and faculty of desiring a thing, craving for a thing, willing a thing—so persistently and so—so inexorably—that at last it has to happen? Don't you believe that?

Hilda (*with an indefinable expression in her eyes*). If that is so, we shall see, one of these days, whether *I* am one of the chosen.

Solness. It is not one's self alone that can do such great things. Oh, no—the helpers and the servers—they must do their part too, if it is to be of any good. But they never come of themselves. One has to call upon them very persistently—inwardly, you understand.

Hilda. What are these helpers and servers?

Solness. Oh, we can talk about that some other time. For the present, let us keep to this business of the fire.

Hilda. Don't you think that fire would have happened all the same—even without your wishing for it?

Solness. If the house had been old Knut Brovik's, it would never have burnt down so conveniently for him. I am sure of that; for he does not know how to call for the helpers—no, nor for the servers, either. (*Rises in unrest.*)

So you see, Hilda—it is my fault, after all, that the lives of the two little boys had to be sacrificed. And do you think it is not my fault, too, that Aline has never been the woman she should and might have been—and that she most longed to be?

Hilda. Yes, but if it is all the work of those helpers and servers——?

Solness. Who called for the helpers and servers? It was I! And they came and obeyed my will. (*In increasing excitement.*) That is what people call having the luck on your side; but I must tell you what this sort of luck feels like! It feels like a great raw place here on my breast. And the helpers and servers keep on flaying pieces of skin off other people in order to close my sore!—But still the sore is not healed—never, never! Oh, if you knew how it can sometimes gnaw and burn.

Hilda (*looks attentively at him*). You are ill, Mr. Solness. Very ill, I almost think.

Solness. Say mad; for that is what you mean.

Hilda. No, I don't think there is much amiss with your intellect.

Solness. With what then? Out with it!

Hilda. I wonder whether you were not sent into the world with a sickly conscience.

Solness. A sickly conscience? What devilry is that?

Hilda. I mean that your conscience is feeble—too delicately built, as it were—hasn't strength to take a grip of things—to lift and bear what is heavy.

Solness (*growls*). H'm! May I ask, then, what sort of conscience one ought to have?

Hilda. I should like your conscience to be—to be thoroughly robust.

Solness. Indeed? Robust, eh? Is your own conscience robust, may I ask?

Hilda. Yes, I think it is. I have never noticed that it wasn't.

Solness. It has not been put very severely to the test, I should think.

Hilda (with a quivering of the lips). Oh, it was no such simple matter to leave father—I am so awfully fond of him.

Solness. Dear me! for a month or two——

Hilda. I think I shall never go home again.

Solness. Never? Then why did you leave him?

Hilda (half-seriously, half-banteringly). Have **you** forgotten that the ten years are up?

Solness. Oh nonsense. Was anything wrong at home? Eh?

Hilda (quite seriously). It was this impulse within me that urged and goaded me to come—and lured and drew me on, as well.

Solness (eagerly). There we have it! There we have it, Hilda! There is a troll in you too, as in me. For it's the troll in one, you see—it is that that calls to the powers outside us. And then you must give in—whether you will or no.

Hilda. I almost think you are right, Mr. Solness.

Solness (walks about the room). Oh, there are devils innumerable abroad in the world, Hilda, that one never sees!

Hilda. Devils, too?

Solness (stops). Good devils and bad devils; light-haired devils and black-haired devils. If only you could always tell whether it is the light or dark ones that have got hold of you! *(Paces about.)* Ho-ho! Then it would be simple enough.

Hilda (follows him with her eyes). Or if one had a really vigorous, radiantly healthy conscience—so that one dared to do what one would.

Solness (stops beside the console table). I believe, now, that most people are just as puny creatures as I am in that respect.

Hilda. I shouldn't wonder.

Solness (*leaning against the table*). In the sagas—— Have you read any of the old sagas?

Hilda. Oh yes! When I used to read books, I——

Solness. In the sagas you read about vikings, who sailed to foreign lands, and plundered and burned and killed men——

Hilda. And carried off women——

Solness. ——and kept them in captivity——

Hilda. ——took them home in their ships——

Solness. ——and behaved to them like—like the very worst of trolls.

Hilda (*looks straight before her, with a half-veiled look*). I think that must have been thrilling.

Solness (*with a short, deep laugh*). To carry off women, Hilda.

Hilda. To be carried off.

Solness (*looks at her a moment*). Oh, indeed.

Hilda (*as if breaking the thread of the conversation*). But what made you speak of these vikings, Mr. Solness?

Solness. Why, those fellows must have had robust consciences, if you like! When they got home again, they could eat and drink, and be as happy as children. And the women, too! They often would not leave them on any account. Can you understand that, Hilda?

Hilda. Those women I can understand exceedingly well.

Solness. Oho! Perhaps you could do the same yourself?

Hilda. Why not?

Solness. Live—of your own free will—with a ruffian like that?

Hilda. If it was a ruffian I had come to love——

Solness. Could you come to love a man like that?

Hilda. Good heavens, you know very well one can't choose whom one is going to love.

Solness (*looks meditatively at her*). Oh no, I suppose it is the troll within one that's responsible for that.

Hilda (*half-laughing*). And all those blessed devils, that you know so well—both the light-haired and the dark-haired ones.

Solness (*quietly and warmly*). Then I hope with all my heart that the devils will choose carefully for you, Hilda.

Hilda. For me they have chosen already—once and for all.

Solness (*looks earnestly at her*). Hilda—you are like a wild bird of the woods.

Hilda. Far from it. I don't hide myself away under the bushes.

Solness. No, no. There is rather something of the bird of prey in you.

Hilda. That is nearer it—perhaps. (*Very earnestly.*) And why not a bird of prey? Why should not *I* go a-hunting—I, as well as the rest. Carry off the prey I want—if only I can get my claws into it, and do with it as I will.

Solness. Hilda—do you know what you are?

Hilda. Yes, I suppose I am a strange sort of bird.

Solness. No. You are like a dawning day. When I look at you—I seem to be looking towards the sunrise.

Hilda. Tell me, Mr. Solness—are you certain that you have never called me to you? Inwardly, you know?

Solness (*softly and slowly*). I almost think I must have.

Hilda. What did you want with me?

Solness. You are the younger generation, Hilda.

Hilda (*smiles*). That younger generation that you are so afraid of?

Solness (*nods slowly*). And which, in my heart, I yearn towards so deeply.

[HILDA *rises, goes to the little table, and fetches* RAGNAR BROVIK'S *portfolio.*

Hilda (*holds out the portfolio to him*). We were talking of these drawings——

Solness (*shortly, waving them away*). Put those things away! I have seen enough of them.

Hilda. Yes, but you have to write your approval on them.

Solness. Write my approval on them? Never!

Hilda. But the poor old man is lying at death's door! Can't you give him and his son this pleasure before they are parted? And perhaps he might get the commission to carry them out, too.

Solness. Yes, that is just what he would get. He has made sure of that—has my fine gentleman!

Hilda. Then, good heavens—if that is so—can't you tell the least little bit of a lie for once in a way?

Solness. A lie? (*Raging.*) Hilda—take those devil's drawings out of my sight!

Hilda (*draws the portfolio a little nearer to herself*). Well, well, well—don't bite me.—You talk of trolls—but I think you go on like a troll yourself. (*Looks around.*) Where do you keep your pen and ink?

Solness. There is nothing of the sort in here.

Hilda (*goes towards the door*). But in the office where that young lady is——

Solness. Stay where you are, Hilda!—I ought to tell a lie, you say. Oh yes, for the sake of his old father I might well do that—for in my time I have crushed him, trodden him under foot——

Hilda. Him, too?

Solness. I needed room for myself. But this Ragnar—he must on no account be allowed to come to the front.

Hilda. Poor fellow, there is surely no fear of that. If he has nothing in him——

Solness (*comes closer, looks at her, and whispers*). If Ragnar Brovik gets his chance, he will strike me to the earth. Crush me—as I crushed his father.

Hilda. Crush you? Has he the ability for that?

Solness. Yes, you may depend upon it he has the ability! He is the younger generation that stands ready to knock at my door—to make an end of Halvard Solness.

Hilda (*looks at him with quiet reproach*). And yet you would bar him out. Fie, Mr. Solness!

Solness. The fight I have been fighting has cost heart's blood enough.—And I am afraid, too, that the helpers and servers will not obey me any longer.

Hilda. Then you must go ahead without them. There is nothing else for it.

Solness. It is hopeless, Hilda. The luck is bound to turn. A little sooner or a little later. Retribution is inexorable.

Hilda (*in distress, putting her hands over her ears*). Don't talk like that! Do you want to kill me? To take from me what is more than my life?

Solness. And what is that?

Hilda. The longing to see you great. To see you, with a wreath in your hand, high, high up upon a church-tower. (*Calm again.*) Come, out with your pencil now. You must have a pencil about you?

Solness (*takes out his pocket-book*). I have one here.

Hilda (*lays the portfolio on the sofa-table*). Very well. Now let us two sit down here, Mr. Solness. (SOLNESS *seats himself at the table.* HILDA *stands behind him, leaning over the back of the chair.*) And now we will write on the drawings. We must write very, very nicely and cordially—for this horrid Ruar—or whatever his name is.

Solness (*writes a few words, turns his head and looks at her*). Tell me one thing, Hilda.

Hilda. Yes!

Solness. If you have been waiting for me all these ten years——

Hilda. What then?

Solness. Why have you never written to me? Then I could have answered you.

Hilda (*hastily*). No, no, no! That was just what I did not want.

Solness. Why not?

Hilda. I was afraid the whole thing might fall to pieces.

—But we were going to write on the drawings, Mr. Solness.

Solness. So we were.

Hilda (*bends forward and looks over his shoulder while he writes*). Mind now, kindly and cordially! Oh how I hate —how I hate this Ruald——

Solness (*writing*). Have you never really cared for any one, Hilda?

Hilda (*harshly*). What do you say?

Solness. Have you never cared for any one?

Hilda. For any one else, I suppose you mean?

Solness (*looks up at her*). For any one else, yes. Have you never? In all these ten years? Never?

Hilda. Oh yes, now and then. When I was perfectly furious with you for not coming.

Solness. Then you did take an interest in other people, too?

Hilda. A little bit—for a week or so. Good heavens, Mr. Solness, you surely know how such things come about.

Solness. Hilda—what is it you have come for?

Hilda. Don't waste time talking. The poor old man might go and die in the meantime.

Solness. Answer me, Hilda. What do you want of me?

Hilda. I want my kingdom.

Solness. H'm——

He gives a rapid glance towards the door on the left, and then goes on writing on the drawings. At the same moment MRS. SOLNESS *enters; she has some packages in her hand.*

Mrs. Solness. Here are a few things I have got for you, Miss Wangel. The large parcels will be sent later on.

Hilda. Oh, how very, very kind of you!

Mrs. Solness. Only my simple duty. Nothing more than that.

Solness (*reading over what he has written*). Aline!

Mrs. Solness. Yes?

Solness. Did you notice whether the—the book-keeper was out there?

Mrs. Solness. Yes, of course, she was out there.

Solness (*puts the drawings in the portfolio*). H'm——

Mrs. Solness. She was standing at the desk, as she always is—when *I* go through the room.

Solness (*rises*). Then I'll give this to her, and tell her that——

Hilda (*takes the portfolio from him*). Oh, no, let me have the pleasure of doing that! (*Goes to the door, but turns.*) What is her name?

Solness. Her name is Miss Fosli.

Hilda. Pooh, that sounds too cold! Her Christian name, I mean?

Solness. Kaia—I believe.

Hilda (*opens the door and calls out*). Kaia, come in here! Make haste! Mr. Solness wants to speak to you.

KAIA FOSLI *appears at the door.*

Kaia (*looking at him in alarm*). Here I am——?

Hilda (*handing her the portfolio*). See here, Kaia! You can take this home; Mr. Solness has written on them now.

Kaia. Oh, at last!

Solness. Give them to the old man as soon as you can.

Kaia. I will go straight home with them.

Solness. Yes, do. Now Ragnar will have a chance of building for himself.

Kaia. Oh, may he come and thank you for all——?

Solness (*harshly*). I won't have any thanks! Tell him that from me.

Kaia. Yes, I will——

Solness. And tell him at the same time that henceforward I do not require his services—nor yours either.

Kaia (*softly and quiveringly*). Not mine either?

Solness. You will have other things to think of now, and to attend to; and that is a very good thing for you. Well, go home with the drawings now, Miss Fosli. At once! Do you hear?

Kaia (as before). Yes, Mr. Solness. (*She goes out.*)

Mrs. Solness. Heavens! what deceitful eyes she has.

Solness. She? That poor little creature?

Mrs. Solness. Oh—I can see what I can see, Halvard. —— Are you really dismissing them?

Solness. Yes.

Mrs. Solness. Her as well?

Solness. Was not that what you wished?

Mrs. Solness. But how can you get on without her——? Oh, well, no doubt you have some one else in reserve, Halvard.

Hilda (playfully). Well, I for one am not the person to stand at that desk.

Solness. Never mind, never mind—it will be all right, Aline. Now all you have to do is to think about moving into our new home—as quickly as you can. This evening we will hang up the wreath—(*Turns to Hilda*)—right on the very pinnacle of the tower. What do you say to that, Miss Hilda?

Hilda (looks at him with sparkling eyes). It will be splendid to see you so high up once more.

Solness. Me!

Mrs. Solness. For heaven's sake, Miss Wangel, don't imagine such a thing! My husband!—when he always gets so dizzy!

Hilda. He get dizzy! No, I know quite well he does not!

Mrs. Solness. Oh yes, indeed he does.

Hilda. But I have seen him with my own eyes right up at the top of a high church-tower!

Mrs. Solness. Yes, I hear people talk of that; but it is utterly impossible——

Solness (vehemently). Impossible—impossible, yes! But there I stood all the same!

Mrs. Solness. Oh, how can you say so, Halvard? Why,

you can't even bear to go out on the second-story balcony here. You have always been like that.

Solness. You may perhaps see something different this evening.

Mrs. Solness (in alarm). No, no, no! Please God I shall never see that. I will write at once to the doctor—and I am sure he won't let you do it.

Solness. Why, Aline——!

Mrs. Solness. Oh, you know you're ill, Halvard. This proves it! Oh God—Oh God! *(She goes hastily out to the right.)*

Hilda (looks intently at him). Is it so, or is it not?

Solness. That I turn dizzy?

Hilda. That my master builder dares not—cannot—climb as high as he builds?

Solness. Is that the way you look at it?

Hilda. Yes.

Solness. I believe there is scarcely a corner in me that is safe from you.

Hilda (looks towards the bow-window). Up there, then. Right up there——

Solness (approaches her). You might have the topmost room in the tower, Hilda—there you might live like a princess.

Hilda (indefinably, between earnest and jest). Yes, that is what you promised me.

Solness. Did I really?

Hilda. Fie, Mr. Solness! You said I should be a princess, and that you would give me a kingdom. And then you went and——Well!

Solness (cautiously). Are you quite certain that this is not a dream—a fancy, that has fixed itself in your mind?

Hilda (sharply). Do you mean that you did not do it?

Solness. I scarcely know myself. *(More softly.)* But now I know so much for certain, that I——

Hilda. That you——? Say it at once!

Solness. —that I ought to have done it.

Hilda (exclaims with animation). Don't tell me you can ever be dizzy!

Solness. This evening, then, we will hang up the wreath —Princess Hilda.

Hilda (with a bitter curve of the lips). Over your new home, yes.

Solness. Over the new house, which will never be a home for me.

[*He goes out through the garden door.*

Hilda (looks straight in front of her with a far-away expression, and whispers to herself. The only words audible are)—frightfully thrilling——

ACT III

The large, broad verandah of SOLNESS's *dwelling-house. Part
of the house, with outer door leading to the verandah,
is seen to the left. A railing along the verandah to the
right. At the back, from the end of the verandah, a
flight of steps leads down to the garden below. Tall old
trees in the garden spread their branches over the verandah and towards the house. Far to the right, in among
the trees, a glimpse is caught of the lower part of the
new villa, with scaffolding round so much as is seen of
the tower. In the background the garden is bounded by
an old wooden fence. Outside the fence, a street with
low, tumble-down cottages.*

Evening sky with sun-lit clouds.

*On the verandah, a garden bench stands along the wall of the
house, and in front of the bench a long table. On the
other side of the table, an arm-chair and some stools.
All the furniture is of wicker-work.*

MRS. SOLNESS, *wrapped in a large white crape shawl, sits
resting in the arm-chair and gazes over to the right.
Shortly after,* HILDA WANGEL *comes up the flight of
steps from the garden. She is dressed as in the last act,
and wears her hat. She has in her bodice a little nosegay
of small common flowers.*

Mrs. Solness (turning her head a little). Have you been
round the garden, Miss Wangel?

Hilda. Yes, I have been taking a look at it.

Mrs. Solness. And found some flowers too, I see.

70

Hilda. Yes, indeed! There are such heaps of them in among the bushes.

Mrs. Solness. Are there really? Still? You see I scarcely ever go there.

Hilda (closer). What! Don't you take a run down into the garden every day, then?

Mrs. Solness (with a faint smile). I don't "run" anywhere, nowadays.

Hilda. Well, but do you not go down now and then to look at all the lovely things there?

Mrs. Solness. It has all become so strange to me. I am almost afraaid to see it again.

Hilda. Your own garden!

Mrs. Solness. I don't feel that it is mine any longer.

Hilda. What do you mean——?

Mrs. Solness. No, no, it is not—not as it was in my mother's and father's time. They have taken away so much—so much of the garden, Miss Wangel. Fancy—they have parcelled it out—and built houses for strangers—people that I don't know. And they can sit and look in upon me from their windows.

Hilda (with a bright expression). Mrs. Solness!

Mrs. Solness. Yes!

Hilda. May I stay here with you a little?

Mrs. Solness. Yes, by all means, if you care to.

> [HILDA *moves a stool close to the arm-chair and sits down.*

Hilda. Ah—here one can sit and sun oneself like a cat.

Mrs. Solness (lays her hand softly on HILDA's *neck).* It is nice of you to be willing to sit with me. I thought you wanted to go in to my husband.

Hilda. What should I want with him?

Mrs. Solness. To help him, I thought.

Hilda. No, thank you. And besides, he is not in. He is over there with the workmen. But he looked so fierce that I did not care to talk to him.

Mrs. Solness. He is so kind and gentle in reality.

Hilda. He!

Mrs. Solness. You do not really know him yet, Miss Wangel.

Hilda (looks affectionately at her). Are you pleased at the thought of moving over to the new house?

Mrs. Solness. I ought to be pleased; for it is what Halvard wants——

Hilda. Oh, not just on that account, surely.

Mrs. Solness. Yes, yes, Miss Wangel; for it is only my duty to submit myself to him. But very often it is dreadfully difficult to force one's mind to obedience.

Hilda. Yes, that must be difficult indeed.

Mrs. Solness. I can tell you it is—when one has so many faults as I have——

Hilda. When one has gone through so much trouble as you have——

Mrs. Solness. How do you know about that?

Hilda. Your husband told me.

Mrs. Solness. To me he very seldom mentions these things.—Yes, I can tell you I have gone through more than enough trouble in my life, Miss Wangel.

Hilda (looks sympathetically at her and nods slowly). Poor Mrs. Solness. First of all there was the fire——

Mrs. Solness (with a sigh). Yes, everything that was mine was burnt.

Hilda. And then came what was worse.

Mrs. Solness (looking inquiringly at her). Worse?

Hilda. The worst of all.

Mrs. Solness. What do you mean?

Hilda (softly). You lost the two little boys.

Mrs. Solness. Oh yes, the boys. But, you see, that was a thing apart. That was a dispensation of Providence; and in such things one can only bow in submission—yes, and be thankful, too.

Hilda. Then you are so?

Mrs. Solness. Not always, I am sorry to say. I know well enough that it is my duty—but all the same I cannot.

Hilda. No, no, I think that is only natural.

Mrs. Solness. And often and often I have to remind myself that it was a righteous punishment for me——

Hilda. Why?

Mrs. Solness. Because I had not fortitude enough in misfortune.

Hilda. But I don't see that——

Mrs. Solness. Oh, no, no, Miss Wangel—do not talk to me any more about the two little boys. We ought to feel nothing but joy in thinking of them: for they are so happy —so happy now. No, it is the small losses in life that cut one to the heart—the loss of all that other people look upon as almost nothing.

Hilda (lays her arms on Mrs. Solness's *knees, and looks up at her affectionately).* Dear Mrs. Solness—tell me what things you mean!

Mrs. Solness. As I say, only little things. All the old portraits were burnt on the walls. And all the old silk dresses were burnt, that had belonged to the family for generations and generations. And all mother's and grandmother's lace—that was burnt, too. And only think—the jewels, too! (*Sadly.*) And then all the dolls.

Hilda. The dolls?

Mrs. Solness (choking with tears). I had nine lovely dolls.

Hilda. And they were burnt, too?

Mrs. Solness. All of them. Oh, it was hard—so hard for me.

Hilda. Had you put by all these dolls, then? Ever since you were little?

Mrs. Solness. I had not put them by. The dolls and I had gone on living together.

Hilda. After you were grown up?

Mrs. Solness. Yes, long after that.

Hilda. After you were married, too?

Mrs. Solness. Oh yes, indeed. So long as he did not see it——. But they were all burnt up, poor things. No one thought of saving them. Oh, it is so miserable to think of. You mustn't laugh at me, Miss Wangel.

Hilda. I am not laughing in the least.

Mrs. Solness. For you see, in a certain sense, there was life in them, too. I carried them under my heart—like little unborn children.

DR. HERDAL, *with his hat in his hand, comes out through the door, and observes* MRS. SOLNESS *and* HILDA.

Dr. Herdal. Well, Mrs. Solness, so you are sitting out here catching cold?

Mrs. Solness. I find it so pleasant and warm here to-day.

Dr. Herdal. Yes, yes. But is there anything going on here? I got a note from you.

Mrs. Solness (rises). Yes, there is something I must talk to you about.

Dr. Herdal. Very well; then perhaps we had better go in. (*To* HILDA.) Still in your mountaineering dress, Miss Wangel?

Hilda (gaily, rising). Yes—in full uniform! But to-day I am not going climbing and breaking my neck. We two will stop quietly below and look on, doctor.

Dr. Herdal. What are we to look on at?

Mrs. Solness (softly, in alarm, to HILDA.) Hush, hush—for God's sake! He is coming. Try to get that idea out of his head. And let us be friends, Miss Wangel. Don't you think we can?

Hilda (throws her arms impetuously round MRS. SOLNESS'S *neck*). Oh, if we only could!

Mrs. Solness (gently disengages herself). There, there, there! There he comes, doctor. Let me have a word with you.

Dr. Herdal. Is it about him?

Mrs. Solness. Yes, to be sure it's about him. Do come in.

She and the doctor enter the house.   Next moment SOLNESS
comes up from the garden by the flight of steps.   A se-
rious look comes over HILDA'*s face.*

Solness (*glances at the house-door, which is closed cau-*
tiously from within).   Have you noticed, Hilda, that as soon
as I come, she goes?

Hilda.   I have noticed that as soon as you come, you
make her go.

Solness.   Perhaps so.   But I cannot help it.   (*Looks ob-*
servantly at her.)   Are you cold, Hilda?   I think you look
cold.

Hilda.   I have just come up out of a tomb.

Solness.   What do you mean by that?

Hilda.   That I have got chilled through and through, Mr.
Solness.

Solness (*slowly*).   I believe I understand——

Hilda.   What brings you up here just now?

Solness.   I caught sight of you from over there.

Hilda.   But then you must have seen her too?

Solness.   I knew she would go at once if I came.

Hilda.   Is it very painful for you that she should avoid
you in this way?

Solness.   In one sense, it's a relief as well.

Hilda.   Not to have her before your eyes?

Solness.   Yes.

Hilda.   Not to be always seeing how heavily the loss of
the little boys weighs upon her?

Solness.   Yes.   Chiefly that.

> [HILDA *drifts across the verandah with her hands*
> *behind her back, stops at the railing and looks*
> *out over the garden.*

Solness (*after a short pause*).   Did you have a long talk
with her?

> [HILDA *stands motionless and does not answer.*

Solness.   Had you a long talk, I asked?

> [HILDA *is silent as before.*

Solness. What was she talking about, Hilda?

[HILDA *continues silent.*

Solness. Poor Aline! I suppose it was about the little boys.

Hilda (*a nervous shudder runs through her; then she nods hurriedly once or twice*).

Solness. She will never get over it—never in this world. (*Approaches her.*) Now you are standing there again like a statue; just as you stood last night.

Hilda (*turns and looks at him, with great serious eyes*). I am going away.

Solness (*sharply*). Going away!

Hilda. Yes.

Solness. But I won't allow you to!

Hilda. What am I to do here now?

Solness. Simply to be here, Hilda!

Hilda (*measures him with a look*). Oh, thank you. You know it wouldn't end there.

Solness (*heedlessly*). So much the better!

Hilda (*vehemently*). I cannot do any harm to one whom I know! I can't take away anything that belongs to her.

Solness. Who wants you to do that?

Hilda (*continuing*). A stranger, yes! for that is quite a different thing! A person I have never set eyes on. But one that I have come into close contact with——! Oh no! Oh no! Ugh!

Solness. Yes, but I never proposed you should.

Hilda. Oh, Mr. Solness, you know quite well what the end of it would be. And that is why I am going away.

Solness. And what is to become of me when you are gone? What shall I have to live for then?—After that?

Hilda (*with the indefinable look in her eyes*). It is surely not so hard for you. You have your duties to her. Live for those duties.

Solness. Too late. These powers—these—these——

Hilda. ——devils——

Solness. Yes, these devils! And the troll within me as well—they have drawn all the life-blood out of her. (*Laughs in desperation.*) They did it for my happiness! Yes, yes! (*Sadly.*) And now she is dead—for my sake. And I am chained alive to a dead woman. (*In wild anguish.*) I—I who cannot live without joy in life!

> [HILDA *moves round the table and seats herself on the bench, with her elbows on the table, and her head supported by her hands.*

Hilda (*sits and looks at him awhile*). What will you build next?

Solness (*shakes his head*). I don't believe I shall build much more.

Hilda. Not those cosy, happy homes for mother and father, and for the troop of children?

Solness. I wonder whether there will be any use for such homes in the coming time.

Hilda. Poor Mr. Solness! And you have gone all these ten years—and staked your whole life—on that alone.

Solness. Yes, you may well say so, Hilda.

Hilda (*with an outburst*). Oh, it all seems to me so foolish—so foolish!

Solness. All what?

Hilda. Not to be able to grasp at your own happiness— at your own life! Merely because some one you know happens to stand in the way!

Solness. One whom you have no right to set aside.

Hilda. I wonder whether one really has not the right! And yet, and yet——. Oh, if one could only sleep the whole thing away!

> [*She lays her arms flat on the table, rests the left side of her head on her hands, and shuts her eyes.*

Solness (*turns the arm-chair and sits down at the table*). Had you a cosy, happy home—up there with your father, Hilda?

Hilda (without stirring, answers as if half asleep). I had only a cage.

Solness. And you are determined not to go back to it?

Hilda (as before). The wild bird never wants to go into the cage.

Solness. Rather range through the free air——

Hilda (still as before). The bird of prey loves to range——

Solness (lets his eyes rest on her). If only one had the viking-spirit in life——

Hilda (in her usual voice; opens her eyes but does not move). And the other thing? Say what that was!

Solness. A robust conscience.

> [HILDA *sits erect on the bench, with animation. Her eyes have once more the sparkling expression of gladness.*

Hilda (nods to him). I know what you are going to build next!

Solness. Then you know more than I do, Hilda.

Hilda. Yes, builders are such stupid people.

Solness. What is it to be then?

Hilda (nods again). The castle.

Solness. What castle?

Hilda. My castle, of course.

Solness. Do you want a castle now?

Hilda. Don't you owe me a kingdom, I should like to know?

Solness. You say I do.

Hilda. Well—you admit you owe me this kingdom. And you can't have a kingdom without a royal castle, I should think!

Solness (more and more animated). Yes, they usually go together.

Hilda. Good! Then build it for me! This moment!

Solness (laughing). Must you have that on the instant, too?

Hilda. Yes, to be sure! For the ten years are up now, and I am not going to wait any longer. So—out with the castle, Mr. Solness!

Solness. It's no light matter to owe you anything, Hilda.

Hilda. You should have thought of that before. It is too late now. So—(*tapping the table*)—the castle on the table! It is my castle! I will have it at once!

Solness (*more seriously, leans over towards her, with his arms on the table*). What sort of castle have you imagined, Hilda?

[*Her expression becomes more and more veiled. She seems gazing inwards at herself.*

Hilda (*slowly*). My castle shall stand on a height—on a very great height—with a clear outlook on all sides, so that I can see far—far around.

Solness. And no doubt it is to have a high tower!

Hilda. A tremendously high tower. And at the very top of the tower there shall be a balcony. And I will stand out upon it——

Solness (*involuntarily clutches at his forehead*). How can you like to stand at such a dizzy height——?

Hilda. Yes, I wlll, right up there will I stand and look down on the other people—on those that are building churches, and homes for mother and father and the troop of children. And you may come up and look on at it, too.

Solness (*in a low tone*). Is the builder to be allowed to come up beside the princess?

Hilda. If the builder will.

Solness (*more softly*). Then I think the builder will come.

Hilda (*nods*). The builder—he will come.

Solness. But he will never be able to build any more. Poor builder!

Hilda (*animated*). Oh yes, he will! We two will set to work together. And then we will build the loveliest—the very loveliest—thing in all the world.

Solness (*intently*). Hilda—tell me what that is!

Hilda (*looks smilingly at him, shakes her head a little, pouts, and speaks as if to a child*). Builders—they are such very—very stupid people.

Solness. Yes, no doubt they are stupid. But now tell me what it is—the loveliest thing in the world—that we two are to build together?

Hilda (*is silent a little while, then says with an indefinable expression in her eyes*). Castles in the air.

Solness. Castles in the air?

Hilda (*nods*). Castles in the air, yes! Do you know what sort of thing a castle in the air is?

Solness. It is the loveliest thing in the world, you say.

Hilda (*rises with vehemence, and makes a gesture of repulsion with her hand*). Yes, to be sure it is! Castles in the air—they are so easy to take refuge in. And so easy to build, too—(*looks scornfully at him*)—especially for the builders who have a—a dizzy conscience.

Solness (*rises*). After this day we two will build together, Hilda.

Hilda (*with a half-dubious smile*). A real castle in the air?

Solness. Yes. One with a firm foundation under it.

RAGNAR BROVIK *comes out from the house. He is carrying a large, green wreath with flowers and silk ribbons.*

Hilda (*with an outburst of pleasure*). The wreath! Oh, that will be glorious!

Solness (*in surprise*). Have you brought the wreath, Ragnar?

Ragnar. I promised the foreman I would.

Solness (*relieved*). Ah, then I suppose your father is better?

Ragnar. No.

Solness. Was he not cheered by what I wrote?

Ragnar. It came too late.

Solness. Too late!

Ragnar. When she came with it he was unconscious. He had had a stroke.

Solness. Why, then, you must go home to him! You must attend to your father!

Ragnar. He does not need me any more.

Solness. But surely you ought to be with him.

Ragnar. She is sitting by his bed.

Solness (rather uncertainly). Kaia?

Ragnar (looking darkly at him). Yes—Kaia.

Solness. Go home, Ragnar—both to him and to her. Give me the wreath.

Ragnar (suppresses a mocking smile). You don't mean that you yourself——?

Solness. I will take it down to them myself. (*Takes the wreath from him.*) And now you go home; we don't require you to-day.

Ragnar. I know you do not require me any more; but to-day I shall remain.

Solness. Well, remain then, since you are bent upon it.

Hilda (at the railing). Mr. Solness, I will stand here and look on at you.

Solness. At me!

Hilda. It will be fearfully thrilling.

Solness (in a low tone). We will talk about that presently, Hilda.

[*He goes down the flight of steps with the wreath, and away through the garden.*

Hilda (looks after him, then turns to Ragnar). I think you might at least have thanked him.

Ragnar. Thanked him? Ought I to have thanked him?

Hilda. Yes, of course you ought!

Ragnar. I think it is rather you I ought to thank.

Hilda. How can you say such a thing?

Ragnar (without answering her). But I advise you to take care, Miss Wangel! For you don't know him rightly yet.

Hilda (*ardently*). Oh, no one knows him as I do!

Ragnar (*laughs in exasperation*). Thank him, when he has held me down year after year! When he made father disbelieve in me—made me disbelieve in myself! And all merely that he might——!

Hilda (*as if divining something*). That he might——? Tell me at once!

Ragnar. That he might keep her with him.

Hilda (*with a start towards him*). The girl at the desk.

Ragnar. Yes.

Hilda (*threateningly, clenching her hands*). That is not true! You are telling falsehoods about him!

Ragnar. I would not believe it either until to-day—when she said so herself.

Hilda (*as if beside herself*). What did she say? I will know! At once! at once!

Ragnar. She said that he had taken possession of her mind—her whole mind—centred all her thoughts upon himself alone. She says that she can never leave him—that she will remain here, where he is——

Hilda (*with flashing eyes*). She will not be allowed to!

Ragnar (*as if feeling his way*). Who will not allow her?

Hilda (*rapidly*). He will not either!

Ragnar. Oh no—I understand the whole thing now. After this, she would merely be—in the way.

Hilda. You understand nothing—since you can talk like that! No, *I* will tell you why he kept hold of her.

Ragnar. Well then, why?

Hilda. In order to keep hold of you.

Ragnar. Has he told you so?

Hilda. No, but it is so. It must be so! (*Wildly.*) I will—I will have it so!

Ragnar. And at the very moment when you came—he let her go.

Hilda. It was you—you that he let go; What do you suppose he cares about strange women like her?

Ragnar (*reflects*). Is it possible that all this time he has been afraid of me?

Hilda. He afraid! I would not be so conceited if I were you.

Ragnar. Oh, he must have seen long ago that I had something in me, too. Besides—cowardly—that is just what he is, you see.

Hilda. He! Oh yes, I am likely to believe that!

Ragnar. In a certain sense he is cowardly—he, the great master builder. He is not afraid of robbing others of their life's happiness—as he has done both for my father and for me. But when it comes to climbing up a paltry bit of scaffolding—he will do anything rather than that.

Hilda. Oh, you should just have seen him high, high up —at the dizzy height where I once saw him.

Ragnar. Did you see that?

Hilda. Yes, indeed I did. How free and great he looked as he stood and fastened the wreath to the church vane!

Ragnar. I know that he ventured that, once in his life— one solitary time. It is a legend among us younger men. But no power on earth would induce him to do it again.

Hilda. To-day he will do it again!

Ragnar (*scornfully*). Yes, I daresay!

Hilda. We shall see it!

Ragnar. That neither you nor I will see.

Hilda (*with uncontrollable vehemence*). I will see it! I will and must see it!

Ragnar. But he will not do it. He simply dare not do it. For you see he cannot get over this infirmity—master builder though he be.

MRS. SOLNESS *comes from the house on to the verandah.*

Mrs. Solness (*looks around*). Is he not here? Where has he gone to?

Ragnar. Mr. Solness is down with the men.

Hilda. He took the wreath with him.

Mrs. Solness (*terrified*). Took the wreath with him! Oh,

God! oh God! Brovik—you must go down to him! **Get**
him to come back here!

Ragnar. Shall I say you want to speak to him, Mrs.
Solness?

Mrs. Solness. Oh yes, do!—No, no—don't say that *I*
want anything! You can say that somebody is here, and
that he must come at once.

Ragnar. Good. I will do so, Mrs. Solness.

> [*He goes down the flight of steps and away through
> the garden.*

Mrs. Solness. Oh, Miss Wangel, you can't think how
anxious I feel about him.

Hilda. Is there anything in this to be so terribly frightened about?

Mrs. Solness. Oh yes; surely you can understand. Just
think, if he were really to do it! If he should take it into
his head to climb up the scaffolding!

Hilda (*eagerly*). Do you think he will?

Mrs. Solness. Oh, one can never tell what he might take
into his head. I am afraid there is nothing he mightn't
think of doing.

Hilda. Aha! Perhaps you too think that he is—well——?

Mrs. Solness. Oh, I don't know what to think about him
now. The doctor has been telling me all sorts of things;
and putting it all together with several things I have heard
him say——

DR. HERDAL *looks out, at the door.*

Dr. Herdal. Is he not coming soon?

Mrs. Solness. Yes, I think so. I have sent for him at
any rate.

Dr. Herdal (*advancing*). I am afraid you will have to
go in, my dear lady——

Mrs. Solness. Oh no! Oh no! I shall stay out here and
wait for Halvard.

Dr. Herdal. But some ladies have just come to call on
you——

Mrs. Solness. Good heavens, that too! And just at this moment!

Dr. Herdal. They say they positively must see the ceremony.

Mrs. Solness. Well, well, I suppose I must go to them after all. It is my duty.

Hilda. Can't you ask the ladies to go away?

Mrs. Solness. No, that would never do. Now that they are here, it is my duty to see them. But do you stay out here in the meantime—and receive him when he comes.

Dr. Herdal. And try to occupy his attention as long as possible——

Mrs. Solness. Yes, do, dear Miss Wangel. Keep a firm hold of him as ever you can.

Hilda. Would it not be best for you to do that?

Mrs. Solness. Yes; God knows that is my duty. But when one has duties in so many directions——

Dr. Herdal (*looks towards the garden*). There he is coming.

Mrs. Solness. And I have to go in!

Dr. Herdal (*to Hilda*). Don't say anything about my being here.

Hilda. Oh no! I daresay I shall find something else to talk to Mr. Solness about.

Mrs. Solness. And be sure you keep firm hold of him. I believe you can do it best.

> [MRS. SOLNESS *and* DR. HERDAL *go into the house.* HILDA *remains standing on the verandah.* SOLNESS *comes from the garden, up the flight of steps.*

Solness. Somebody wants me, I hear.

Hilda. Yes; it is I, Mr. Solness.

Solness. Oh, is it you, Hilda? I was afraid it might be Aline or the Doctor.

Hilda. You are very easily frightened, it seems!

Solness. Do you think so?

Hilda. Yes; people say that you are afraid to climb about—on the scaffoldings, you know.

Solness. Well, that is quite a special thing.

Hilda. Then it is true that you are afraid to do it?

Solness. Yes, I am.

Hilda. Afraid of falling down and killing yourself?

Solness. No, not of that.

Hilda. Of what, then?

Solness. I am afraid of retribution, Hilda.

Hilda. Of retribution? (*Shakes her head.*) I don't understand that.

Solness. Sit down and I will tell you something.

Hilda. Yes, do! At once!

    [*She sits on a stool by the railing, and looks expectantly at him.*

Solness (*throws his hat on the table*). You know that I began by building churches.

Hilda (*nods*). I know that well.

Solness. For, you see, I came as a boy from a pious home in the country; and so it seemed to me that this church-building was the noblest task I could set myself.

Hilda. Yes, yes.

Solness. And I venture to say that I built those poor little churches with such honest and warm and heartfelt devotion that—that——

Hilda. That——? Well?

Solness. Well, that I think that he ought to have been pleased with me.

Hilda. He? What he?

Solness. He who was to have the churches, of course! He to whose honour and glory they were dedicated.

Hilda. Oh, indeed! But are you certain, then, that—that he was not—pleased with you?

Solness (*scornfully*). He pleased with me! How can you talk so, Hilda? He who gave the troll in me leave to lord it just as it pleased. He who bade them be at hand to serve me, both day and night—all these—all these——

Hilda. Devils——

Solness. Yes, of both kinds. Oh no, he made me feel clearly enough that he was not pleased with me. (*Mysteriously.*) You see, that was really the reason why he made the old house burn down.

Hilda. Was that why?

Solness. Yes, don't you understand? He wanted to give me the chance of becoming an accomplished master in my own sphere—so that I might build all the more glorious churches for him. At first I did not understand what he was driving at; but all of a sudden it flashed upon me.

Hilda. When was that?

Solness. It was when I was building the church-tower up at Lysanger.

Hilda. I thought so.

Solness. For you see, Hilda—up there, amidst those new surroundings, I used to go about musing and pondering within myself. Then I saw plainly why he had taken my little children from me. It was that I should have nothing else to attach myself to. No such thing as love and happiness, you understand. I was to be only a master builder—nothing else. And all my life long I was to go on building for him. (*Laughs.*) But I can tell you nothing came of that!

Hilda. What did you do, then?

Solness. First of all, I searched and tried my own heart——

Hilda. And then?

Solness. Then I did the impossible—I no less than he.

Hilda. The impossible?

Solness. I had never before been able to climb up to a great, free height. But that day I did it.

Hilda (*leaping up*). Yes, yes, you did!

Solness. And when I stood there, high over everything, and was hanging the wreath over the vane, I said to him:

Hear me now, thou Mighty One! From this day forward I will be a free builder—I, too, in my sphere—just as thou in thine. I will never more build churches for thee— only homes for human beings.

Hilda (*with great sparkling eyes*). That was the song that I heard through the air!

Solness. But afterwards his turn came.

Hilda. What do you mean by that?

Solness (*looks despondently at her*). Building homes for human beings—is not worth a rap, Hilda.

Hilda. Do you say that now?

Solness. Yes, for now I see it. Men have no use for these homes of theirs—to be happy in. And I should not have had any use for such a home, if I had had one. (*With a quiet, bitter laugh.*) See, that is the upshot of the whole affair, however far back I look. Nothing really built; nor anything sacrificed for the chance of building. Nothing, nothing! the whole is nothing.

Hilda. Then you will never build anything more?

Solness (*with animation*). On the contrary, I am just going to begin!

Hilda. What, then? What will you build? Tell me at once!

Solness. I believe there is only one possible dwelling-place for human happiness—and that is what I am going to build now.

Hilda (*looks fixedly at him*). Mr. Solness—you mean our castle?

Solness. The castles in the air—yes.

Hilda. I am afraid you would turn dizzy before we got half-way up.

Solness. Not if I can mount hand in hand with you, Hilda.

Hilda (*with an expression of suppressed resentment*). Only with me? Will there be no others of the party?

Solness. Who else should there be?

Hilda. Oh—that girl—that Kaia at the desk. Poor thing—don't you want to take her with you too?

Solness. Oho! Was it about her that Aline was talking to you?

Hilda. Is it so—or is it not?

Solness (vehemently). I will not answer such a question. You must believe in me, wholly and entirely!

Hilda. All these ten years I have believed in you so utterly—so utterly.

Solness. You must go on believing in me!

Hilda. Then let me see you stand free and high up!

Solness (sadly). Oh Hilda—it is not every day that I can do that.

Hilda (passionately). I will have you do it! I will have it! (*Imploringly.*) Just once more, Mr. Solness! Do the impossible once again!

Solness (stands and looks deep into her eyes). If I try it, Hilda, I will stand up there and talk to him as I did that time before.

Hilda (in rising excitement). What will you say to him?

Solness. I will say to him: Hear me, Mighty Lord— thou may'st judge me as seems best to thee. But hereafter I will build nothing but the loveliest thing in the world——

Hilda (carried away). Yes—yes—yes!

Solness. —build it together with a princess, whom I love——

Hilda. Yes, tell him that! Tell him that!

Solness. Yes. And then I will say to him: Now I shall go down and throw my arms round her and kiss her——

Hilda. —many times! Say that!

Solness. —many, many times, I will say.

Hilda. And then——?

Solness. Then I will wave my hat—and come down to the earth—and do as I said to him.

Hilda (with outstretched arms). Now I see you again as I did when there was song in the air.

Solness (looks at her with his head bowed). How have you become what you are, Hilda?

Hilda. How have you made me what I am?

Solness (shortly and firmly). The princess shall have her castle.

Hilda (jubilant, clapping her hands). Oh, Mr. Solness——! My lovely, lovely castle. Our castle in the air!

Solness. On a firm foundation.

> [*In the street a crowd of people has assembled, vaguely seen through the trees. Music of wind-instruments is heard far away behind the new house.*
>
> Mrs. Solness, *with a fur collar round her neck,* Doctor Herdal *with her white shawl on his arm, and some ladies, come out on the verandah.* Ragnar Brovik *comes at the same time up from the garden.*

Mrs. Solness (to Ragnar*).* Are we to have music, too?

Ragnar. Yes. It's the band of the Masons' Union. (*To* Solness.) The foreman asked me to tell you that he is ready now to go up with the wreath.

Solness (takes his hat). Good. I will go down to him myself.

Mrs. Solness (anxiously). What have you to do down there, Halvard?

Solness (curtly). I must be down below with the men.

Mrs. Solness. Yes, down below—only down below.

Solness. That is where I always stand—on everyday occasions.

> [*He goes down the flight of steps and away through the garden.*

Mrs. Solness (calls after him over the railing). But do beg the man to be careful when he goes up? Promise me that, Halvard!

Dr. Herdal (to Mrs Solness). Don't you see that I was right? He has given up all thought of that folly.

Mrs. Solness. Oh, what a relief! Twice workmen have

fallen, and each time they were killed on the spot. (*Turns to* HILDA.) Thank you, Miss Wangel, for having kept such a firm hold upon him. I should never have been able to manage him.

Dr. Herdal (*playfully*). Yes, yes, Miss Wangel, you know how to keep firm hold on a man, when you give your mind to it.

> [MRS. SOLNESS *and* DR. HERDAL *go up to the ladies, who are standing nearer to the steps and looking over the garden.* HILDA *remains standing beside the railing in the foreground.* RAGNAR *goes up to her.*

Ragnar (*with suppressed laughter, half whispering*). Miss Wangel—do you see all those young fellows down in the street?

Hilda. Yes.

Ragnar. They are my fellow students, come to look at the master.

Hilda. What do they want to look at him for?

Ragnar. They want to see how he daren't climb to the top of his own house.

Hilda. Oh, that is what those boys want, is it?

Ragnar (*spitefully and scornfully*). He has kept us down so long—now we are going to see him keep quietly down below himself.

Hilda. You will not see that—not this time.

Ragnar (*smiles*). Indeed! Then where shall we see him?

Hilda. High—high up by the vane! That is where you will see him!

Ragnar (*laughs*). Him! Oh yes, I daresay!

Hilda. His will is to reach the top—so at the top you shall see him.

Ragnar. His will, yes; that I can easily believe. But he simply cannot do it. His head would swim round, long, long before he got half-way. He would have to crawl down again on his hands and knees.

Dr. Herdal (points across). Look! There goes the fore-man up the ladders.

Mrs. Solness. And of course he has the wreath to carry, too. Oh, I do hope he will be careful!

Ragnar (stares incredulously and shouts). Why, but it's——

Hilda (breaking out in jubilation). It is the master builder himself!

Mrs. Solness (screams with terror). Yes, it is Halvard! Oh, my great God——! Halvard! Halvard!

Dr. Herdal. Hush! Don't shout to him!

Mrs. Solness (half beside herself). I must go to him! I must get him to come down again!

Dr. Herdal (holds her). Don't move, any of you! Not a sound!

Hilda (immovable, follows SOLNESS *with her eyes)*. He climbs and climbs. Higher and higher! Higher and higher! Look! Just look!

Ragnar (breathless). He must turn now. He can't possibly help it.

Hilda. He climbs and climbs. He will soon be at the top now.

Mrs. Solness. Oh, I shall die of terror. I cannot bear to see it.

Dr. Herdal. Then don't look up at him.

Hilda. There he is standing on the topmost planks. Right at the top!

Dr. Herdal. Nobody must move! Do you hear?

Hilda (exulting, with quiet intensity). At last! At last! Now I see him great and free again!

Ragnar (almost voiceless). But this is im——

Hilda. So I have seen him all through these ten years. How secure he stands! Frightfully thrilling all the same. Look at him! Now he is hanging the wreath round the vane.

Ragnar. I feel as if I were looking at something utterly impossible.

Hilda. Yes, it is the impossible that he is doing now! (*With the indefinable expression in her eyes.*) Can you see any one else up there with him?

Ragnar. There is no one else.

Hilda. Yes, there is one he is striving with.

Ragnar. You are mistaken.

Hilda. Then do you hear no song in the air, either?

Ragnar. It must be the wind in the tree-tops.

Hilda. *I* hear a song—a mighty song! (*Shouts in wild jubilation and glee.*) Look, look! Now he is waving his hat! He is waving it to us down here! Oh, wave, wave back to him. For now it is finished! (*Snatches the white shawl from the Doctor, waves it, and shouts up to* SOLNESS.) Hurrah for Master Builder Solness!

Dr. Herdal. Stop! Stop! For God's sake——!

> [*The ladies on the verandah wave their pocket-handkerchiefs, and the shouts of "Hurrah" are taken up in the street below. Then they are suddenly silenced, and the crowd bursts out into a shriek of horror. A human body, with planks and fragments of wood, is vaguely perceived crashing down behind the trees.*

Mrs. Solness and the Ladies (*at the same time*). He is falling! He is falling!

> [MRS. SOLNESS *totters, falls backwards, swooning, and is caught, amid cries and confusion, by the ladies. The crowd in the street breaks down the fence and storms into the garden. At the same time* DR. HERDAL, *too, rushes down thither. A short pause.*

Hilda (*stares fixedly upwards and says, as if petrified*). My Master Builder.

Ragnar (*supports himself, trembling, against the railing*). He must be dashed to pieces—killed on the spot.

One of the Ladies (whilst Mrs. Solness *is carried into the house).* Run down for the doctor——

Ragnar. I can't stir a foot——

Another Lady. Then call to some one!

Ragnar (tries to call out). How is it? Is he alive?

A Voice (below in the garden). Mr. Solness is dead!

Other Voices (nearer). The head is all crushed.—He fell right into the quarry.

Hilda (turns to Ragnar, *and says quietly).* I can't see him up there now.

Ragnar. This is terrible. So, after all, he could not do it.

Hilda (as if in quiet spell-bound triumph). But he mounted right to the top. And I heard harps in the air. *(Waves her shawl in the air, and shrieks with wild intensity.)* My—my Master Builder!

PILLARS OF SOCIETY
(1877)

A PLAY IN FOUR ACTS

DRAMATIS PERSONÆ

KARSTEN BERNICK, a shipbuilder.
MRS. BERNICK, his wife.
OLAF, their son, thirteen years old.
MARTHA BERNICK, Karsten Bernick's sister.
JOHAN TÖNNESEN, Mrs. Bernick's younger brother.
LONA HESSEL, Mrs. Bernick's elder half-sister.
HILMAR TÖNNESEN, Mrs. Bernick's cousin.
DINA DORF, a young girl living with the Bernicks.
RÖRLUND, a schoolmaster.
RUMMEL, a merchant.
VIGELAND,
SANDSTAD, } tradesmen.
KRAP, Bernick's confidential clerk.
AUNE, foreman of Bernick's shipbuilding yard.
MRS. RUMMEL.
HILDA RUMMEL, her daughter.
MRS. HOLT.
NETTA HOLT, her daughter.
MRS. LYNGE.
Townsfolk and visitors, foreign sailors, steamboat
    passengers, etc., etc.

*(The action takes place at the Bernicks' house in
    one of the smaller coast towns in Norway.)*

ACT I.

(SCENE.—*A spacious garden-room in the* BERNICKS' *house. In the foreground on the left is a door leading to* BERNICK'S *business room; farther back in the same wall, a similar door. In the middle of the opposite wall is a large entrance-door, which leads to the street. The wall in the background is almost wholly composed of plate-glass; a door in it opens upon a broad flight of steps which lead down to the garden; a sun-awning is stretched over the steps. Below the steps a part of the garden is visible, bordered by a fence with a small gate in it. On the other side of the fence runs a street, the opposite side of which is occupied by small wooden houses painted in bright colours. It is summer, and the sun is shining warmly. People are seen, every now and then, passing along the street and stopping to talk to one another; others going in and out of a shop at the corner; etc., etc.*

In the room a gathering of ladies is seated round a table. MRS. BERNICK *is presiding; on her left side are* MRS. HOLT *and her daughter* NETTA, *and next to them* MRS. RUMMEL *and* HILDA RUMMEL. *On* MRS. BERNICK'S *right are* MRS. LYNGE, MARTHA BERNICK *and* DINA DORF. *All the ladies are busy working. On the table lie great piles of linen garments and other articles of clothing, some half finished and some merely cut out. Farther back, at a small table on which two pots of flowers and a glass of sugared water are standing,* RÖRLUND *is sitting, reading aloud from a book with gilt edges, but only loud enough for the spectators to catch a*

word now and then.   Out in the garden OLAF BERNICK *is
running about and shooting at a target with a toy crossbow.*

After a moment AUNE *comes in quietly through the door
on the right.   There is a slight interruption in the reading.*
MRS. BERNICK *nods to him and points to the door on the
left.* AUNE *goes quietly across, knocks softly at the door of*
BERNICK'S *room, and after a moment's pause knocks again.*
KRAP *comes out of the room, with his hat in his hand and
some papers under his arm.*)

Krap.   Oh, it was you knocking?

Aune.   Mr. Bernick sent for me.

Krap.   He did; but he cannot see you. He has deputed
me to tell you—

Aune.   Deputed you?   All the same, I would much
rather—

Krap.   —deputed me to tell you what he wanted to say to
you. You must give up these Saturday lectures of yours to
the men.

Aune.   Indeed?   I supposed I might use my own time—

Krap.   You must not use your own time in making the
men useless in working hours. Last Saturday you were talking to them of the harm that would be done to the workmen
by our new machines and the new working methods at the
yard. What makes you do that?

Aune.   I do it for the good of the community.

Krap.   That's curious, because Mr. Bernick says it is dis-
organising the community.

Aune.   My community is not Mr. Bernick's, Mr. Krap!
As president of the Industrial Association, I must—

Krap.   You are, first and foremost, president of Mr. Bernick's shipbuilding yard; and, before everything else, you
have to do your duty to the community known as the firm of
Bernick & Co.; that is what every one of us lives for. Well,
now you know what Mr. Bernick had to say to you.

Aune.   Mr. Bernick would not have put it that way, Mr.
Krap! But I know well enough whom I have to thank for

this. It is that damned American boat. Those fellows expect to get work done here the way they are accustomed to it over there, and that—

Krap Yes, yes, but I can't go into all these details. You know now what Mr. Bernick means, and that is sufficient. Be so good as to go back to the yard; probably you are needed there. I shall be down myself in a little while.— Excuse me, ladies! (*Bows to the ladies and goes out through the garden and down the street.* AUNE *goes quietly out to the right.* RÖRLUND, *who has continued his reading during the foregoing conversation, which has been carried on in low tones, has now come to the end of the book, and shuts it with a bang.*)

Rörlund. There, my dear ladies, that is the end of it.

Mrs. Rummel. What an instructive tale!

Mrs. Holt. And such a good moral!

Mrs. Bernick. A book like that really gives one something to think about.

Rörlund. Quite so; it presents a salutary contrast to what, unfortunately, meets our eyes every day in the newspapers and magazines. Look at the gilded and painted exterior displayed by any large community, and think what it really conceals!—emptiness and rottenness, if I may say so; no foundation of morality beneath it. In a word, these large communities of ours now-a-days are whited sepulchres.

Mrs. Holt. How true! How true!

Mrs. Rummel. And for an example of it we need look no farther than at the crew of the American ship that is lying here just now.

Rörlund. Oh, I would rather not speak of such offscourings of humanity as that. But even in higher circles—what is the case there? A spirit of doubt and unrest on all sides; minds never at peace, and instability characterising all their behaviour. Look how completely family life is undermined over there! Look at their shameless love of casting doubt on even the most serious truths!

Dina (without looking up from her work.) But are there not many big things done there too?

Rörlund. Big things done—? I do not understand—.

Mrs. Holt (in amazement). Good gracious, Dina—!

Mrs. Rummel (in the same breath). Dina, how can you—?

Rörlund. I think it would scarcely be a good thing for us if such "big things" became the rule here. No, indeed, we ought to be only too thankful that things are as they are in this country. It is true enough that tares grow up amongst our wheat here too, alas; but we do our best conscientiously to weed them out as well as we are able. The important thing is to keep society pure, ladies—to ward off all the hazardous experiments that a restless age seeks to force upon us.

Mrs. Holt. And there are more than enough of them in the wind, unhappily.

Mrs. Rummel. Yes, you know last year we only by a hair's breadth escaped the project of having a railway here.

Mrs. Bernick. Ah, my husband prevented that.

Rörlund. Providence, Mrs. Bernick. You may be certain that your husband was the instrument of a higher Power when he refused to have anything to do with the scheme.

Mrs. Bernick. And yet they said such horrible things about him in the newspapers! But we have quite forgotten to thank you, Mr. Rörlund. It is really more than friendly of you to sacrifice so much of your time to us.

Rörlund. Not at all. This is holiday time, and—

Mrs. Bernick. Yes, but it is a sacrifice all the same, Mr. Rörlund.

Rörlund (drawing his chair nearer). Don't speak of it, my dear lady. Are you not all of you making some sacrifice in a good cause?—and that willingly and gladly? These poor fallen creatures for whose rescue we are working may be compared to soldiers wounded on the field of battle; you, ladies, are the kind-hearted sisters of mercy who prepare the lint for these stricken ones, lay the bandages softly on their wounds, heal them and cure them—

Mrs. Bernick. It must be a wonderful gift to be able to see everything in such a beautiful light.

Rörlund. A good deal of it is inborn in one—but it can be to a great extent acquired, too. All that is needful is to see things in the light of a serious mission in life. (*To* MARTHA:) What do you say, Miss Bernick? Have you not felt as if you were standing on firmer ground since you gave yourself up to your school work?

Martha. I really do not know what to say. There are times, when I am in the schoolroom down there, that I wish I were far away out on the stormy seas.

Rörlund. That is merely temptation, dear Miss Bernick. You ought to shut the doors of your mind upon such disturbing guests as that. By the "stormy seas"—for of course you do not intend me to take your words literally—you mean the restless tide of the great outer world, where so many are shipwrecked. Do you really set such store on the life you hear rushing by outside? Only look out into the street. There they go, walking about in the heat of the sun, perspiring and tumbling about over their little affairs. No, we undoubtedly have the best of it, who are able to sit here in the cool and turn our backs on the quarter from which disturbance comes.

Martha. Yes, I have no doubt you are perfectly right—

Rörlund. And in a house like this—in a good and pure home, where family life shows in its fairest colours—where peace and harmony rule— (*To* MRS. BERNICK:) What are you listening to, Mrs. Bernick?

Mrs. Bernick (who has turned towards the door of BERNICK'S *room*). They are talking very loud in there.

Rörlund. Is there anything particular going on?

Mrs. Bernick. I don't know. I can hear that there is somebody with my husband.

(HILMAR TÖNNESEN, *smoking a cigar, appears in the door-*

way on the right, but stops short at the sight of the company of ladies.)

Hilmar.　Oh, excuse me—　(*Turns to go back.*)

Mrs. Bernick.　No, Hilmar, come along in; you are not disturbing us.　Do you want something?

Hilmar.　No, I only wanted to look in here.—Good morning, ladies.　(*To* MRS. BERNICK.)　Well, what is the result?

Mrs. Bernick.　Of what?

Hilmar.　Karsten has summoned a meeting, you know.

Mrs. Bernick.　Has he?　What about?

Hilmar.　Oh, it is this railway nonsense over again.

Mrs. Rummel.　Is it possible?

Mrs. Bernick.　Poor Karsten, is he to have more annoyance over that?

Rörlund.　But how do you explain that, Mr. Tönnesen? You know that last year Mr. Bernick made it perfectly clear that he would not have a railway here.

Hilmar.　Yes, that is what I thought, too; but I met Krap, his confidential clerk, and he told me that the railway project had been taken up again, and that Mr. Bernick was in consultation with three of our local capitalists.

Mrs. Rummel.　Ah, I was right in thinking I heard my husband's voice.

Hilmar.　Of course Mr. Rummel is in it, and so are Sandstad and Michael Vigeland—"Saint Michael," as they call him.

Rörlund.　Ahem!

Hilmar.　I beg your pardon, Mr. Rörlund?

Mrs. Bernick.　Just when everything was so nice and peaceful.

Hilmar.　Well, as far as I am concerned, I have not the slightest objection to their beginning their squabbling again. It will be a little diversion, anyway.

Rörlund.　I think we can dispense with that sort of diversion.

Hilmar.　It depends how you are constituted.　Certain

natures feel the lust of battle now and then. But unfortunately life in a country town does not offer much in that way, and it isn't given to every one to—(*turns the leaves of the book* RÖRLUND *has been reading*). "Woman as the Handmaid of Society." What sort of drivel is this?

Mrs. Bernick. My dear Hilmar, you must not say that. You certainly have not read the book.

Hilmar. No, and I have no intention of reading it, either.

Mrs. Bernick. Surely you are not feeling quite well today.

Hilmar. No, I am not.

Mrs. Bernick. Perhaps you did not sleep well last night?

Hilmar. No, I slept very badly. I went for a walk yesterday evening for my health's sake; and I finished up at the club and read a book about a Polar expedition. There is something bracing in following the adventures of men who are battling with the elements.

Mrs. Rummel. But it does not appear to have done you much good, Mr. Tönnesen.

Hilmar. No, it certainly did not. I lay all night tossing about, only half asleep, and dreamt that I was being chased by a hideous walrus.

Olaf (*who meanwhile has come up the steps from the garden*). Have you been chased by a walrus, uncle?

Hilmar. I dreamt it, you duffer! Do you mean to say you are still playing about with that ridiculous bow? Why don't you get hold of a real gun?

Olaf. I should like to, but—

Hilmar. There is some sense in a thing like that; it is always an excitement every time you fire it off.

Olaf. And then I could shoot bears, uncle. But daddy won't let me.

Mrs. Bernick. You really mustn't put such ideas into his head, Hilmar.

Hilmar. Hm!—it's a nice breed we are educating up now-a-days, isn't it! We *talk* a great deal about manly sports, goodness knows—but we only play with the question, all the same; there is never any serious inclination for the bracing discipline that lies in facing danger manfully. Don't stand pointing your crossbow at me, blockhead—it might go off.

Olaf. No, uncle, there is no arrow in it.

Hilmar. You don't know that there isn't—there may be, all the same. Take it away, I tell you!—Why on earth have you never gone over to America on one of your father's ships? You might have seen a buffalo hunt then, or a fight with Red Indians.

Mrs. Bernick. Oh, Hilmar—!

Olaf. I should like that awfully, uncle; and then perhaps I might meet Uncle Johan and Aunt Lona.

Hilmar. Hm!—Rubbish.

Mrs. Bernick. You can go down into the garden again now, Olaf.

Olaf. Mother, may I go out into the street too?

Mrs. Bernick. Yes, but not too far, mind.

(OLAF *runs down into the garden and out through the gate in the fence.*)

Rörlund. You ought not to put such fancies into the child's head, Mr. Tönnesen.

Hilmar. No, of course he is destined to be a miserable stay-at-home, like so many others.

Rörlund. But why do you not take a trip over there yourself?

Hilmar. I? With my wretched health? Of course I get no consideration on that account. But putting that out of the question, you forget that one has certain obligations to perform towards the community of which one forms a part. There must be *some one* here to hold aloft the banner of the Ideal.—Ugh, there he is shouting again!

The Ladies. Who is shouting?

Hilmar. I am sure I don't know. They are raising their voices so loud in there that it gets on my nerves.

Mrs. Bernick. I expect it is my husband, Mr. Tönnesen. But you must remember he is so accustomed to addressing large audiences—

Rörlund. I should not call the others low-voiced, either.

Hilmar. Good Lord, no!—not on any question that touches their pockets. Everything here ends in these petty material considerations. Ugh!

Mrs. Bernick. Anyway, that is a better state of things than it used to be when everything ended in mere frivolity.

Mrs. Lynge. Used things really to be as bad as that here?

Mrs. Rummel. Indeed they were, Mrs. Lynge. You may think yourself lucky that you did not live here then.

Mrs. Holt. Yes, times have changed, and no mistake. When I look back to the days when I was a girl—

Mrs. Rummel. Oh, you need not look back more than fourteen or fifteen years. God forgive us, what a life we led! There used to be a Dancing Society and a Musical Society—

Mrs. Bernick. And the Dramatic Club. I remember it very well.

Mrs. Rummel. Yes, that was where your play was performed, Mr. Tönnesen?

Hilmar (*from the back of the room*). What, what?

Rörlund. A play by Mr. Tönnesen?

Mrs. Rummel. Yes, it was long before you came here, Mr. Rörlund. And it was only performed once.

Mrs. Lynge. Was that not the play in which you told me you took the part of a young man's sweetheart, Mrs. Rummel?

Mrs. Rummel (*glancing towards* RÖRLUND). I? I really cannot remember, Mrs. Lynge. But I remember well all the riotous gaiety that used to go on.

Mrs. Holt. Yes, there were houses I could name in which two large dinner-parties were given in one week.

Mrs. Lynge. And surely I have heard that a touring theatrical company came here, too?

Mrs. Rummel. Yes, that was the worst thing of the lot—

Mrs. Holt (*uneasily*). Ahem!

Mrs. Rummel. Did you say a theatrical company? No, I don't remember that at all.

Mrs. Lynge. Oh yes, and I have been told they played all sorts of mad pranks. What is really the truth of those stories?

Mrs. Rummel. There is practically no truth in them, Mrs. Lynge.

Mrs. Holt. Dina, my love, will you give me that linen?

Mrs. Bernick (*at the same time*). Dina, dear, will you go and ask Katrine to bring us our coffee?

Martha. I will go with you, Dina.

(DINA *and* MARTHA *go out by the farther door on the left.*)

Mrs. Bernick (*getting up*). Will you excuse me for a few minutes? I think we will have our coffee outside. (*She goes out to the verandah and sets to work to lay a table.* RÖRLUND *stands in the doorway talking to her.* HILMAR *sits outside, smoking.*)

Mrs. Rummel (*in a low voice*). My goodness, Mrs. Lynge, how you frightened me!

Mrs. Lyne. I?

Mrs. Holt. Yes, but you know it was you that began it, Mrs. Rummel.

Mrs. Rummel. I? How can you say such a thing, Mrs. Holt? Not a syllable passed my lips!

Mrs. Lynge. But what does it all mean?

Mrs. Rummel. What made you begin to talk about—? Think—did you not see that Dina was in the room?

Mrs. Lynge. Dina? Good gracious, is there anything wrong with—?

Mrs. Holt. And in this house, too! Did you not know it was Mrs. Bernick's brother—?

Mrs. Lynge. What about him? I know nothing about it at all; I am quite new to the place, you know.

Mrs. Rummel. Have you not heard that—? Ahem! (*To*

her daughter.) Hilda, dear, you can go for a little stroll in the garden.

Mrs. Holt. You go too, Netta. And be very kind to poor Dina when she comes back. (HILDA *and* NETTA *go out into the garden.*)

Mrs. Lynge. Well, what about Mrs. Bernick's brother?

Mrs. Rummel. Don't you know the dreadful scandal about him?

Mrs. Lynge. A dreadful scandal about Mr. Tönnesen?

Mrs. Rummel. Good Heavens, no. Mr. Tönnesen is her cousin, of course, Mrs. Lynge. I am speaking of her brother——

Mrs. Holt. The wicked Mr. Tönnesen——

Mrs. Rummel. His name was Johan. He ran away to America.

Mrs. Holt. Had to run away, you must understand.

Mrs. Lynge. Then it is he the scandal is about?

Mrs. Rummel. Yes; there was something—how shall I put it?—there was something of some kind between him and Dina's mother. I remember it all as if it were yesterday. Johan Tönnesen was in old Mrs. Bernick's office then; Karsten Bernick had just come back from Paris—he had not yet become engaged——

Mrs. Lynge. Yes, but what was the scandal?

Mrs. Rummel. Well, you must know that Möller's company were acting in the town that winter——

Mrs. Holt. And Dorf, the actor, and his wife were in the company. All the young men in the town were infatuated with her.

Mrs. Rummel. Yes, goodness knows how they could think *her* pretty. Well, Dorf came home late one evening——

Mrs. Holt. Quite unexpectedly.

Mrs. Rummel. And found his—. No, really it isn't a thing one can talk about.

Mrs. Holt. After all, Mrs. Rummel, he didn't find anything, because the door was locked on the inside.

Mrs. Rummel. Yes, that is just what I was going to say
—he found the door locked. And—just think of it—the
man that was in the house had to jump out of the window.

Mrs. Holt. Right down from an attic window.

Mrs. Lynge. And that was Mrs. Bernick's brother?

Mrs. Rummel. Yes, it was he.

Mrs. Lynge. And that was why he ran away to America?

Mrs. Holt. Yes, he had to run away, you may be sure.

Mrs. Rummel. Because something was discovered afterwards that was nearly as bad; just think—he had been
making free with the cash-box—

Mrs. Holt. But, you know, no one was certain of that,
Mrs. Rummel; perhaps there was no truth in the rumour.

Mrs. Rummel. Well, I must say—! Wasn't it known
all over the town? Did not old Mrs. Bernick nearly go
bankrupt as the result of it? However, God forbid *I* should
be the one to spread such reports.

Mrs. Holt. Well, anyway, Mrs. Dorf didn't get the
money, because she—

Mrs. Lynge. Yes, what happened to Dina's parents afterwards?

Mrs. Rummel. Well, Dorf deserted both his wife and
his child. But madam was impudent enough to stay here
a whole year. Of course she had not the face to appear at
the theatre any more, but she kept herself by taking in washing and sewing—

Mrs. Holt. And then she tried to set up a dancing school.

Mrs. Rummel. Naturally that was no good. What
parents would trust their children to such a woman? But
it did not last very long. The fine madam was not accustomed to work; she got something wrong with her lungs and
died of it.

Mrs. Lynge. What a horrible scandal!

Mrs. Rummel. Yes, you can imagine how hard it was
upon the Bernicks. It is the dark spot among the sunshine

of their good fortune, as Rummel once put it. So never speak about it in this house, Mrs. Lynge.

Mrs. Holt. And for heaven's sake never mention the step-sister, either!

Mrs. Lynge. Oh, so Mrs. Bernick has a step-sister, too?

Mrs. Rummel. *Had,* luckily; for the relationship between them is all over now. She was an extraordinary person too! Would you believe it, she cut her hair short, and used to go about in men's boots in bad weather!

Mrs. Holt. And when her step-brother—the black sheep —had gone away, and the whole town naturally was talking about him—what do you think she did? She went out to America to him!

Mrs. Rummel. Yes, but remember the scandal *she* caused before she went, Mrs. Holt!

Mrs. Holt. Hush, don't speak of it.

Mrs. Lynge. My goodness, did she create a scandal too?

Mrs. Rummel. I think you ought to hear it, Mrs. Lynge. Mr. Bernick had just got engaged to Betty Tönnesen, and the two of them went arm in arm into her aunt's room to tell her the news——

Mrs. Holt. The Tönnesens' parents were dead, you know——

Mrs. Rummel. When, suddenly, up got Lona Hessel from her chair and gave our refined and well-bred Karsten Bernick such a box on the ear that his head swam.

Mrs. Lynge. Well, I am sure I never—

Mrs. Holt. It is absolutely true.

Mrs. Rummel. And then she packed her box and went away to America.

Mrs. Lynge. I suppose she had had her eye on him for herself.

Mrs. Rummel. Of course she had. She imagined that he and she would make a match of it when he came back from Paris.

Mrs. Holt. The idea of her thinking such a thing!

Karsten Bernick—a man of the world and the pink of courtesy—a perfect gentleman—the darling of all the ladies—

Mrs. Rummel. And, with it all, such an excellent young man, Mrs. Holt—so moral.

Mrs. Lynge. But what has this Miss Hessel made of herself in America?

Mrs. Rummel. Well, you see, over that (as my husband once put it) has been drawn a veil which one should hesitate to lift.

Mrs. Lynge. What do you mean?

Mrs. Rummel. She no longer has any connection with the family, as you may suppose; but this much the whole town knows, that she has sung for money in drinking saloons over there——

Mrs. Holt. And has given lectures in public——

Mrs. Rummel. And has published some mad kind of book.

Mrs. Lynge. You don't say so!

Mrs. Rummel. Yes, it is true enough that Lona Hessel is one of the spots on the sun of the Bernick family's good fortune. Well, now you know the whole story, Mrs. Lynge. I am sure I would never have spoken about it except to put you on your guard.

Mrs. Lynge. Oh, you may be sure I shall be most careful. But that poor child Dina Dorf! I am truly sorry for her.

Mrs. Rummel. Well, really it was a stroke of good luck for her. Think what it would have meant if she had been brought up by such parents! Of course we did our best for her, every one of us, and gave her all the good advice we could. Eventually Miss Bernick got her taken into this house.

Mrs. Holt. But she has always been a difficult child to deal with. It is only natural—with all the bad example she had had before her. A girl of that sort is not like one of our own; one must be lenient with her.

Mrs. Rummel. Hush—here she comes. (*In a louder voice.*) Yes, Dina is really a clever girl. Oh, is that you, Dina? We are just putting away the things.

Mrs. Holt. How delicious your coffee smells, my dear Dina. A nice cup of coffee like that—.

Mrs. Bernick (calling in from the verandah.) Will you come out here? (*Meanwhile* MARTHA *and* DINA *have helped the maid to bring out the coffee. All the ladies seat themselves on the verandah, and talk with a great show of kindness to* DINA. *In a few moments* DINA *comes back into the room and looks for her sewing.*

Mrs. Bernick (from the coffee table). Dina, won't you—?

Dina. No, thank you. (*Sits down to her sewing.* MRS. BERNICK *and* RÖRLUND *exchange a few words; a moment afterwards he comes back into the room, makes a pretext for going up to the table, and begins speaking to* DINA *in low tones.*)

Rörlund. Dina.

Dina. Yes?

Rörlund. Why don't you want to sit with the others?

Dina. When I came in with the coffee, I could see from the strange lady's face that they had been talking about me.

Rörlund. But did you not see as well how agreeable she was to you out there?

Dina. That is just what I will not stand!

Rörlund. You are very self-willed, Dina.

Dina. Yes.

Rörlund. But why?

Dina. Because it is my nature.

Rörlund. Could you not try to alter your nature?

Dina. No.

Rörlund. Why not?

Dina (looking at him). Because I am one of the "poor fallen creatures," you know.

Rörlund. For shame, Dina.

Dina. So was my mother.

Rörlund. Who has spoken to you about such things?

Dina. No one; they never do. Why don't they? They all handle me in such a gingerly fashion, as if they thought I should go to pieces if they— Oh, how I hate all this kind-heartedness.

Rörlund. My dear Dina, I can quite understand that you feel repressed here, but—

Dina. Yes; if only I could get right away from here. I could make my own way quite well, if only I did not live amongst people who are so—so—

Rörlund. So what?

Dina. So proper and so moral.

Rörlund. Oh but, Dina, you don't mean that.

Dina. You know quite well in what sense I mean it. Hilda and Netta come here every day, to be exhibited to me as good examples. I can never be so beautifully be-haved as they; I don't *want* to be. If only I were right away from it all, I should grow to be worth something.

Rörlund. But you are worth a great deal, Dina dear.

Dina. What good does that do me here?

Rörlund. Get right away, you say? Do you mean it seriously?

Dina. I would not stay here a day longer, if it were not for you.

Rörlund. Tell me, Dina—why is it that you are fond of being with me?

Dina. Because you teach me so much that is beautiful.

Rörlund. Beautiful? Do you call the little I can teach you, beautiful?

Dina. Yes. Or perhaps, to be accurate, it is not that you teach me anything; but when I listen to you talking I see beautiful visions.

Rörlund. What do you mean exactly when you call a thing beautiful?

Dina. I have never thought it out.

Rörluna. Think it out now, then. What do you understand by a beautiful thing?

Dina. A beautiful thing is something that is great—and far off.

Rörlund. Hm!—Dina, I am so deeply concerned about you, my dear.

Dina. Only that?

Rörlund. You know perfectly well that you are dearer to me than I can say.

Dina. If I were Hilda or Netta, you would not be afraid to let people see it.

Rörlund. Ah, Dina, you can have no idea of the number of things I am forced to take into consideration. When it is a man's lot to be a moral pillar of the community he lives in, he cannot be too circumspect. If only I could be certain that people would interpret my motives properly— But no matter for that; you must, and shall be, helped to raise yourself. Dina, is it a bargain between us that when I come—when circumstances allow me to come—to you and say: "Here is my hand," you will take it and be my wife? Will you promise me that, Dina?

Dina. Yes.

Rörlund. Thank you, thank you! Because for my part, too—oh, Dina, I love you so dearly. Hush! Some one is coming. Dina—for my sake—go out to the others. (*She goes out to the coffee table. At the same moment* RUMMEL, SANDSTAD *and* VIGELAND *come out of* BERNICK'S *room, followed by* BERNICK, *who has a bundle of papers in his hand.*)

Bernick. Well, then, the matter is settled.

Vigeland. Yes, I hope to goodness it is.

Rummel. It is settled, Bernick. A Norseman's word stands as firm as the rocks on Dovrefjeld, you know!

Bernick. And no one must falter, no one give way, no matter what opposition we meet with.

Rummel. We will stand or fall together, Bernick.

Hilmar (*coming in from the verandah*). Fall? If I

may ask, isn't it the railway scheme that is going to fall?

Bernick. No, on the contrary, it is going to proceed—

Rummel. Full steam, Mr. Tönnesen.

Hilmar (coming nearer). Really?

Rörlund. How is that?

Mrs. Bernick (at the verandah door). Karsten dear, what is it that—?

Bernick. My dear Betty, how can it interest you? (*To the three men.*) We must get out lists of subscribers, and the sooner the better. Obviously our four names must head the list. The positions we occupy in the community make it our duty to make ourselves as prominent as possible in the affair.

Sandstad. Obviously, Mr. Bernick.

Rummel. The thing *shall* go through, Bernick; I swear it shall.

Bernick. Oh, I have not the least anticipation of failure. We must see that we work, each one among the circle of his own acquaintances; and if we can point to the fact that the scheme is exciting a lively interest in all ranks of society, then it stands to reason that our Municipal Corporation will have to contribute its share.

Mrs. Bernick. Karsten, you really must come out here and tell us—

Bernick. My dear Betty, it is an affair that does not concern ladies at all.

Hilmar. Then you are really going to support this railway scheme after all?

Bernick. Yes, naturally.

Rörlund. But last year, Mr. Bernick—

Bernick. Last year it was quite another thing. At that time it was a question of a line along the coast—

Vigeland. Which would have been quite superfluous, Mr. Rörlund; because, of course, we have our steamboat service——

Sandstad. And would have been quite unreasonably costly——

Rummel. Yes, and would have absolutely ruined certain important interests in the town.

Bernick. The main point was that it would not have been to the advantage of the community as a whole. That is why I opposed it, with the result that the inland line was resolved upon.

Hilmar. Yes, but surely that will not touch the towns about here.

Bernick. It will eventually touch *our* town, my dear Hilmar, because we are going to build a branch line here.

Hilmar. Aha—a new scheme, then?

Rummel. Yes, isn't it a capital scheme? What?

Rörlund. Hm!——

Vigeland. There is no denying that it looks as though Providence had just planned the configuration of the country to suit a branch line.

Rörlund. Do you really mean it, Mr. Vigeland?

Bernick. Yes, I must confess it seems to me as if it had been the hand of Providence that caused me to take a journey on business this spring, in the course of which I happened to traverse a valley through which I had never been before. It came across my mind like a flash of lightning that this was where we could carry a branch line down to our town. I got an engineer to survey the neighbourhood, and have here the provisional calculations and estimate; so there is nothing to hinder us.

Mrs. Bernick (who is still with the other ladies at the verandah door). But, my dear Karsten, to think that you should have kept it all a secret from us!

Bernick. Ah, my dear Betty, I knew you would not have been able to grasp the exact situation. Besides, I have not mentioned it to a living soul till to-day. But now the decisive moment has come, and we must work openly and with all our might. Yes, even if I have to risk all I have for its sake, I mean to push the matter through.

Rummel. And we will back you up, Bernick; you may rely upon that.

Rörlund. Do you really promise us so much, then, from this undertaking, gentlemen?

Bernick. Yes, undoubtedly. Think what a lever it will be to raise the status of our whole community. Just think of the immense tracts of forest-land that it will make accessible; think of all the rich deposits of minerals we shall be able to work; think of the river with one waterfall above another! Think of the possibilities that open out in the way of manufactories!

Rörlund. And are you not afraid that an easier intercourse with the depravity of the outer world—?

Bernick. No, you may make your mind quite easy on that score, Mr. Rörlund. Our little hive of industry rests now-a-days, God be thanked, on such a sound moral basis; we have all of us helped to drain it, if I may use the expression; and that we will continue to do, each in his degree. You, Mr. Rörlund, will continue your richly blessed activity in our schools and our homes. We, the practical men of business, will be the support of the community by extending its welfare within as wide a radius as possible; and our women—yes, come nearer, ladies, you will like to hear it—our women, I say, our wives and daughters—you, ladies, will work on undisturbed in the service of charity, and moreover will be a help and a comfort to your nearest and dearest, as my dear Betty and Martha are to me and Olaf— (*Looks round him.*) Where is Olaf to-day?

Mrs. Bernick. Oh, in the holidays it is impossible to keep him at home.

Bernick. I have no doubt he is down at the shore again. You will see he will end by coming to some harm there.

Hilmar. Bah! A little sport with the forces of nature—

Mrs. Rummel. Your family affection is beautiful, Mr. Bernick!

Bernick. Well, the family is the kernel of society. A good home, honoured and trusty friends, a little snug family circle where no disturbing elements can cast their shadow— (KRAP *comes in from the right, bringing letters and papers*).

Krap. The foreign mail, Mr. Bernick—and a telegram from New York.

Bernick (*taking the telegram*). Ah—from the owners of the "Indian Girl."

Rummel. Is the mail in? Oh, then you must excuse me.

Vigeland. And me too.

Sandstad. Good day, Mr. Bernick.

Bernick. Good day, good day, gentlemen. And remember, we have a meeting this afternoon at five o'clock.

The Three Men. Yes—quite so—of course. (*They go out to the right.*)

Bernick (*who has read the telegram*). This is thoroughly American! Absolutely shocking!

Mrs. Bernick. Good gracious, Karsten, what is it?

Bernick. Look at this, Krap! Read it!

Krap (*reading*). "Do the least repairs possible. Send over 'Indian Girl' as soon as she is ready to sail; good time of year; at a pinch her cargo will keep her afloat." Well, I must say—

Rörlund. You see the state of things in these vaunted great communities!

Bernick. You are quite right; not a moment's consideration for human life, when it is a question of making a profit. (*To* KRAP:) Can the "Indian Girl" go to sea in four—or five—days?

Krap. Yes, if Mr. Vigeland will agree to our stopping work on the "Palm Tree" meanwhile.

Bernick. Hm—he won't. Well, be so good as to look through the letters. And look here, did you see Olaf down at the quay?

Krap. No, Mr. Bernick. (*Goes into* BERNICK'S *room.*)

Bernick (*looking at the telegram again*). These gentlemen think nothing of risking eight men's lives—

Hilmar. Well, it is a sailor's calling to brave the elements: it must be a fine tonic to the nerves to be like that, with only a thin plank between one and the abyss—

Bernick. I should like to see the ship-owner amongst us who would condescend to such a thing! There is not one that would do it—not a single one! (*Sees* OLAF *coming up to the house.*) Ah, thank Heaven, here he is, safe and sound. (OLAF, *with a fishing-line in his hand, comes running up the garden and in through the verandah.*)

Olaf. Uncle Hilmar, I have been down and seen the steamer.

Bernick. Have you been down to the quay again?

Olaf. No, I have only been out in a boat. But just think, Uncle Hilmar, a whole circus company has come on shore, with horses and animals; and there were such lots of passengers.

Mrs. Rummel. No, are we really to have a circus?

Rörlund. We? I certainly have no desire to see it.

Mrs. Rummel. No, of course I don't mean *we*, but—

Dina. I should like to see a circus very much.

Olaf. So should I.

Hilmar. You are a duffer. Is that anything to see? Mere tricks. No, it would be something quite different to see the Gaucho careering over the Pampas on his snorting mustang. But, Heaven help us, in these wretched little towns of ours—

Olaf (*pulling at* MARTHA'S *dress*). Look, Aunt Martha! Look, there they come!

Mrs. Holt. Good Lord, yes—here they come.

Mrs. Lynge. Ugh, what horrid people!

(*A number of passengers and a whole crowd of townsfolk are seen coming up the street.*)

Mrs. Rummel. They *are* a set of mountebanks, certainly. Just look at that woman in the grey dress, Mrs. Holt—the one with a knapsack over her shoulder.

Mrs. Holt. Yes—look—she has slung it on the handle of her parasol. The manager's wife, I expect.

Mrs. Rummel. And there is the manager himself, no doubt! He looks a regular pirate. Don't look at him, Hilda!

Mrs. Holt. Nor you, Netta!

Olaf. Mother, the manager is bowing to us.

Bernick. What?

Mrs. Bernick. What are you saying, child?

Mrs. Rummel. Yes, and—good heavens—the woman is bowing to us too.

Bernick. That is a little *too* cool!

Martha (exclaims involuntarily). Ah—!

Mrs. Bernick. What is it, Martha?

Martha. Nothing, nothing. I thought for a moment—

Olaf (shrieking with delight). Look, look, there are the rest of them, with the horses and animals! And there are the Americans, too! All the sailors from the "Indian Girl"! (*The strains of "Yankee Doodle," played on a clarinet and a drum, are heard.*)

Hilmar (stopping his ears). Ugh, ugh, ugh!

Rörlund. I think we ought to withdraw ourselves from sight a little, ladies; we have nothing to do with such goings on. Let us go to our work again.

Mrs. Bernick. Do you think we had better draw the curtains?

Rörlund. Yes, that is exactly what I meant.

(*The ladies resume their places at the work-table;* RÖR-
LUND *shuts the verandah door, and draws the curtains over it and over the windows, so that the room be- comes half dark.*)

Olaf (peeping out through the curtains). Mother, the manager's wife is standing by the fountain now, washing her face.

Mrs. Bernick. What? In the middle of the market- place?

Mrs. Rummel. And in broad daylight, too!

Hilmar. Well, I must say if I were travelling across a desert waste and found myself beside a well, I am sure I should not stop to think whether— Ugh, that frightful clarinet!

Rörlund. It is really high time the police interfered.

Bernick. Oh no! we must not be too hard on foreigners. Of course these folk have none of the deep-seated instincts of decency which restrain us within proper bounds. Suppose they do behave outrageously, what does it concern us? Fortunately this spirit of disorder, that flies in the face of all that is customary and right, is absolutely a stranger to our community, if I may say so— What is this! (LONA HESSEL *walks briskly in from the door on the right.*)

The Ladies (*in low, frightened tones.*) The circus woman! The manager's wife!

Mrs. Bernick. Heavens, what does this mean!

Martha (*jumping up*). Ah—!

Lona. How do you do, Betty dear! How do you do, Martha! How do you do, brother-in-law!

Mrs. Bernick (*with a cry*). Lona—!

Bernick (*stumbling backwards*). As sure as I am alive—!

Mrs. Holt. Mercy on us—!

Mrs. Rummel. It cannot possibly be—!

Hilmar. Well! Ugh!

Mrs. Bernick. Lona—! Is it really—?

Lona. Really me? Yes, indeed it is; you may fall on my neck if you like.

Hilmar. Ugh, ugh!

Mrs. Bernick. And coming back here as—?

Mrs. Bernick. And actually mean to appear in—?

Lona. Appear? Appear in what?

Bernick. Well, I mean—in the circus—

Lona. Ha, ha, ha! Are you mad, brother-in-law? Do you think I belong to the circus troupe? No; certainly I have turned my hand to a good many things, and made a fool of myself in a good many ways—

Mrs. Rummel. Hm!—

Lona. But I have never tried circus riding.

Bernick. Then you are not—?

Mrs. Bernick. Thank Heaven!

Lona. No, we travelled like other respectable folk — second-class, certainly, but we are accustomed to that.

Mrs. Bernick. We, did you say?

Bernick (*taking a step forward*). Whom do you mean by "we"?

Lona. I and the child, of course.

The Ladies (*with a cry*). The child!

Hilmar. What!

Rörlund. I really must say—!

Mrs. Bernick. But what do you mean, Lona?

Lona. I mean John, of course; I have no other child, as far as I know, but John—or Johan, as you used to call him.

Mrs. Bernick. Johan!

Mrs. Rummel (*in an undertone, to* Mrs. Lynge). The scapegrace brother!

Bernick (*hesitatingly*). Is Johan with you?

Lona. Of course he is; I certainly would not come without him. Why do you look so tragical? And why are you sitting here in the gloom, sewing white things? There has not been a death in the family, has there?

Rörlund. Madam, you find yourself in the Society for Fallen Women—

Lona (*half to herself*). What? Can these nice, quiet-looking ladies possibly be—?

Mrs. Rummel. Well, really—!

Lona. Oh, I understand! But, bless my soul, that is surely Mrs. Rummel? And Mrs. Holt sitting there too! Well, we three have not grown younger since the last time we met. But listen now, good people; let the Fallen Women wait for a day—they will be none the worse for that. A joyful occasion like this—

Rörlund. A home-coming is not always a joyful occasion.

Lona. Indeed? How do you read your Bible, Mr. Parson?

Rörlund. I am not a parson.

Lona. Oh, you will grow into one, then. But—faugh!—this moral linen of yours smells tainted—just like a winding-sheet. I am accustomed to the air of the prairies, let me tell you.

Bernick (wiping his forehead). Yes, it certainly is rather close in here.

Lona. Wait a moment; we will resurrect ourselves from this vault. (*Pulls the curtains to one side.*) We must have broad daylight in here when the boy comes. Ah, you will see a boy then that has washed himself—

Hilmar. Ugh!

Lona (opening the verandah door and window). I should say, *when* he has washed himself up at the hotel—for on the boat he got piggishly dirty.

Hilmar. Ugh, ugh!

Lona. Ugh! Why, surely isn't that—? (*Points at* HILMAR *and asks the others:*) Is *he* still loafing about here saying "Ugh"?

Hilmar. I do not loaf; it is the state of my health that keeps me here.

Rörlund. Ahem! Ladies, I do not think—

Lona (who has noticed OLAF). Is he yours, Betty? Give me a paw, my boy! Or are you afraid of your ugly old aunt?

Rörlund (putting his book under his arm). Ladies, I do not think any of us is in the mood for any more work to-day. I suppose we are to meet again to-morrow?

Lona (while the others are getting up and taking their leave). Yes, let us. I shall be on the spot.

Rörlund You? Pardon me, Miss Hessel, but what do you propose to do in *our* Society?

Lona. I will let some fresh air into it, Mr. Parson.

ACT II

(SCENE.—*The same room.* MRS. BERNICK *is sitting alone at the work-table, sewing.* BERNICK *comes in from the right, wearing his hat and gloves and carrying a stick.*)

Mrs. Bernick. Home already, Karsten?

Bernick. Yes, I have made an appointment with a man.

Mrs. Bernick (*with a sigh*). Oh yes, I suppose Johan is coming up here again.

Bernick. With a *man*, I said. (*Lays down his hat.*) What has become of all the ladies to-day?

Mrs. Bernick. Mrs. Rummel and Hilda hadn't time to come.

Bernick. Oh!—did they send any excuse?

Mrs. Bernick. Yes, they had so much to do at home.

Bernick. Naturally. And of course the others are not coming either?

Mrs. Bernick. No, something has prevented them to-day, too.

Bernick. I could have told you that, beforehand. Where is Olaf?

Mrs. Bernick. I let him go out a little with Dina.

Bernick. Hm—she is a giddy little baggage. Did you see how she at once started making a fuss of Johan yesterday?

Mrs. Bernick. But, my dear Karsten, you know Dina knows nothing whatever of—

Bernick. No, but in any case Johan ought to have had sufficient tact not to pay her any attention. I saw quite well, from his face, what Vigeland thought of it.

Mrs. Bernick (laying her sewing down on her lap). Karsten, can you imagine what his object is in coming here?

Bernick. Well—I know he has a farm over there, and I fancy he is not doing particularly well with it; *she* called attention yesterday to the fact that they were obliged to travel second class—

Mrs. Bernick. Yes, I am afraid it must be something of that sort. But to think of her coming with him? She! After the deadly insult she offered him!

Bernick. Oh, don't think about that ancient history.

Mrs. Bernick. How can I help thinking of it just now? After all, he is my brother—still, it is not on his account that I am distressed, but because of all the unpleasantness it would mean for you. Karsten, I am so dreadfully afraid—

Bernick. Afraid of what?

Mrs. Bernick. Isn't it possible that they may send him to prison for stealing that money from your mother?

Bernick. What rubbish! Who can prove that the money *was* stolen?

Mrs. Bernick. The whole town knows it, unfortunately; and you know you said yourself—

Bernick. I said nothing. The town knows nothing whatever about the affair; the whole thing was no more than idle rumour.

Mrs. Bernick. How magnanimous you are, Karsten!

Bernick. Do not let us have any more of these reminiscences, please! You don't know how you torture me by raking up all that. (*Walks up and down; then flings his stick away from him.*) And to think of their coming home now—just now, when it is particularly necessary for me that I should stand well in every respect with the town and with the Press. Our newspaper men will be sending paragraphs to the papers in the other towns about here. Whether I receive them well, or whether I receive them ill, it will all be discussed and talked over. They will rake up all those old stories—as you do. In a community like ours—(*Throws his gloves down on the table.*) And I have not a soul here to whom I can talk about it and to whom I can go for support.

Mrs. Bernick. No one at all, Karsten?

Bernick. No—who is there? And to have them on my shoulders just at this moment! Without a doubt they will create a scandal in some way or another—she, in particular. It is simply a calamity to be connected with such folk in any way!

Mrs. Bernick. Well, *I* can't help their—

Bernick. What can't you help? Their being your relations? No, that is quite true.

Mrs. Bernick. And I did not ask them to come home.

Bernick. That's it—go on! "I did not ask them to come home; I did not write to them; I did not drag them home by the hair of their heads!" Oh, I know the whole rigmarole by heart.

Mrs. Bernick (bursting into tears). You need not be so unkind—

Bernick. Yes, that's right—begin to cry, so that our neighbours may have that to gossip about too. Do stop being so foolish, Betty. Go and sit outside; some one may come in here. I don't suppose you want people to see the lady of the house with red eyes? It would be a nice thing, wouldn't it, if the story got about that— There, I hear some one in the passage. (*A knock is heard at the door.*) Come in! (MRS. BERNICK *takes her sewing and goes out down the garden steps.* AUNE *comes in from the right.*)

Aune. Good-morning, Mr. Bernick.

Bernick. Good-morning. Well, I suppose you can guess what I want you for?

Aune. Mr. Krap told me yesterday that you were not pleased with—

Bernick. I am displeased with the whole management of

the yard, Aune. The work does not get on as quickly as it ought. The "Palm Tree" ought to have been under sail long ago. Mr. Vigeland comes here every day to complain about it; he is a difficult man to have with one as part owner.

Aune. The "Palm Tree" can go to sea the day after to-morrow.

Bernick. At last. But what about the American ship, the "Indian Girl," which has been laid up here for five weeks and—

Aune. The American ship? I understood that, before everything else, we were to work our hardest to get your own ship ready.

Bernick. I gave you no reason to think so. You ought to have pushed on as fast as possible with the work on the American ship also; but you have not.

Aune. Her bottom is completely rotten, Mr. Bernick; the more we patch it, the worse it gets.

Bernick. That is not the reason. Krap has told me the whole truth. You do not understand how to work the new machines I have provided—or rather, you will not try to work them.

Aune. Mr. Bernick, I am well on in the fifties; and ever since I was a boy I have been accustomed to the old way of working—

Bernick. We cannot work that way now-a-days. You must not imagine, Aune, that it is for the sake of making profit; I do not need that, fortunately; but I own consideration to the community I live in, and to the business I am at the head of. I must take the lead in progress, or there would never be any.

Aune. I welcome progress too, Mr. Bernick.

Bernick. Yes, for your own limited circle—for the working class. Oh, I know what a busy agitator you are; you make speeches, you stir people up; but when some concrete instance of progress presents itself—as now, in the case of our machines—you do not want to have anything to do with it; you are afraid.

Aune. Yes, I really am afraid, Mr. Bernick. I am afraid for the number of men who will have the bread taken out of their mouths by these machines. You are very fond, sir, of talking about the consideration we owe to the community; it seems to me, however, that the community has its duties too. Why should science and capital venture to introduce these new discoveries into labour, before the community has had time to educate a generation up to using them?

Bernick. You read and think too much, Aune; it does you no good, and that is what makes you dissatisfied with your lot.

Aune. It is not, Mr. Bernick; but I cannot bear to see one good workman dismissed after another, to starve because of these machines.

Bernick. Hm! When the art of printing was discovered, many a quill-driver was reduced to starvation.

Aune. Would you have admired the art so greatly if you had been a quill-driver in those days, sir?

Bernick. I did not send for you to argue with you. I sent for you to tell you that the "Indian Girl" must be ready to put to sea the day after to-morrow.

Aune. But, Mr. Bernick—

Bernick. The day after to-morrow, do you hear?—at the same time as our own ship, not an hour later. I have good reasons for hurrying on the work. Have you seen to-day's papers? Well, then you know the pranks these American sailors have been up to again. The rascally pack is turning the whole town upside down. Not a night passes without some brawling in the taverns or the streets—not to speak of other abominations.

Aune. Yes, they certainly are a bad lot.

Bernick. And who is it that has to bear the blame for all this disorder? It is I! Yes, it is I who have to suffer for it. These newspaper fellows are making all sorts of covert insinuations because we are devoting all our energies to the "Palm Tree." I, whose task in life it is to influence my fellow-citizens by the force of example, have to endure this sort of thing cast in my face. I am not going to stand that. I have no fancy for having my good name smirched in that way.

Aune. Your name stands high enough to endure that and a great deal more, sir.

Bernick. Not just now. At this particular moment I have need of all the respect and goodwill my fellow-citizens can give me. I have a big undertaking on the stocks, as you probably have heard; but, if it should happen that evil-disposed persons succeeded in shaking the absolute confidence I enjoy, it might land me in the greatest difficulties. That is why I want, at any price, to avoid these shameful innuendoes in the papers, and that is why I name the day after to-morrow as the limit of the time I can give you.

Aune. Mr. Bernick, you might just as well name this afternoon as the limit.

Bernick. You mean that I am asking an impossibility?

Aune. Yes, with the hands we have now at the yard.

Bernick. Very good; then we must look about elsewhere.

Aune. Do you really mean, sir, to discharge still more of your old workmen?

Bernick. No, I am not thinking of that.

Aune. Because I think it would cause bad blood against you both among the townsfolk and in the papers, if you did that.

Bernick. Very probably; therefore we will not do it. But, if the "Indian Girl" is not ready to sail the day after to-morrow, I shall discharge *you*.

Aune (with a start). Me! (*He laughs.*) You are joking, Mr. Bernick.

Bernick. I should not be so sure of that, if I were you.

Aune. Do you mean that you can contemplate discharging *me*?—Me, whose father and grandfather worked in your yard all their lives, as I have done myself—?

Bernick. Who is it that is forcing me to do it?

Aune. You are asking what is impossible, Mr. Bernick.

Bernick. Oh, where there's a will there's a way. Yes or no; give me a decisive answer, or consider yourself discharged on the spot.

Aune (coming a step nearer to him). Mr. Bernick, have you ever realised what discharging an old workman means? You think he can look about for another job. Oh, yes, he can do that; but does that dispose of the matter? You should just be there once, in the house of a workman who has been discharged, the evening he comes home bringing all his tools with him.

Bernick. Do you think I am discharging you with a light heart? Have I not always been a good master to you?

Aune. So much the worse, Mr. Bernick. Just for that very reason those at home will not blame *you*; they will say nothing to me, because they dare not; but they will look at me when I am not noticing, and think that I must have deserved it. You see, sir, that is—that is what I cannot bear. I am a mere nobody, I know; but I have always been accustomed to stand first in my own home. My humble home is a little community too, Mr. Bernick—a little community which I have been able to support and maintain because my wife has believed in me and because my children have believed in me. And now it is all to fall to pieces.

Bernick. Still, if there is nothing else for it, the lesser must go down before the greater; the individual must be sacrificed to the general welfare. I can give you no other answer; and that, and no other, is the way of the world. You are an obstinate man, Aune! You are opposing me, not because you cannot do otherwise, but because you will not exhibit the superiority of machinery over manual labour.

Aune. And you will not be moved, Mr. Bernick, because you know that if you drive me away you will at all events have given the newspapers proof of your good-will.

Bernick. And suppose that were so? I have told you what it means for me—either bringing the Press down on my back, or making them well-disposed to me at a moment when I am working for an object which will mean the advancement of the general welfare. Well, then, can I do otherwise than as I am doing? The question, let me tell you, turns upon this—whether your home is to be supported, as you put it, or whether hundreds of new homes are to be prevented from existing—hundreds of homes that will never be built, never have a fire lighted on their hearth, unless I succeed in carrying through the scheme I am working for now. That is the reason why I have given you your choice.

Aune. Well, if that is the way things stand, I have nothing more to say.

Bernick. Hm—my dear Aune, I am extremely grieved to think that we are to part.

Aune. We are not going to part, Mr. Bernick.

Bernick. How is that?

Aune. Even a comomn man like myself has something he is bound to maintain.

Bernick. Quite so, quite so—then I presume you think you may promise—?

Aune. The "Indian Girl" shall be ready to sail the day after to-morrow. (*Bows and goes out to the right.*)

Bernick. Ah, I have got the better of that obstinate fellow! I take it as a good omen. (HILMAR *comes in through the garden door, smoking a cigar.*)

Hilmar (*as he comes up the steps to the verandah*). Good-morning, Betty! Good-morning, Karsten!

Mrs. Bernick. Good-morning.

Hilmar. Ah, I see you have been crying, so I suppose you know all about it too?

Mrs. Bernick. Know all about what?

Hilmar. That the scandal is in full swing. Ugh!

Bernick. What do you mean?

Hilmar (*coming into the room*). Why, that our two friends from America are displaying themselves about the streets in the company of Dina Dorf.

Mrs. Bernick (*coming in after him*). Hilmar, is it possible?

Hilmar. Yes, unfortunately, it is quite true. Lona was even so wanting in tact as to call after me, but of course I appeared not to have heard her.

Bernick. And no doubt all this has not been unnoticed.

Hilmar. You may well say that. People stood still and looked at them. It spread like wildfire through the town —just like a prairie fire out West. In every house people were at the windows waiting for the procession to pass, cheek by jowl behind the curtains—ugh! Oh, you must excuse me, Betty, for saying "ugh"—this has got on my nerves. If it is going on, I shall be forced to think about getting right away from here.

Mrs. Bernick. But you should have spoken to him and represented to him that—

Hilmar. In the open street? No, excuse me, I could not do that. To think that the fellow should dare to show himself in the town at all! Well, we shall see if the Press doesn't put a stopper on him; yes—forgive me, Betty, but—

Bernick. The Press, do you say? Have you heard a hint of anything of the sort?

Hilmar. There *are* such things flying about. When I left here yesterday evening I looked in at the club, because I did not feel well. I saw at once, from the sudden silence that fell when I went in, that our American couple had been the subject of conversation. Then that impudent newspaper fellow, Hammer, came in and congratulated me at the top of his voice on the return of my rich cousin.

Bernick. Rich?

Hilmar. Those were his words. Naturally I looked him up and down in the manner he deserved, and gave him to understand that I knew nothing about Johan Tönnesen's being rich. "Really," he said, "that is very remarkable. People usually get on in America when they have something to start with, and I believe your cousin did not go over there quite empty-handed."

Bernick. Hm—now will you oblige me by—

Mrs. Bernick (distressed). There, you see, Karsten—

Hilmar. Anyhow, I have spent a sleepless night because of them. And here he is, walking about the streets as if nothing were the matter. Why couldn't he disappear for good and all? It really is insufferable how hard some people are to kill.

Mrs. Bernick. My dear Hilmar, what are you saying?

Hilmar. Oh, nothing. But here this fellow escapes with a whole skin from railway accidents and fights with Californian grizzlies and Blackfoot Indians—has not even been scalped— Ugh, here they come!

Bernick (looking down the street). Olaf is with them too!

Hilmar. Of course! They want to remind everybody that they belong to the best family in the town. Look there!—look at the crowd of loafers that have come out of the chemist's to stare at them and make remarks. My nerves really won't stand it; how a man is to be expected to keep the banner of the Ideal flying under such circumstances, I—

Bernick. They are coming here. Listen, Betty; it is my particular wish that you should receive them in the friendliest possible way.

Mrs. Bernick. Oh, may I, Karsten?

Bernick. Certainly, certainly—and you too, Hilmar. It is to be hoped they will not stay here very long; and when we are quite by ourselves—no allusions to the past; we must not hurt their feelings in any way.

Mrs. Bernick. How magnanimous you are, Karsten!

Bernick. Oh, don't speak of that.

Mrs. Bernick. But you must let me thank you; and you must forgive me for being so hasty. I am sure you had every reason to—

Bernick. Don't talk about it, please!

Hilmar. Ugh!

(JOHAN TÖNNESON *and* DINA *come up through the garden, followed by* LONA *and* OLAF.)

Lona. Good-morning, dear people!

Johan. We have been out having a look round the old place, Karsten.

Bernick. So I hear. Greatly altered, is it not?

Lona. Mr. Bernick's great and good works everywhere. We have been up into the Recreation Ground you have presented to the town—

Bernick. Have you been *there*?

Lona. "The gift of Karsten Bernick," as it says over the gateway. You seem to be responsible for the whole place here.

Johan. Splendid ships you have got, too. I met my old schoolfellow, the captain of the "Palm Tree."

Lona. And you have built a new school-house too; and I hear that the town has to thank you for both the gas supply and the water supply.

Bernick. Well, one ought to work for the good of the community one lives in.

Lona. That is an excellent sentiment, brother-in-law; but it is a pleasure, all the same, to see how people appreciate you. I am not vain, I hope; but I could not resist reminding one or two of the people we talked to that we were relations of yours.

Hilmar. Ugh!

Lona. Do you say "ugh" to that?

Hilmar. No, I said "ahem."

Lona. Oh, poor chap, you may say that if you like. But are you all by yourselves to-day?

Bernick. Yes, we are by ourselves to-day.

Lona. Ah, yes, we met a couple of members of your Morality Society up at the market; they made out they were very busy. You and I have never had an opportunity for a good talk yet. Yesterday you had your three pioneers here, as well as the parson—

Hilmar. The schoolmaster.

Lona. I call him the parson. But now tell me what you think of *my* work during these fifteen years? Hasn't he grown a fine fellow? Who would recognise the madcap that ran away from home?

Hilmar. Hm!

Johan. Now, Lona, don't brag too much about me.

Lona. Well, I can tell you I am precious proud of him. Goodness knows it is about the only thing I have done in my life; but it does give me a sort of right to exist. When I think, Johan, how we two began over there with nothing but our four bare fists—

Hilmar. Hands.

Lona. I say fists; and they were dirty fists—

Hilmar. Ugh!

Lona. And empty, too.

Hilmar. Empty? Well, I must say—

Lona. What must you say?

Bernick. Ahem!

Hilmar. I must say—ugh! (*Goes out through the garden.*)

Lona. What is the matter with the man?

Bernick. Oh, do not take any notice of him; his nerves are rather upset just now. Would you not like to take a look at the garden? You have not been down there yet, and I have got an hour to spare.

Lona. With pleasure. I can tell you my thoughts have been with you in this garden many and many a time.

Mrs. Bernick. We have made a great many alterations there too, as you will see. (BERNICK, MRS. BERNICK, *and* LONA *go down to the garden, where they are visible every now and then during the following scene.*)

Olaf (*coming to the verandah door*). Uncle Hilmar, do you know what uncle Johan asked me? He asked me if I would go to America with him.

Hilmar. You, you duffer, who are tied to your mother's apron strings—!

Olaf. Ah, but I won't be that any longer. You will see, when I grow big—

Hilmar. Oh, fiddlesticks! You have no really serious bent towards the strength of character necessary to—

(*They go down to the garden.* DINA *meanwhile has taken off her hat and is standing at the door on the right, shaking the dust off her dress.*)

Johan (*to* DINA). The walk has made you pretty warm.

Dina. Yes, it was a splendid walk. I have never had such a splendid walk before.

Johan. Do you not often go for a walk in the morning?

Dina. Oh, yes—but only with Olaf.

Johan. I see.—Would you rather go down into the garden than stay here?

Dina. No, I would rather stay here.

Johan. So would I. Then shall we consider it a bargain that we are to go for a walk like this together every morning?

Dina. No, Mr. Tönnesen, you mustn't do that.

Johan. What mustn't I do? You promised, you know.

Dina. Yes, but—on second thoughts—you mustn't go out with me.

Johan. But why not?

Dina. Of course, you are a stranger—you cannot understand; but I must tell you—

Johan. Well?

Dina. No, I would rather not talk about it.

Johan. Oh, but you must; you can talk to me about whatever you like.

Dina. Well, I must tell you that I am not like the other young girls here. There is something—something or other about me. That is why you mustn't.

Johan. But I do not understand anything about it. You have not done anything wrong?

Dina. No, not I, but— No, I am not going to talk any more about it now. You will hear about it from the others, sure enough.

Johan. Hm !

Dina. But there is something else I want very much to ask you.

Johan. What is it?

Dina. I suppose it is easy to make a position for oneself over in America?

Johan. No, it is not always easy; at first you often have to rough it and work very hard.

Dina. I should be quite ready to do that.

Johan. You?

Dina. I can work now; I am strong and healthy; **and** Aunt Martha taught me a lot.

Johan. Well, hang it, come back with us !

Dina. Ah, now you are only making fun of me; you said that to Olaf too. But what I wanted to know is if people are so very—so very moral over there?

Johan. Moral?

Dina. Yes; I mean are they as—as proper and as well-behaved as they are here?

Johan. Well, at all events they are not so bad as people here make out. You need not be afraid on that score.

Dina. You don't understand me. What I want to hear is just that they are *not* so proper and so moral.

Johan. Not? What would you wish them to be, then?

Dina. I would wish them to be natural.

Johan. Well, I believe that is just what they are.

Dina. Because in that case I should get on if I went there.

Johan. You would, for certain!—and that is why you must come back with us.

Dina. No, I don't want to go with you; I must go alone. Oh, I would make something of my life; I would get on—

Bernick (*speaking to* LONA *and his wife at the foot of the garden steps*). Wait a moment—I will fetch it, Betty dear; you might so easily catch cold. (*Comes into the room and looks for his wife's shawl*).

Mrs. Bernick (*from outside*). You must come out too, Johan; we are going down to the grotto.

Bernick. No, I want Johan to stay here. Look here, Dina; you take my wife's shawl and go with them. Johan is going to stay here with me, Betty dear. I want to hear how he is getting on over there.

Mrs. Bernick. Very well—then you will follow us; you know where you will find us. (MRS. BERNICK, LONA *and* DINA *go out through the garden, to the left.* BERNICK *looks after them for a moment, then goes to the farther door on the left and locks it, after which he goes up to* JOHAN, *grasps both his hands, and shakes them warmly.*)

Bernick. Johan, now that we are alone, you must let me thank you.

Johan. Oh, nonsense!

Bernick. My home and all the happiness that it means to me—my position here as a citizen—all these I owe to you.

Johan. Well, I am glad of it, Karsten; some good came of that mad story after all, then.

Bernick (*grasping his hands again*). But still you must let me thank you! Not one in ten thousand would have done what you did for me.

Johan. Rubbish! Weren't we, both of us, young and thoughtless? One of us had to take the blame, you know.

Bernick. But surely the guilty one was the proper one to do that?

Johan. Stop! At the moment the innocent one happened to be the proper one to do it. Remember, I had no ties— I was an orphan; it was a lucky chance to get free from the drudgery of the office. You, on the other hand, had your old mother still alive; and, besides that, you had just become secretly engaged to Betty, who was devoted to you. What would have happened between you and her if it had come to her ears?

Bernick. That is true enough, but still—

Johan. And wasn't it just for Betty's sake that you broke off your acquaintance with Mrs. Dorf? Why, it was merely in order to put an end to the whole thing that you were up there with her that evening.

Bernick. Yes, that unfortunate evening when that drunken creature came home! Yes, Johan, it was for Betty's sake; but, all the same, it was splendid of you to let all the appearances go against you, and to go away.

Johan. Put your scruples to rest, my dear Karsten. We agreed that it should be so; you had to be saved, and you were my friend. I can tell you, I was uncommonly proud of that friendship. Here was I, drudging away like a miserable stick-in-the-mud, when you came back from your grand tour abroad, a great swell who had been to London and to Paris; and you chose me for your chum, although I was four years younger than you—it is true it was because you were courting Betty, I understand that now—but I *was* proud of it! Who would not have been? Who would not willingly have sacrificed himself for you?—especially as it only meant a month's talk in the town, and enabled me to get away into the wide world.

Bernick. Ah, my dear Johan, I must be candid and tell you that the story is not so completely forgotten yet.

Johan. Isn't it? Well, what does that matter to me, once I am back over there on my farm again?

Bernick. Then you mean to go back?

Johan. Of course.

Bernick. But not immediately, I hope?

Johan. As soon as possible. It was only to humour Lona that I came over with her, you know.

Bernick. Really? How so?

Johan. Well, you see, Lona is no longer young, and lately she began to be obsessed with home-sickness; but she never would admit it. (*Smiles.*) How could she venture to risk leaving such a flighty fellow as me alone, who before I was nineteen had been mixed up in—

Bernick. Well, what then?

Johan. Well, Karsten, now I am coming to a confession that I am ashamed to make.

Bernick. You surely haven't confided the truth to her?

Johan. Yes. It was wrong of me, but I could not do otherwise. You can have no conception what Lona has been to me. You never could put up with her; but she has been like a mother to me. The first year we were out there, when things went so badly with us, you have no idea how she worked! And when I was ill for a long time, and could earn nothing and could not prevent her, she took to singing ballads in taverns, and gave lectures that people laughed at; and then she wrote a book that she has both laughed and cried over since then—all to keep the life in me. Could I look on when in the winter she, who had toiled and drudged for me, began to pine away? No, Karsten, I couldn't. And so I said, "You go home for a trip, Lona; don't be afraid for me, I am not so flighty as you think." And so—the end of it was that she had to know.

Bernick. And how did she take it?

Johan. Well, she thought, as was true, that as I knew I was innocent nothing need prevent me from taking a trip over here with her. But make your mind easy; Lona will let nothing out, and I shall keep my mouth shut as I did before.

Bernick. Yes, yes—I rely on that.

Johan. Here is my hand on it. And now we will say no

more about that old story; luckily it is the only mad prank either of us has been guilty of, I am sure. I want thoroughly to enjoy the few days I shall stay here. You cannot think what a delightful walk we had this morning. Who would have believed that that little imp, who used to run about here and play angels' parts on the stage—! But tell me, my dear fellow, what became of her parents afterwards?

Bernick. Oh, my boy, I can tell you no more than I wrote to you immediately after you went away. I suppose you got my two letters?

Johan. Yes, yes, I have them both. So that drunken fellow deserted her?

Bernick. And drank himself to death afterwards.

Johan. And *she* died soon afterwards, too?

Bernick. She was proud; she betrayed nothing, and would accept nothing.

Johan. Well, at all events you did the right thing by taking Dina into your house.

Bernick. I suppose so. As a matter of fact it was Martha that brought that about.

Johan. So it was Martha? By the way, where is she to-day?

Bernick. She? Oh, when she hasn't her school to look after, she has her sick people to see to.

Johan. So it was Martha who interested herself in her.

Bernick. Yes, you know Martha has always had a certain liking for teaching; so she took a post in the Board-school. It was very ridiculous of her.

Johan. I thought she looked very worn yesterday; I should be afraid her health was not good enough for it.

Bernick. Oh, as far as her health goes, it is all right enough. But it is unpleasant for me; it looks as though I, her brother, were not willing to support her.

Johan. Support her? I thought she had means enough of her own.

Bernick. Not a penny. Surely you remember how badly

off our mother was when you went away? She carried things on for a time with my assistance, but naturally I could not put up with that state of affairs permanently. I made her take me into the firm, but even then things did not go well. So I had to take over the whole business myself, and when we made up our balance-sheet it became evident that there was practically nothing left as my mother's share. And when mother died soon afterwards, of course Martha was left penniless.

Johan. Poor Martha!

Bernick. Poor! Why? You surely do not suppose I let her want for anything? No, I venture to say I am a good brother. Of course she has a home here with us; her salary as a teacher is more than enough for her to dress on; what more could she want?

Johan. Hm—that is not our idea of things in America.

Bernick. No, I dare say not—in such a revolutionary state of society as you find there. But in our small circle—in which, thank God, depravity has not gained a footing, up to now at all events—women are content to occupy a seemly, as well as modest, position. Moreover, it is Martha's own fault; I mean, she might have been provided for long ago, if she had wished.

Johan. You mean she might have married?

Bernick. Yes, and married very well, too. She has had several good offers—curiously enough, when you think that she is a poor girl, no longer young, and, besides, quite an insignificant person.

Johan. Insignificant?

Bernick. Oh, I am not blaming her for that. I most certainly would not wish her otherwise. I can tell you it is always a good thing to have a steady-going person like that in a big house like this—some one you can rely on in any contingency.

Johan. Yes, but what does *she*—?

Bernick. She? How? Oh well, of course *she* has plenty

to interest herself in; she has Betty and Olaf and me. People should not think first of themselves—women least of all. We have all got some community, great or small, to work for. That is my principle, at all events. (*Points to* KRAP, *who has come in from the right.*) Ah, here is an example of it, ready to hand. Do you suppose that it is my own affairs that are absorbing me just now? By no means. (*Eagerly to* KRAP.) Well?

Krap (*in an undertone, showing him a bundle of papers*). Here are all the sale contracts, completed.

Bernick. Capital! Splendid!—Well, Johan, you must really excuse me for the present. (*In a low voice, grasping his hand.*) Thanks, Johan, thanks! And rest assured that anything I can do for you— Well, of course you understand. Come along, Krap. (*They go into* BERNICK'S *room.*)

Johan (*looking after them for a moment*). Hm! (*Turns to go down to the garden. At the same moment* MARTHA *comes in from the right, with a little basket over her arm.*) Martha!

Martha. Ah, Johan—is it you?

Johan. Out so early?

Martha. Yes. Wait a moment; the others are just coming. (*Moves towards the door on the left.*)

Johan. Martha, are you always in such a hurry?

Martha. I?

Johan. Yesterday you seemed to avoid me, so that I never managed to have a word with you—we two old playfellows.

Martha. Ah, Johan; that is many, many years ago.

Johan. Good Lord—why, it is only fifteen years ago, no more and no less. Do you think I have changed so much?

Martha. You? Oh yes, you have changed too, although—

Johan. What do you mean?

Martha. Oh, nothing.

Johan. You do not seem to be very glad to see me again.

Martha. I have waited so long, Johan—too long.

Johan. Waited? For me to come?

Martha. Yes.

Johan. And why did you think I would come?

Martha. To atone for the wrong you had done.

Johan. I?

Martha. Have you forgotten that it was through you that a woman died in need and in shame? Have you forgotten that it was through you that the best years of a young girl's life were embittered?

Johan. And you can say such things to me? Martha, has your brother never—?

Martha. Never what?

Johan. Has he never—oh, of course, I mean has he never so much as said a word in my defence?

Martha. Ah, Johan, you know Karsten's high principles.

Johan. Hm—! Oh, of course; I know my old friend Karsten's high principles! But really this is— Well, well. I was having a talk with him just now. He seems to me to have altered considerably.

Martha. How can you say that? I am sure Karsten has always been an excellent man.

Johan. Yes, that was not exactly what I meant—but never mind. Hm! Now I understand the light you have seen me in; it was the return of the prodigal that you were waiting for.

Martha. Johan, I will tell you what light I have seen you in. (*Points down to the garden.*) Do you see that girl playing on the grass down there with Olaf? That is Dina. Do you remember that incoherent letter you wrote me when you went away? You asked me to believe in you. I have believed in you, Johan. All the horrible things that were rumoured about you after you had gone must have been done through being led astray—from thoughtlessness,

Johan. What do you mean?

Martha. Oh, you understand me well enough—not a word more of that. But of course you had to go away and begin afresh—a new life. Your duties here which you never remembered to undertake—or never were able to undertake—I have undertaken for you. I tell you this, so that you shall not have that also to reproach yourself with. I have been a mother to that much-wronged child; I have brought her up as well as I was able.

Johan. And have wasted your whole life for that reason.

Martha. It has not been wasted. But you have come late, Johan.

Johan. Martha—if only I could tell you— Well, at all events let me thank you for your loyal friendship.

Martha (*with a sad smile*). Hm.—Well, we have had it out now, Johan. Hush, some one is coming. Good bye, I can't stay now. (*Goes out through the farther door on the left.* LONA *comes in from the garden, followed by* MRS. BERNICK.)

Mrs. Bernick. But, good gracious, Lona—what are you thinking of?

Lona. Let me be, I tell you! I must and will speak to him.

Mrs. Bernick. But it would be a scandal of the worst sort! Ah, Johan—still here?

Lona. Out with you, my boy; don't stay here indoors; go down into the garden and have a chat with Dina.

Johan. I was just thinking of doing so.

Mrs. Bernick. But—

Lona. Look here, Johan—have you had a good look at Dina?

Johan. I should think so!

Lona. Well, look at her to some purpose, my boy That would be somebody for *you!*

Mrs. Bernick. But, Lona!

Johan. Somebody for me?

Lona. Yes, to look at, I mean. Be off with you!

Johan. Oh, I don't need any pressing. (*Goes down into the garden.*)

Mrs. Bernick. Lona, you astound me! You cannot possibly be serious about it?

Lona. Indeed I am. Isn't she sweet and healthy and honest? She is exactly the wife for Johan. She is just what he needs over there; it will be a change from an old stepsister.

Mrs. Bernick. Dina? Dina Dorf? But think—

Lona. I think first and foremost of the boy's happiness. because, help him I must; he has not much idea of that sort of thing; he has never had much of an eye for girls or women.

Mrs. Bernick. He? Johan? Indeed I think we have had only too sad proofs that—

Lona. Oh, devil take all those stupid stories! Where is Karsten? I mean to speak to him.

Mrs. Bernick. Lona, you must not do it, I tell you!

Lona. I am going to. If the boy takes a fancy to her— and she to him—then they shall make a match of it. Karsten is such a clever man, he must find some way to bring it about.

Mrs. Bernick. And do you think these American indecencies will be permitted here?

Lona. Bosh, Betty!

Mrs. Bernick. Do you think a man like Karsten, with his strictly moral way of thinking—

Lona. Pooh! he is not so terribly moral.

Mrs. Bernick. What have you the audacity to say?

Lona. I have the audacity to say that Karsten is not any more particularly moral than anybody else.

Mrs. Bernick. So you still hate him as deeply as that! But what are you doing here, if you have never been able to forget that? I cannot understand how you dare look him in the face after the shameful insult you put upon him in the old days.

Lona. Yes, Betty, that time I did forget myself badly.

Mrs. Bernick. And to think how magnanimously he has

forgiven you—he, who had never done any wrong! It was not *his* fault that you encouraged yourself with hopes. But since then you have always hated me too. (*Bursts into tears.*) You have always grudged me my good fortune. And now you come here to heap all this on my head—to let the whole town know what sort of family I have brought Karsten into. Yes, it is me that it all falls upon, and that is what you want. Oh, it is abominable of you. (*Goes out by the door on the left, in tears.*)

Lona (*looking after her*). Poor Betty! (BERNICK *comes in from his room. He stops at the door to speak to* KRAP.)

Bernick. Yes, that is excellent, Krap—capital! Send twenty pounds to the fund for dinners to the poor. (*Turns round.*) Lona! (*Comes forward.*) Are you alone? Is Betty not coming in?

Lona. No. Would you like me to call her?

Bernick. No, no—not at all. Oh, Lona, you don't know how anxious I have been to speak openly to you—after having begged for your forgiveness.

Lona. Look here, Karsten—do not let us be sentimental; it doesn't suit us.

Bernick. You *must* listen to me, Lona. I know only too well how much appearances are against me, as you have learnt all about that affair with Dina's mother. But I swear to you that it was only a temporary infatuation; I was really, truly and honestly, in love with you once.

Lona. Why do you think I have come home?

Bernick. Whatever you have in your mind, I entreat you to do nothing until I have exculpated myself. I can do that, Lona; at all events I can excuse myself.

Lona. Now you are frightened. You once were in love with me, you say. Yes, you told me that often enough in your letters; and perhaps it was true, too—in a way—as long as you were living out in the great, free world which gave you the courage to think freely and greatly. Perhaps **you** found in me a little more character and strength of will and independence than in most of the folk at home here. And then we kept it secret between us; nobody could make fun of your bad taste.

Bernick. Lona, how can you think—?

Lona. But when you came back—when you heard the gibes that were made at me on all sides—when you noticed how people laughed at what they called my absurdities—

Bernick. You were regardless of people's opinion at that time.

Lona. Chiefly to annoy the petticoated and trousered prudes that one met at every turn in the town. And then, when you met that seductive young actress—

Bernick. It was a boyish escapade—nothing more; I swear to you that there was no truth in a tenth part of the rumours and gossip that went about.

Lona. Maybe. But then, when Betty came home—a pretty young girl, idolised by every one—and it became known that she would inherit all her aunt's money and that I would have nothing—

Bernick. That is just the point, Lona; and now you shall have the truth without any beating about the bush. I did not love Betty then; I did not break off my engagement with you because of any new attachment. It was entirely for the sake of the money. I needed it; I *had* to make sure of it.

Lona. And you have the face to tell me that?

Bernick. Yes, I have. Listen, Lona.

Lona. And yet you wrote to me that an unconquerable passion for Betty had overcome you—invoked my magnanimity—begged me, for Betty's sake, to hold my tongue about all that had been between us.

Bernick. I *had* to, I tell you.

Lona. Now, by Heaven, I don't regret that I forgot myself as I did that time!

Bernick. Let me tell you the plain truth of how things stood with me then. My mother, as you remember, was at the head of the business, but she was absolutely without any business ability whatever. I was hurriedly summoned home from Paris; times were critical, and they relied on me to set things straight. What did I find? I found—and you must keep this a profound secret—a house on the brink of ruin. Yes—as good as on the brink of ruin, this old respected house which had seen three generations of us. What else could I—the son, the only son—do than look about for some means of saving it?

Lona. And so you saved the house of Bernick at the cost of a woman.

Bernick. You know quite well that Betty was in love with me.

Lona. But what about me?

Bernick. Believe me, Lona, you would never have been happy with me.

Lona. Was it out of consideration for my happiness that you sacrificed me?

Bernick. Do you suppose I acted as I did from selfish motives? If I had stood alone then, I would have begun all over again with cheerful courage. But you do not understand how the life of a man of business, with his tremendous responsibilities, is bound up with that of the business which falls to his inheritance. Do you realise that the prosperity or the ruin of hundreds—of thousands—depends on him? Can you not take into consideration the fact that the whole community in which both you and I were born would have been affected to the most dangerous extent if the house of Bernick had gone to smash?

Lona. Then is it for the sake of the community that you have maintained your position these fifteen years upon a lie?

Bernick. Upon a lie?

Lona. What does Betty know of all this that underlies her union with you?

Bernick. Do you suppose that I would hurt her feelings to no purpose by disclosing the truth?

Lona. To no purpose, you say? Well, well—you are a man of business; you ought to understand what is to the purpose. But listen to me, Karsten— *I* am going to speak the plain truth now. Tell me, are you really happy?

Bernick. In my family life, do you mean?

Lona. Yes.

Bernick. I am, Lona. You have not been a self-sacrificing friend to me in vain. I can honestly say that I have grown happier every year. Betty is good and willing; and if I were to tell you how, in the course of years, she has learnt to model her character on the lines of my own—

Lona. Hm!

Bernick. At first, of course, she had a whole lot of romantic notions about love; she could not reconcile herself to the idea that, little by little, it must change into a quiet comradeship.

Lona. But now she is quite reconciled to that?

Bernick. Absolutely. As you can imagine, daily intercourse with me has had no small share in developing her character. Every one, in their degree, has to learn to lower their own pretensions, if they are to live worthily of the community to which they belong. And Betty, in her turn, has gradually learnt to understand this; and that is why our home is now a model to our fellow-citizens.

Lona. But your fellow-citizens know nothing about the lie?

Bernick. The lie?

Lona. Yes—the lie you have persisted in for these fifteen years.

Bernick. Do you mean to say that you call that—?

Lona. I call it a lie—a threefold lie; first of all there is the lie towards me, then the lie towards Betty, and then the lie towards Johan.

Bernick. Betty has never asked me to speak.

Lona. Because she has known nothing.

Bernick. And *you* will not demand it—out of consideration for her.

Lona. Oh, no—I shall manage to put up with their gibes well enough; I have broad shoulders.

Bernick. And Johan will not demand it either; he has promised me that.

Lona. But you yourself, Karsten. Do you feel within yourself no impulse urging you to shake yourself free of this lie?

Bernick. Do you suppose that of my own free will I would sacrifice my family happiness and my position in the world?

Lona. What right have you to the position you hold?

Bernick. Every day during these fifteen years I have earned some little right to it—by my conduct, and by what I have achieved by my work.

Lona. True, you have achieved a great deal by your work, for yourself as well as for others. You are the richest and most influential man in the town; nobody in it dares do otherwise than defer to your will, because you are looked upon as a man without spot or blemish; your home is regarded as a model home, and your conduct as a model of conduct. But all this grandeur, and you with it, is founded on a treacherous morass. A moment may come and a word may be spoken—and you and all your grandeur will be engulfed in the morass, if you do not save yourself in time.

Bernick. Lona—what is your object in coming here?

Lona. I want to help you to get firm ground under your feet, Karsten.

Bernick. Revenge!—you want to revenge yourself! I suspected it. But you won't succeed! There is only one person here that can speak with authority, and he will be silent.

Lona. You mean Johan?

Bernick. Yes, Johan. If any one else accuses me, I shall deny everything. If any one tries to crush me, I shall fight for my life. But you will never succeed in that, let me tell you! The one who could strike me down will say nothing —and is going away.

(RUMMEL *and* VIGELAND *come in from the right.*)

Rummell. Good-morning, my dear Bernick, good-morning. You must come up with us to the Commercial Association. There is a meeting about the railway scheme, you know.

Bernick. I cannot. It is impossible just now.

Vigeland. You really must, Mr. Bernick.

Rummel. Bernick, you must. There is an opposition to us on foot. Hammer, and the rest of those who believe in a line along the coast, are declaring that private interests are at the back of the new proposals.

Bernick. Well, then, explain to them—

Vigeland. Our explanations have no effect, Mr. Bernick.

Rummel. No, no, you must come yourself. Naturally, no one would dare to suspect you of such duplicity.

Lona. I should think not.

Bernick. I cannot, I tell you; I am not well. Or, at all events, wait—let me pull myself together. (RÖRLUND *comes in from the right.*)

Rörlund. Excuse me, Mr. Bernick, but I am terribly upset.

Bernick. Why, what is the matter with you?

Rörlund. I must put a question to you, Mr. Bernick. Is it with your consent that the young girl who has found a shelter under your roof shows herself in the open street in the company of a person who—

Lona. What person, Mr. Parson?

Rörlund. With the person from whom, of all others in the world, she ought to be kept farthest apart!

Lona. Ha! ha!

Rörlund. Is it with your consent, Mr. Bernick?

Bernick (*looking for his hat and gloves*). I know nothing about it. You must excuse me; I am in a great hurry. I am due at the Commercial Association.

(HILMAR *comes up from the garden and goes over to the farther door on the left.*)

Hilmar. Betty, Betty, I want to speak to you.

Mrs. Bernick (*coming to the door*). What is it?

Hilmar. You ought to go down into the garden and put a stop to the flirtation that is going on between a certain person and Dina Dorf! It has quite got on my nerves to listen to them.

Lona. Indeed! And what has the certain person been saying?

Hilmar. Oh, only that he wishes she would go off to America with him. Ugh!

Rörlund. Is it possible?

Mrs. Bernick. What do you say?

Lona. But that would be perfectly splendid!

Bernick. Impossible! You cannot have heard aright.

Hilmar. Ask him yourself, then. Here comes the pair of them. Only, leave me out of it, please.

Bernick (*to* RUMMEL *and* VIGELAND). I will follow you —in a moment. (RUMMEL *and* VIGELAND *go out to the right.* JOHAN *and* DINA *come up from the garden.*)

Johan. Hurrah, Lona, she is going with us!

Mrs. Bernick. But, Johan—are you out of your senses?

Rörlund. Can I believe my ears! Such an atrocious scandal! By what arts of seduction have you—?

Johan. Come, come, sir—what are you saying?

Rörlund. Answer me, Dina; do you mean to do this—entirely of your own free will?

Dina. I must get away from here.

Rörlund. But with *him!*—with *him!*

Dina. Can you tell me of any one else here who would have the courage to take me with him?

Rörlund. Very well, then—you shall learn who he is.

Johan. Do not speak!

Bernick. Not a word more!

Rörlund. If I did not, I should be unworthy to serve a

community of whose morals I have been appointed a guardian, and should be acting most unjustifiably towards this young girl, in whose upbringing I have taken a material part, and who is to me—

Johan. Take care what you are doing!

Rörlund. She *shall* know! Dina, this is the man who was the cause of all your mother's misery and shame.

Bernick. Mr. Rörlund—?

Dina. He! (*To Johan.*) Is this true?

Johan. Karsten, you answer.

Bernick. Not a word more! Do not let us say another word about it to-day.

Dina. Then it is true.

Rörlund. Yes, it is true. And more than that—this fellow, whom you were going to trust, did not run away from home empty-handed; ask him about old Mrs. Bernick's cashbox—Mr. Bernick can bear witness to that!

Lona. Liar!

Bernick. Ah!—

Mrs. Bernick. My God! my God!

Johan (*rushing at* Rörlund *with uplifted arm.*) And you dare to—

Lona (*restraining him.*) Do not strike him, Johan!

Rörlund. That is right, assault me! But the truth will out; and it *is* the truth—Mr. Bernick has admitted it, and the whole town knows it. Now, Dina, you know him. (*A short silence.*)

Johan (*softly, grasping* Bernick *by the arm*). Karsten, Karsten, what have you done?

Mrs. Bernick (*in tears*). Oh, Karsten, to think that I should have mixed you up in all this disgrace!

Sandstad (*coming in hurriedly from the right, and calling out, with his hand still on the door-handle*). You positively *must* come now, Mr. Bernick. The fate of the whole railway 's hanging by a thread.

Bernick (*abstractedly*). What is it? What have I to—

Lona (earnestly and with emphasis). You have to go and be a pillar of society, brother-in-law.

Sandstad. Yes, come along; we need the full weight of your moral excellence on our side.

Johan (aside to BERNICK). Karsten, we will have a talk about this to-morrow. (*Goes out through the garden.* BER-NICK, *looking half dazed, goes out to the right with* SAND-STAD.)

ACT III

(SCENE.—*The same room.* BERNICK, *with a cane in his hand and evidently in a great rage, comes out of the farther room on the left, leaving the door half-open behind him.*)

Bernick (*speaking to his wife, who is in the other room*). There! I have given it him in earnest now; I don't think he will forget that thrashing! What do you say?—And *I* say that you are an injudicious mother! You make excuses for him, and countenance any sort of rascality on his part.— Not rascality? What do you call it, then? Slipping out of the house at night, going out in a fishing boat, staying away till well on in the day, and giving me such a horrible fright when I have so much to worry me! And then the young scamp has the audacity to threaten that he will run away! Just let him try it!—You? No, very likely; you don't trouble yourself much about what happens to him. I really believe that if he were to get killed—! Oh, really? Well, *I* have work to leave behind me in the world; I have no fancy for being left childless.—Now, do not raise objections, Betty; it shall be as I say—he is confined to the house. (*Listens.*) Hush; do not let any one notice anything. (KRAP *comes in from the right.*)

Krap. Can you spare me a moment, Mr. Bernick?

Bernick (*throwing away the cane*). Certainly, certainly. Have you come from the yard?

Krap. Yes. Ahem—!

Bernick. Well? Nothing wrong with the "Palm Tree," I hope?

Krap. The "Palm Tree" can sail to-morrow, but—

Bernick. It is the "Indian Girl," then?　I had a suspicion that that obstinate fellow—

Krap. The "Indian Girl" can sail to-morrow, too; but I am sure she will not get very far.

Bernick. What do you mean?

Krap. Excuse me, sir; that door is standing ajar, and I think there is some one in the other room—

Bernick (*shutting the door*). There, then!　But what is this that no one else must hear?

Krap. Just this—that I believe Aune intends to let the "Indian Girl" go to the bottom with every mother's son on board.

Bernick.　Good God!—what makes you think that?

Krap. I cannot account for it any other way, sir.

Bernick. Well, tell me as briefly as you can—

Krap. I will.　You know yourself how slowly the work has gone on in the yard since we got the new machines and the new inexperienced hands?

Bernick. Yes, yes.

Krap. But this morning, when I went down there, I noticed that the repairs to the American boat had made extraordinary progress; the great hole in the bottom—the rotten patch, you know—

Bernick. Yes, yes—what about it?

Krap. Was completely repaired—to all appearance, at any rate—covered up—looked as good as new.　I heard that Aune himself had been working at it by lantern light the whole night.

Bernick. Yes, yes—well?

Krap. I turned it over in my head for a bit; the hands were away at breakfast, so I found an opportunity to have a look round the boat, both outside and in, without any one's seeing me.　I had a job to get down to the bottom through the cargo, but I learnt the truth.　There is something very suspicious going on, Mr. Bernick.

Bernick. I cannot believe it, Krap. I cannot and will not believe such a thing of Aune.

Krap. I am very sorry—but it is the simple truth. Something very suspicious is going on. No new timbers put in, as far as I could see, only stopped up and tinkered at, and covered over with sailcloth and tarpaulins and that sort of thing—an absolute fraud. The "Indian Girl" will never get to New York; she will go to the bottom like a cracked pot.

Bernick. This is most horrible! But what can be his object, do you suppose?

Krap. Probably he wants to bring the machines into discredit—wants to take his revenge—wants to force you to take the old hands on again.

Bernick. And to do this he is willing to sacrifice the lives of all on board.

Krap. He said the other day that there were no men on board the "Indian Girl"—only wild beasts.

Bernick. Yes, but—apart from that—has he no regard for the great loss of capital it would mean?

Krap. Aune does not look upon capital with a very friendly eye, Mr. Bernick.

Bernick. That is perfectly true; he is an agitator and a fomentor of discontent; but such an unscrupulous thing as this— Look here, Krap; you must look into the matter once more. Not a word of it to any one. The blame will fall on our yard if any one hears anything of it.

Krap. Of course, but—

Bernick. When the hands are away at their dinner you must manage to get down there again; I must have absolute certainty about it.

Krap. You shall, sir; but, excuse me, what do you propose to do?

Bernick. Report the affair, naturally. We cannot, of course, let ourselves become accomplices in such a crime. I could not have such a thing on my conscience. Moreover, it will make a good impression, both on the Press and on the public in general, if it is seen that I set all personal interests aside and let justice take its course.

Krap. Quite true, Mr. Bernick.

Bernick. But first of all I must be absolutely certain. And meanwhile, do not breathe a word of it—

Krap. Not a word, sir. And you shall have your certainty. (*Goes out through the garden and down the street.*)

Bernick (*half aloud*). Shocking!—But no, it is impossible!—inconceivable!

(*As he turns to go into his room,* HILMAR *comes in from the right.*)

Hilmar. Good morning, Karsten. Let me congratulate you on your triumph at the Commercial Association yesterday.

Bernick. Thank you.

Hilmar. It was a brilliant triumph, I hear; the triumph of intelligent public spirit over selfishness and prejudice— something like a raid of French troops on the Kabyles. It is astonishing that after that unpleasant scene here, you could—

Bernick. Yes, yes—quite so.

Hilmar. But the decisive battle has not been fought yet.

Bernick. In the matter of the railway, do you mean?

Hilmar. Yes; I suppose you know the trouble that Hammer is brewing?

Bernick (*anxiously*). No, what is that?

Hilmar. Oh, he is greatly taken up with the rumour that is going round, and is preparing to dish up an article about it.

Bernick. What rumour?

Hilmar. About the extensive purchase of property along the branch line, of course.

Bernick. What? Is there such a rumour as that going about?

Hilmar. It is all over the town. I heard it at the club

when I looked in there. They say that one of our lawyers has quietly bought up, on commission, all the forest land, all the mining land, all the waterfalls—

Bernick. Don't they say whom it was for?

Hilmar. At the club they thought it must be for some company, not connected with this town, that has got a hint of the scheme you have in hand, and has made haste to buy before the price of these properties went up. Isn't it villainous?—ugh!

Bernick. Villainous?

Hilmar. Yes, to have strangers putting their fingers into our pie—and one of our own local lawyers lending himself to such a thing! And now it will be outsiders that will get all the profits!

Bernick. But, after all, it is only an idle rumour.

Hilmar. Meanwhile people are believing it, and to-morrow or next day I have no doubt Hammer will nail it to the counter as a fact. There is a general sense of exasperation in the town already. I heard several people say that if the rumour were confirmed they would take their names off the subscription lists.

Bernick. Impossible!

Hilmar. Is it? Why do you suppose these mercenary-minded creatures were so willing to go into the undertaking with you? Don't you suppose they have scented profit for themselves—

Bernick. It is impossible, I am sure; there is so much public spirit in our little community—

Hilmar. In our community? Of course you are a confirmed optimist, and so you judge others by yourself. But I, who am a tolerably experienced observer—! There isn't a single soul in the place—excepting ourselves, of course—not a single soul in the place who holds up the banner of the Ideal. (*Goes towards the verandah.*) Ugh, I can see them there!

Bernick. See whom?

Hilmar. Our two friends from America. (*Looks out to the right.*) And who is that they are walking with? As I am alive, if it is not the captain of the "Indian Girl." Ugh!

Bernick. What can they want with *him?*

Hilmar. Oh, he is just the right company for them. He looks as if he had been a slave-dealer or a pirate; and who knows what the other two may have been doing all these years.

Bernick. Let me tell you that it is grossly unjust to think such things about them.

Hilmar. Yes—you are an optimist. But here they are, bearing down upon us again; so I will get away while there is time. (*Goes towards the door on the left.* LONA *comes in from the right.*)

Lona. Oh, Hilmar, am I driving you away?

Hilmar. Not at all; I am in rather a hurry! I want to have a word with Betty. (*Goes into the farthest room on the left.*)

Bernick (*after a moment's silence*). Well, Lona?

Lona. Yes?

Bernick. What do you think of me to-day?

Lona. The same as I did yesterday. A lie more or less—

Bernick. I must enlighten you about it. Where has Johan gone?

Lona. He is coming; he had to see a man first.

Bernick. After what you heard yesterday, you will understand that my whole life will be ruined if the truth comes to light.

Lona. I can understand that.

Bernick. Of course, it stands to reason that *I* was not guilty of the crime there was so much talk about here.

Lona. That stands to reason. But who was the thief?

Bernick. There was no thief. There was no money stolen—not a penny.

Lona. How is that?

Bernick. Not a penny, I tell you.

Lona. But those rumours? How did that shameful rumour get about that Johan—

Bernick. Lona, I think I can speak to you as I could to no one else. I will conceal nothing from you. *I* was partly to blame for spreading the rumour.

Lona. You? You could act in that way towards a man who for your sake—!

Bernick. Do not condemn me without bearing in mind how things stood at that time. I told you about it yesterday. I came home and found my mother involved in a mesh of injudicious undertakings; we had all manner of bad luck—it seemed as if misfortunes were raining upon us, and our house was on the verge of ruin. I was half reckless and half in despair. Lona, I believe it was mainly to deaden my thoughts that I let myself drift into that entanglement that ended in Johan's going away.

Lona. Hm—

Bernick. You can well imagine how every kind of rumour was set on foot after he and you had gone. People began to say that it was not his first piece of folly—that Dorf had received a large sum of money to hold his tongue and go away; other people said that she had received it. At the same time it was obvious that our house was finding it difficult to meet its obligations. What was more natural than that scandal-mongers should find some connection between these two rumours? And as the woman remained here, living in poverty, people declared that he had taken the money with him to America; and every time rumour mentioned the sum, it grew larger.

Lona. And you, Karsten—?

Bernick. I grasped at the rumour like a drowning man at a straw.

Lona. You helped to spread it?

Bernick. I did not contradict. Our creditors had begun to be pressing, and I had the task of keeping them quiet. The result was the dissipating of any suspicion as to the stability of the firm; people said that we had been hit by a temporary piece of ill-luck—that all that was necessary was that they should not press us—only give us time and every creditor would be paid in full.

Lona. And every creditor was paid in full?

Bernick. Yes, Lona, that rumour saved our house and made me the man I now am.

Lona. That is to say, a lie has made you the man you now are.

Bernick. Whom did it injure at the time? It was Johan's intention never to come back.

Lona. You ask whom it injured. Look into your own heart, and tell me if it has not injured you.

Bernick. Look into any man's heart you please, and you will always find, in every one, at least one black spot which he has to keep concealed.

Lona. And you call yourselves pillars of society!

Bernick. Society has none better.

Lona. And of what consequence is it whether such a society be propped up or not? What does it all consist of? Show and lies—and nothing else. Here are you, the first man in the town, living in grandeur and luxury, powerful and respected—you, who have branded an innocent man as a criminal.

Bernick. Do you suppose I am not deeply conscious of the wrong I have done him? And do you suppose I am not ready to make amends to him for it?

Lona. How? By speaking out?

Bernick. Would you have the heart to insist on that?

Lona. What else can make amends for such a wrong?

Bernick. I am rich, Lona; Johan can demand any sum he pleases—

Lona. Yes, offer him money, and you will hear what he will say.

Bernick. Do you know what he intends to do?

Lona. No; since yesterday he has been dumb. He looks

as if this had made a grown man of him all at once.

Bernick. I must talk to him.

Lona. Here he comes. (JOHAN *comes in from the right.*)

Bernick (*going towards him.*) Johan—!

Johan (*motioning him away*). Listen to me first. Yesterday morning I gave you my word that I would hold my tongue.

Bernick. You did.

Johan. But then I did not know—

Bernick. Johan, only let me say a word or two to explain the circumstances—

Johan. It is unnecessary; I understand the circumstances perfectly. The firm was in a dangerous position at the time; I had gone off, and you had my defenceless name and reputation at your mercy. Well, I do not blame you so very much for what you did; we were young and thoughtless in those days. But now I have need of the truth, and now you must speak.

Bernick. And just now I have need of all my reputation for morality, and therefore I *cannot* speak.

Johan. I don't take much account of the false reports you spread about me; it is the other thing that you must take the blame of. I shall make Dina my wife, and here—here in your town—I mean to settle down and live with her.

Lona. Is that what you mean to do?

Bernick. With Dina? Dina as your wife?—in this town?

Johan. Yes, here and nowhere else. I mean to stay here to defy all these liars and slanderers. But before I can win her you must exonerate me.

Bernick. Have you considered that, if I confess to the one thing, it will inevitably mean making myself responsible for the other as well? You will say that I can show by our books that nothing dishonest happened? But I cannot; our books were not so accurately kept in those days. And even if I could, what good would it do? Should I not in any case be pointed at as the man who had once saved himself by an untruth, and for fifteen years had allowed that untruth and all its consequences to stand without having raised a finger to demolish it? You do not know our community very much, or you would realise that it would ruin me utterly.

Johan. I can only tell you that I mean to make Mrs. Dorf's daughter my wife, and live with her in this town.

Bernick (wiping the perspiration from his forehead). Listen to me, Johan—and you too, Lona. The circumstances I am in just now are quite exceptional. I am situated in such a way that if you aim this blow at me you will not only destroy me, but will also destroy a great future, rich in blessings, that lies before the community which, after all, was the home of your childhood.

Johan. And if I do not aim this blow at you, I shall be destroying all my future happiness with my own hand.

Lona. Go on, Karsten.

Bernick. I will tell you, then. It is mixed up with the railway project, and the whole thing is not quite so simple as you think. I suppose you have heard that last year there was some talk of a railway line along the coast? Many influential people backed up the idea—people in the town and the suburbs, and especially the Press; but I managed to get the proposal quashed, on the ground that it would have injured our steamboat trade along the coast.

Lona. Have you any interest in the steamboat trade?

Bernick. Yes. But no one ventured to suspect me on that account; my honoured name fully protected me from that. For the matter of that, I could have stood the loss; but the place could not have stood it. So the inland line was decided upon. As soon as that was done, I assured myself—without saying anything about it—that a branch line could be laid to the town.

Lona. Why did you say nothing about it, Karsten?

Bernick. Have you heard the rumours of extensive buying up of forest lands, mines and waterfalls—?

Johan. Yes, apparently it is some company from another part of the country—

Bernick. As these properties are situated at present, they are as good as valueless to their owners, who are scattered about the neighbourhood; they have therefore been sold comparatively cheap. If the purchaser had waited till the branch line began to be talked of, the proprietors would have asked exorbitant prices.

Lona. Well—what then?

Bernick. Now I am going to tell you something that can be construed in different ways—a thing to which, in our community, a man could only confess provided he had an untarnished and honoured name to take his stand upon.

Lona. Well?

Bernick. It is I that have bought up the whole of them.

Lona. You?

Johan. On your own account?

Bernick. On my own account. If the branch line becomes an accomplished fact, I am a millionaire; if it does not, I am ruined.

Lona. It is a big risk, Karsten.

Bernick. I have risked my whole fortune on it.

Lona. I am not thinking of your fortune; but if it comes to light that—

Bernick. Yes, that is the critical part of it. With the unblemished and honoured name I have hitherto borne, I can take the whole thing upon my shoulders, carry it through, and say to my fellow-citizens: "See, I have taken this risk for the good of the community."

Lona. Of the community?

Bernick. Yes; and not a soul will doubt my motives.

Lona. Then some of those concerned in it have acted more openly—without any secret motives or considerations.

Bernick. Who?

Lona. Why, of course Rummel and Sandstad and Vigeland.

Bernick. To get them on my side I was obliged to let them into the secret.

Lona. And they?

Bernick. They have stipulated for a fifth part of the profits as their share.

Lona. Oh, these pillars of society!

Bernick. And isn't it society itself that forces us to use these underhand means? What would have happened, if I had not acted secretly? Everybody would have wanted to have a hand in the undertaking; the whole thing would have been divided up, mismanaged and bungled. There is not a single man in the town except myself who is capable of directing so big an affair as this will be. In this country, almost without exception, it is only foreigners who have settled here who have the aptitude for big business schemes. That is the reason why my conscience acquits me in the matter. It is only in my hands that these properties can become a real blessing to the many who have to make their daily bread.

Lona. I believe you are right there, Karsten.

Johan. But I have no concern with the many, and my life's happiness is at stake.

Bernick. The welfare of your native place is also at stake. If things come out which cast reflections on my earlier conduct, then all my opponents will fall upon me with united vigour. A youthful folly is never allowed to be forgotten in our community. They would go through the whole of my previous life, bring up a thousand little incidents in it, interpret and explain them in the light of what has been revealed; they would crush me under the weight of rumours and slanders. I should be obliged to abandon the railway scheme; and, if I take my hand off that, it will come to nothing, and I shall be ruined and my life as a citizen will be over.

Lona. Johan, after what we have just heard, you must go away from here and hold your tongue.

Bernick. Yes, yes, Johan—you must!

Johan. Yes, I will go away, and I will hold my tongue; but I shall come back, and then I shall speak.

Bernick. Stay over there, Johan; hold your tongue, and I am willing to share with you—

Johan. Keep your money, but give me back my name and reputation.

Bernick. And sacrifice my own!

Johan. You and your community must get out of that the best way you can. I must and shall win Dina for my wife. And therefore I am going to sail to-morrow in the "Indian Girl"—

Bernick. In the "Indian Girl"?

Johan. Yes. The captain has promised to take me. I shall go over to America, as I say; I shall sell my farm and set my affairs in order. In two months I shall be back.

Bernick. And then you will speak?

Johan. Then the guilty man must take his guilt on himself.

Bernick. Have you forgotten that, if I do that, I must also take on myself guilt that is not mine?

Johan. Who is it that for the last fifteen years has benefited by that shameful rumour?

Bernick. You will drive me to desperation! Well, if you speak, I shall deny everything! I shall say it is a plot against me—that you have come here to blackmail me!

Lona. For shame, Karsten!

Bernick. I am a desperate man, I tell you, and I shall fight for my life. I shall deny everything—everything!

Johan. I have your two letters. I found them in my box among my other papers. This morning I read them again; they are plain enough.

Bernick. And will you make them public?

Johan. If it becomes necessary.

Bernick. And you will be back here in two months?

Johan. I hope so. The wind is fair. In three weeks I

shall be in New York—if the "Indian Girl" does not go to the bottom.

Bernick (*with a start*). Go to the bottom? Why should the "Indian Girl" go to the bottom?

Johan. Quite so—why should she?

Bernick (*scarcely audibly*). Go to the bottom?

Johan. Well, Karsten, now you know what is before you. You must find your own way out. Good-bye! You can say good-bye to Betty for me, although she has not treated me like a sister. But I must see Martha. She shall tell Dina — she shall promise me— (*Goes out through the farther door on the left.*)

Bernick (*to himself*). The "Indian Girl"—? (*Quickly.*) Lona, you *must* prevent that!

Lona. You see for yourself, Karsten—I have no influence over him any longer. (*Follows* JOHAN *into the other room.*)

Bernick (*a prey to uneasy thoughts*). Go to the bottom—?

(AUNE *comes in from the right.*)

Aune. Excuse me, sir, but if it is convenient—

Bernick (*turning round angrily*). What do you want?

Aune. To know if I may ask you a question, sir.

Bernick. Be quick about it, then. What is it?

Aune. I wanted to ask if I am to consider it as certain—absolutely certain—that I should be dismissed from the yard if the "Indian Girl" were not ready to sail to-morrow?

Bernick. What do you mean? The ship *is* ready to sail.

Aune. Yes—it is. But suppose it were not, should I be discharged?

Bernick. What is the use of asking such idle questions?

Aune. Only that I should like to know, sir. Will you answer me that?—should I be discharged?

Bernick. Am I in the habit of keeping my word or not?

Aune. Then to-morrow I should have lost the position I hold in my house and among those near and dear to me—lost my influence over men of my own class—lost all opportunity of doing anything for the cause of the poorer and needier members of the community?

Bernick. Aune, we have discussed all that before.

Aune. Quite so—then the "Indian Girl" will sail.

(*A short silence.*)

Bernick. Look here—it is impossible for me to have my eyes everywhere—I cannot be answerable for everything. You can give me your assurance, I suppose, that the repairs have been satisfactorily carried out?

Aune. You gave me very short grace, Mr. Bernick.

Bernick. But I understand you to warrant the repairs?

Aune. The weather is fine, and it is summer.

(*Another pause.*)

Bernick. Have you anything else to say to me?

Aune. I think not, sir.

Bernick. Then—the "Indian Girl" will sail—

Aune. To-morrow?

Bernick. Yes.

Aune. Very good. (*Bows and goes out.* BERNICK *stands for a moment irresolute; then walks quickly towards the door, as if to call* AUNE *back; but stops, hesitatingly, with his hand on the door-handle. At that moment the door is opened from without, and* KRAP *comes in.*)

Krap (*in a low voice*). Aha, he has been here. Has he confessed?

Bernick. Hm— have you discovered anything?

Krap. What need of that, sir? Could you not see the evil conscience looking out of the man's eyes?

Bernick. Nonsense—such things don't show. Have you discovered anything, I want to know?

Krap. I could not manage it; I was too late. They had already begun hauling the ship out of the dock. But their very haste in doing that plainly shows that—

Bernick. It shows nothing. Has the inspection taken place, then?

Krap. Of course; but—

Bernick. There, you see! And of course they found nothing to complain of?

Krap. Mr. Bernick, you know very well how much this inspection means, especially in a yard that has such a good name as ours has.

Bernick. No matter—it takes all responsibilty off us.

Krap. But, sir, could you really not tell from Aune's manner that—?

Bernick. Aune has completely reassured me, let me tell you.

Krap. And let me tell you, sir, that I am morally certain that—

Bernick. What does this mean, Krap? I see plainly enough that you want to get your knife into this man; but if you want to attack him you must find some other occasion. You know how important it is to me —or, I should say, to the owners—that the "Indian Girl" should sail to-morrow.

Krap. Very well—so be it; but if ever we hear of *that* ship again—hm!

(VIGELAND *comes in from the right.*)

Vigeland. I wish you a very good morning, Mr. Bernick. Have you a moment to spare?

Bernick. At your service, Mr. Vigeland.

Vigeland. I only want to know if you are also of opinion that the "Palm Tree" should sail to-morrow?

Bernick. Certainly; I thought that was quite settled.

Vigeland. Well, the captain came to me just now and told me that storm-signals have been hoisted.

Bernick. Oh! Are we to expect a storm?

Vigeland. A stiff breeze, at all events; but not a contrary wind—just the opposite.

Bernick. Hm—well, what do you say?

Vigeland. I say, as I said to the captain, that the "Palm Tree" is in the hands of Providence. Besides, they are only going across the North Sea at first; and in England freights are running tolerably high just now, so that—

Bernick. Yes, it would probably mean a loss for us if we waited.

Vigeland. Besides, she is a stout ship, and fully insured as well. It is more risky, now, for the "Indian Girl"—

Bernick. What do you mean?

Vigeland. She sails to-morrow, too.

Bernick. Yes, the owners have been in such a hurry, and, besides—

Vigeland. Well, if that old hulk can venture out—and with such a crew, into the bargain—it would be a disgrace to us if we—

Bernick. Quite so. I presume you have the ship's papers with you.

Vigeland. Yes, here they are.

Bernick. Good; then will you go in with Mr. Krap?

Krap. Will you come in here, sir, and we will dispose of them at once.

Vigeland. Thank you—And the issue we leave in the hands of the Almighty, Mr. Bernick. (*Goes with* KRAP *into* BERNICK'S *room.* RÖRLUND *comes up from the garden.*)

Rörlund. At home at this time of day, Mr. Bernick?

Bernick (*lost in thought*). As you see.

Rörlund. It was really on your wife's account I came. I thought she might be in need of a word of comfort.

Bernick. Very likely she is. But I want to have a little talk with you, too.

Rörlund. With the greatest of pleasure, Mr. Bernick. But what is the matter with you? You look quite pale and upset.

Bernick. Really? Do I? Well, what else could you expect—a man so loaded with responsibilties as I am? There is all my own big business—and now the planning of this railway.—But tell me something, Mr. Rörlund; let me put a question to you.

Rörlund. With pleasure, Mr. Bernick.

Bernick. It is about a thought that has occurred to me. Suppose a man is face to face with an undertaking which will concern the welfare of thousands, and suppose it should be necessary to make a sacrifice of one—?

Rörlund. What do you mean?

Bernick. For example, suppose a man were thinking of starting a large factory. He knows for certain—because all his experience has taught him so—that sooner or later a toll of human life will be exacted in the working of that factory.

Rörlund. Yes, that is only too probable.

Bernick. Or, say a man embarks on a mining enterprise. He takes into his service fathers of families and young men in the first flush of their youth. Is it not quite safe to predict that all of them will not come out of it alive?

Rörlund. Yes, unhappily that is quite true.

Bernick. Well—a man in that position will know beforehand that the undertaking he proposes to start must undoubtedly, at some time or other, mean a loss of human life. But the undertaking itself is for the public good; for every man's life that it costs, it will undoubtedly promote the welfare of many hundreds.

Rörlund. Ah, you are thinking of the railway—of all the dangerous excavating and blasting, and that sort of thing—

Bernick. Yes—quite so—I am thinking of the railway. And, besides, the coming of the railway will mean the starting of factories and mines. But do not think, nevertheless—

Rörlund. My dear Mr. Bernick, you are almost over-conscious. What I think is that, if you place the affair in the hands of Providence—

Bernick. Yes—exactly; Providence—

Rörlund. You are blameless in the matter. Go on and build your railway hopefully.

Bernick. Yes, but now I will put a special instance to you. Suppose a charge of blasting-powder had to be exploded in a dangerous place, and that unless it were exploded the line could not be constructed? Suppose the engineer knew that it would cost the life of the workman who lit the fuse, but that it had to be lit, and that it was the engineer's duty to send a workman to do it?

Rörlund. Hm—

Bernick. I know what you will say. It would be a splendid thing if the engineer took the match himself and went and lit the fuse. But that is out of the question, so he must sacrifice a workman.

Rörlund. That is a thing no engineer here would ever do.

Bernick. No engineer in the bigger countries would think twice about doing it.

Rörlund. In the bigger countries? No, I can quite believe it. In those depraved and unprincipled communities—

Bernick. Oh, there is a good deal to be said for those communities.

Rörlund. Can you say that?—you, who yourself—

Bernick. In the bigger communities a man finds space to carry out a valuable project—finds the courage to make some sacrifice in a great cause; but here a man is cramped by all kinds of petty considerations and scruples.

Rörlund. Is human life a petty consideration?

Bernick. When that human life threatens the welfare of thousands.

Rörlund. But you are suggesting cases that are quite inconceivable, Mr. Bernick! I do not understand you at all to-day. And you quote the bigger countries—well, what do they think of human life there? They look upon it simply as part of the capital they have to use. But *we* look at things from a somewhat different moral standpoint, I should hope. Look at our respected shipping industry! Can you name a single one of our ship-owners who would sacrifice a human life for the sake of paltry gain? And then think of those scoundrels in the bigger countries, who for the sake of profit send out freights in one unseaworthy ship after another—

Bernick. I am not talking of unseaworthy ships!

Rörlund. But I am, Mr. Bernick.

Bernick. Yes, but to what purpose? They have nothing to do with the question.—Oh, these small, timid considerations! If a General from this country were to take his men under fire and some of them were shot, I suppose he would have sleepless nights after it! It is not so in other countries. You should hear what that fellow in there says—

Rörlund. He? Who? The American—?

Bernick. Yes. You should hear how in America—

Rörlund. He, in there? And you did not tell me? I shall at once—

Bernick. It's no use; you won't be able to do anything with him.

Rörlund. We shall see. Ah, here he comes. (JOHAN *comes in from the other room.*)

Johan (*talking back through the open door*). Yes, yes, Dina—as you please; but I do not mean to give you up, all the same. I shall come back, and then everything will come right between us.

Rörlund. Excuse me, but what did you mean by that? What is it you propose to do?

Johan. I propose that that young girl, before whom you blackened my character yesterday, shall become my wife.

Rörlund. Your wife? And can you really suppose that—?

Johan. I mean to marry her.

Rörlund. Well, then you shall know the truth. (*Goes to the half-open door.*) Mrs. Bernick, will you be so kind as to come and be a witness—and you too, Miss Martha. And let Dina come. (*Sees* LONA *at the door.*) Ah, you here too?

Lona. Shall I come too?

Rörlund. As many as you please—the more the better.

Bernick. What are you going to do? (LONA, MRS. BERNICK, MARTHA, DINA *and* HILMAR *come in from the other room.*)

Mrs. Bernick. Mr. Rörlund, I have tried my hardest, but I cannot prevent him—

Rörlund. I shall prevent him, Mrs. Bernick. Dina, you are a thoughtless girl, but I do not blame you so greatly. You have too long lacked the necessary moral support that should have sustained you. I blame myself for not having afforded you that support.

Dina. You mustn't speak now!

Mrs. Bernick. What is it?

Rörlund. It is now that I *must* speak, Dina, although your conduct yesterday and to-day has made it ten times more difficult for me. But all other considerations must give way to the necessity for saving you. You remember that I gave you my word; you remember what you promised you would answer when I judged that the right time had come. Now I dare not hesitate any longer, and therefore—. (*Turns to* JOHAN.) This young girl, whom you are persecuting, is my betrothed.

Mrs. Bernick. What?

Bernick. Dina!

Johan. She? Your—?

Martha. No, no, Dina!

Lona. It is a lie!

Johan. Dina—is this man speaking the truth?

Dina (*after a short pause*). Yes.

Rörlund. I hope this has rendered all your arts of seduction powerless. The step I have determined to take for Dina's good I now wish openly proclaimed to every one. I cherish the certain hope that it will not be misinterpreted. And now, Mrs. Bernick, I think it will be best for us to take her away from here, and try to bring back peace and tranquility to her mind.

Mrs. Bernick. Yes, come with me. Oh, Dina—what a lucky girl you are! (*Takes* DINA *out to the left:* RÖRLUND *follows them.*)

Martha. Good-bye, Johan! (*Goes out.*)

Hilmar (*at the verandah door*). Hm—I really must say—

Lona (*who has followed* DINA *with her eyes, to* JOHAN).

Don't be downhearted, my boy! I shall stay here and keep my eye on the parson. (*Goes out to the right.*)

Bernick. Johan, you won't sail in the "Indian Girl" now?

Johan. Indeed I shall.

Bernick. But you won't come back?

Johan. I am coming back.

Bernick. After this? What have you to do here after this?

Johan. Revenge myself on you all; crush as many of you as I can. (*Goes out to the right.* VIGELAND *and* KRAP *come in from* BERNICK'S *room.*)

Vigeland. There, now the papers are in order, Mr. Bernick.

Bernick. Good, good.

Krap (*in a low voice*). And I suppose it is settled that the "Indian Girl" is to sail to-morrow?

Bernick. Yes. (*Goes into his room.* VIGELAND *and* KRAP *go out to the right.* HILMAR *is just going after them, when* OLAF *puts his head carefully out of the door on the left.*)

Olaf. Uncle! Uncle Hilmar!

Hilmar. Ugh, is it you? Why don't you stay upstairs? You know you are confined to the house.

Olaf (*coming a step or two nearer*). Hush! Uncle Hilmar, have you heard the news?

Hilmar. Yes, I have heard that you got a thrashing to-day.

Olaf (*looking threateningly towards his father's room*). He shan't thrash me any more. But have you heard that Uncle Johan is going to sail to-morrow with the Americans?

Hilmar. What has that got to do with you? You had better run upstairs again.

Olaf. Perhaps I shall be going for a buffalo hunt, too, one of these days, uncle.

Hilmar. Rubbish! A coward like you—

Olaf. Yes—just wait! You will learn something to-morrow!

Hilmar. Duffer! (*Goes out through the garden.* OLAF *runs into the room again and shuts the door, as he sees* KRAP *coming in from the right.*)

Krap (*going to the door of* BERNICK'S *room and opening it slightly.*) Excuse my bothering you again, Mr. Bernick; but there is a tremendous storm blowing up. (*Waits a moment, but there is no answer.*) Is the "Indian Girl" to sail, for all that? (*After a short pause, the following is heard.*)

Bernick (*from his room*). The "Indian Girl" is to sail, for all that.

(KRAP *shuts the door and goes out again to the right.*)

ACT IV

(SCENE.—*The same room. The work-table has been taken away. It is a stormy evening and already dusk. Darkness sets in as the following scene is in progress. A man-servant is lighting the chandelier; two maids bring in pots of flowers, lamps and candles, which they place on tables and stands along the walls.* RUMMEL, *in dress clothes, with gloves and a white tie, is standing in the room giving instructions to the servants.*)

Rummel. Only every other candle, Jacob. It must not look as if it were arranged for the occasion—it has to come as a surprise, you know. And all these flowers—? Oh, well, let them be; it will probably look as if they stood there every day. (BERNICK *comes out of his room.*)

Bernick (*stopping at the door.*) What does this mean?

Rummel. Oh dear, is it you! (*To the servants.*) Yes, you might leave us for the present. (*The servants go out.*)

Bernick. But, Rummel, what is the meaning of this?

Rummel. It means that the proudest moment of your life has come. A procession of his fellow-citizens is coming to do honour to the first man of the town.

Bernick. What!

Rummel. In procession—with banners and a band! We ought to have had torches too; but we did not like to risk that in this stormy weather. There will be illuminations—and that always sounds well in the newspapers.

Bernick. Listen, Rummel—I won't have anything to do with this.

Rummel. But it is too late now; they will be here in half-an-hour.

Bernick. But why did you not tell me about this before?

Rummel. Just because I was afraid you would raise objections to it. But I consulted your wife; she allowed me to take charge of the arrangements, while she looks after the refreshments.

Bernick (*listening*). What is that noise? Are they coming already? I fancy I hear singing.

Rummel (*going to the verandah door*). Singing? Oh, that is only the Americans. The "Indian Girl" is being towed out.

Bernick. Towed out? Oh, yes. No, Rummel, I cannot this evening; I am not well.

Rummel. You certainly do look bad. But you must pull yourself together; devil take it—you *must!* Sandstad and Vigeland and I all attach the greatest importance to carrying this thing through. We have got to crush our opponents under the weight of as complete an expression of public opinion as possible. Rumours are getting about the town; our announcement about the purchase of the property cannot be withheld any longer. It is imperative that this very evening—after songs and speeches, amidst the clink of glasses—in a word, in an ebullient atmosphere of festivity—you should inform them of the risk you have incurred for the good of the community. In such an ebullient atmosphere of festivity—as I just now described it—you can do an astonishing lot with the people here. But you must have that atmosphere, or the thing won't go.

Bernick. Yes, yes—

Rummel. And especially when so delicate and ticklish a point has to be negotiated. Well, thank goodness, you have a name that will be a tower of strength, Bernick. But listen now; we must make our arrangements, to some extent. Mr. Hilmar Tönnesen has written an ode to you. It begins very charmingly with the words: "Raise the Ideal's banner high!" And Mr. Rörlund has undertaken the task of making the speech of the evening. Of course you must reply to that.

Bernick. I cannot to-night, Rummel. Couldn't you—?

Rummel. It is impossible, however willing I might be; because, as you can imagine, his speech will be especially addressed to you. Of course it is possible he may say a word or two about the rest of us; I have spoken to Vigeland and Sandstad about it. Our idea is that, in replying, you should propose the toast of "Prosperity to our Community"; Sandstad will say a few words on the subject of harmonious relations between the different strata of society; then Vigeland will express the hope that this new undertaking may not disturb the sound moral basis upon which our community stands; and I propose, in a few suitable words, to refer to the ladies, whose work for the community, though more inconspicuous, is far from being without its importance. But you are not listening to me—

Bernick. Yes—indeed I am. But, tell me, do you think there is a very heavy sea running outside?

Rummel. Why, are you nervous about the "Palm Tree"? She is fully insured, you know.

Bernick. Yes, she is insured; but—

Rummel. And in good repair—and that is the main thing.

Bernick. Hm— Supposing anything does happen to a ship, it doesn't follow that human life will be in danger, does it? The ship and the cargo may be lost—and one might lose one's boxes and papers—

Rummel. Good Lord—boxes and papers are not of much consequence.

Bernick. Not of much consequence! No, no; I only meant— Hush—I hear voices again.

Rummel. It is on board the "Palm Tree."

(VIGELAND *comes in from the right.*)

Vigeland. Yes, they are just towing the "Palm Tree" out. Good evening, Mr. Bernick.

Bernick. And you, as a seafaring man, are still of opinion that—

Vigeland. I put my trust in Providence, Mr. Bernick. Moreover, I have been on board myself and distributed a few small tracts which I hope may carry a blessing with them.

(SANDSTAD *and* KRAP *come in from the right.*)

Sandstad (*to some one at the door*). Well, if that gets through all right, anything will. (*Comes in*). Ah, good evening, good evening!

Bernick. Is anything the matter, Krap?

Krap. I say nothing, Mr. Bernick.

Sandstad. The entire crew of the "Indian Girl" are drunk; I will stake my reputation on it that they won't come out of it alive. (LONA *comes in from the right.*)

Lona. Ah, now I can say his good-byes for him.

Bernick. Is he on board already?

Lona. He will be directly, at any rate. We parted outside the hotel.

Bernick. And he persists in his intention?

Lona. As firm as a rock.

Rummel (*who is fumbling at the window*). Confound these new-fangled contrivances; I cannot get the curtains drawn.

Lona. Do you want them drawn? I thought, on the contrary—

Rummel. Yes, drawn at first, Miss Hessel. You know what is in the wind, I suppose?

Lona. Yes. Let me help you. (*Takes hold of the cords.*) I will draw down the curtains on my brother-in-law—though I would much rather draw them up.

Rummel. You can do that too, later on. When the garden is filled with a surging crowd, then the curtains shall be drawn back, and they will be able to look in upon a surprised and happy family. Citizens' lives should be such that they can live in glass houses! (BERNICK *opens his*

mouth, as though he were going to say something; but he
turns hurriedly away and goes into his room.)

Rummel. Come along, let us have a final consultation.
Come in, too, Mr. Krap; you must assist us with information on one or two points of detail. (*All the men go into*
BERNICK'S *room.* LONA *has drawn the curtains over the*
windows, and is just going to do the same over the open
glass door, when OLAF *jumps down from the room above*
on to the garden steps; he has a wrap over his shoulders
and a bundle in his hand.

Lona. Bless me, child, how you frightened me!

Olaf (*hiding his bundle*). Hush, aunt!

Lona. Did you jump out of the window? Where are
you going?

Olaf. Hush!—don't say anything. I want to go to
Uncle Johan—only on to the quay, you know—only to say
good-bye to him. Good-night, aunt! (*Runs out through*
the garden.)

Lona. No—stop! Olaf—Olaf!

(JOHAN, *dressed for his journey, with a bag over his*
    shoulder, comes warily in by the door on the right.)

Johan. Lona!

Lona (*turning round*). What! Back again?

Johan. I have still a few minutes. I must see her once
more; we cannot part like this. (*The farther door on the*
left opens, and MARTHA *and* DINA, *both with cloaks on,*
and the latter carrying a small travelling-bag in her hand,
come in.)

Dina. Let me go to him! Let me go to him!

Martha. Yes, you shall go to him, Dina!

Dina. There he is!

Johan. Dina!

Dina. Take me with you!

Johan. What—!

Lona. You mean it?

Dina. Yes, take me with you. The other has written

to me that he means to announce to every one this evening—

Johan. Dina—you do not love him?

Dina. I have never loved the man! I would rather drown myself in the fjord than be engaged to him! Oh, how he humiliated me yesterday with his condescending manner! How clear he made it that he felt he was lifting up a poor despised creature to his own level! I do not mean to be despised any longer. I mean to go away. May I go with you?

Johan. Yes, yes—a thousand times, yes!

Dina. I will not be a burden to you long. Only help me to get over there; help me to go the right way about things at first—

Johan. Hurrah, it is all right after all, Dina!

Lona (*pointing to* BERNICK'S *door*). Hush!—gently, gently!

Johan. Dina, I shall look after you.

Dina. I am not going to let you do that. I mean to look after myself; over there, I am sure I can do that. Only let me get away from here. Oh, these women!—you don't know—they have written to me to-day, too—exhorting me to realise my good fortune—impressing on me how magnanimous he has been. To-morrow, and every day afterwards, they would be watching me to see if I were making myself worthy of it all. I am sick and tired of all this goodness!

Johan. Tell me, Dina—is that the only reason you are coming away? Am I nothing to you?

Dina. Yes, Johan, you are more to me than any one else in the world.

Johan. Oh, Dina—!

Dina. Every one here tells me I ought to hate and detest you—that it is my duty; but I cannot see that it is my duty, and shall never be able to.

Lona. No more you shall, my dear!

Martha. No, indeed you shall not; and that is why you shall go with him as his wife.

Johan. Yes, yes!

Lona. What? Give me a kiss, Martha. I never expected that from *you!*

Martha. No, I dare say not; I would not have expected it myself. But I was bound to break out some time! Ah, what we suffer under the tyranny of habit and custom! Make a stand against that, Dina. Be his wife. Let me see you defy all this convention.

Johan. What is your answer, Dina?

Dina. Yes, I will be your wife.

Johan. Dina!

Dina. But first of all I want to work—to make something of myself—as you have done. I am not going to be merely a thing that is taken.

Lona. Quite right—that is the way.

Johan. Very well; I shall wait and hope—

Lona. And win, my boy! But now you must get on board!

Johan. Yes, on board! Ah, Lona, my dear sister, just one word with you. Look here— (*He takes her into the background and talks hurriedly to her.*)

Martha. Dina, you lucky girl, let me look at you, and kiss you once more—for the last time.

Dina. Not for the last time; no, my darling aunt, we shall meet again.

Martha. Never! Promise me, Dina, never to come back! (*Grasps her hands and looks at her.*) Now go to your happiness, my dear child—across the sea. How often, in my schoolroom, I have yearned to be over there! It must be beautiful; the skies are loftier than here—a freer air plays about your head—

Dina. Oh, Aunt Martha, some day you will follow us.

Martha. I? Never—never. I have my little vocation

here, and now I really believe I can live to the full the life that I ought.

Dina. I cannot imagine being parted from you.

Martha. Ah, one can part from much, Dina. (*Kisses her.*) But I hope you may never experience that, my sweet child. Promise me to make him happy.

Dina. I will promise nothing; I hate promises; things must happen as they will.

Martha. Yes, yes, that is true; only remain what you are—true and faithful to yourself.

Dina. I will, aunt.

Lona (*putting into her pocket some papers that* JOHAN *has given her*). Splendid, splendid, my dear boy. But now you must be off.

Johan. Yes, we have no time to waste now. Good-bye, Lona, and thank you for all your love. Good-bye, Martha, and thank you, too, for your loyal friendship.

Martha. Good-bye, Johan! Good-bye, Dina! And may you be happy all your lives! (*She and* LONA *hurry them to the door at the back.* JOHAN *and* DINA *go quickly down the steps and through the garden.* LONA *shuts the door and draws the curtains over it.*

Lona. Now we are alone, Martha. You have lost her and I him.

Martha. You—lost him?

Lona. Oh, I had already half lost him over there. The boy was longing to stand on his own feet; that was why I pretended to be suffering from homesickness.

Martha. So that was it? Ah, then I understand why you came. But he will want you back, Lona.

Lona. An old step-sister—what use will he have for her now? Men break many very dear ties to win their happiness.

Martha. That sometimes is so.

Lona. But we two will stick together. Martha.

Martha. Can I be anything to you?

Lona. Who more so? We two foster-sisters—haven't we both lost our children? Now we are alone.

Martha. Yes, alone. And therefore you ought to know this too—I loved him more than anything in the world.

Lona. Martha! (*Grasps her by the arm.*) Is that true?

Martha. All my existence lies in those words. I have loved him and waited for him. Every summer I waited for him to come. And then he came—but he had no eyes for me.

Lona. You loved him! And it was you yourself that put his happiness into his hands.

Martha. Ought I not to be the one to put his happiness into his hands, since I loved him? Yes, I have loved him. All my life has been for him, ever since he went away. What reason had I to hope, you mean? Oh, I think I had some reason, all the same. But when he came back—then it seemed as if everything had been wiped out of his memory. He had no eyes for me.

Lona. It was Dina that overshadowed you, Martha?

Martha. And it is a good thing she did. At the time he went away, we were of the same age; but when I saw him again—oh, that dreadful moment!—I realised that now I was ten years older than he. He had gone out into the bright sparkling sunshine, and breathed in youth and health with every breath; and here I sat meanwhile, spinning and spinning—

Lona. Spinning the thread of his happiness, Martha.

Martha. Yes, it was a golden thread I spun. No bitterness! We have been two good sisters to him, haven't we, Lona?

Lona (*throwing her arms round her*). Martha!

(BERNICK *comes in from his room.*)

Bernick (*to the other men, who are in his room.*) Yes, yes, arrange it any way you please. When the time comes, I shall be able to— (*Shuts the door.*) Ah, you are here.

Look here, Martha—I think you had better change your dress; and tell Betty to do the same. I don't want anything elaborate, of course—something homely, but neat. But you must make haste.

Lona. And a bright, cheerful face, Martha; your eyes must look happy.

Bernick. Olaf is to come downstairs too; I will have him beside me.

Lona. Hm! Olaf—

Martha. I will give Betty your message. (*Goes out by the farther door on the left.*)

Lona. Well, the great and solemn moment is at hand.

Bernick (walking uneasily up and down). Yes, it is.

Lona. At such a moment I should think a man would feel proud and happy.

Bernick (looking at her). Hm!

Lona. I hear the whole town is to be illuminated.

Bernick. Yes, they have some idea of that sort.

Lona. All the different clubs will assemble with their banners—your name will blaze out in letters of fire—to-night the telegraph will flash the news to every part of the country: "In the bosom of his happy family, Mr. Bernick received the homage of his fellow-citizens as one of the pillars of society."

Bernick. That is so; and they will begin to cheer outside, and the crowd will shout in front of my house until I shall be obliged to go out and bow to them and thank them.

Lona. Obliged to?

Bernick. Do you suppose I shall feel happy at that moment?

Lona. No, I don't suppose you will feel so very happy.

Bernick. Lona, you despise me.

Lona. Not yet.

Bernick. And you have no right to; no right to *despise* me! Lona, you can have no idea how utterly alone I stand in this cramped and stunted community—where I have had, year after year, to stifle my ambition for a fuller life. My work may seem many-sided, but what have I really accomplished? Odds and ends—scraps. They would not stand anything else here. If I were to go a step in advance of the opinions and views that are current at the moment, I should lose all my influence. Do you know what we are —we who are looked upon as pillars of society? We are nothing more nor less than the tools of society.

Lona. Why have you only begun to realise that now?

Bernick. Because I have been thinking a great deal lately—since you came back—and this evening I have thought more seriously than ever before. Oh, Lona, why did not I really know you then—in the old days, I mean?

Lona. And if you had?

Bernick. I should never have let you go; and, if I had had you, I should not be in the position I am in to-night.

Lona. And do you never consider what *she* might have been to you—she whom you chose in my place?

Bernick. I know, at all events, that she has been nothing to me of what I needed.

Lona. Because you have never shared your interests with her; because you have never allowed her full and frank exchange of thoughts with you; because you have allowed her to be borne under by self-reproach for the shame you cast upon one who was dear to her.

Bernick. Yes, yes; it all comes from lying and deceit.

Lona. Then why not break with all this lying and deceit?

Bernick. Now? It is too late now, Lona.

Lona. Karsten, tell me—what gratification does all this show and deception bring you?

Bernick. It brings *me* none. I must disappear some day, and all this community of bunglers with me. But a generation is growing up that will follow us; it is my son that I work for—I am providing a career for *him*. There will come a time when truth will enter into the life of the community, and on that foundation he shall build up a happier existence than his father.

Lona. With a lie at the bottom of it all? Consider what sort of inheritance it is that you are leaving to your son.

Bernick (in tones of suppressed despair). It is a thousand times worse than you think. But surely some day the curse must be lifted; and yet—nevertheless— (*Vehemently.*) How could I bring all this upon my own head! Still, it is done now; I must go on with it now. You *shall* not succeed in crushing me! (HILMAR *comes in hurriedly and agitatedly from the right, with an open letter in his hand.*)

Hilmar. But this is— Betty, Betty!

Bernick. What is the matter? Are they coming already?

Hilmar. No, no—but I must speak to some one immediately. (*Goes out through the farther door on the left.*)

Lona. Karsten, you talk about our having come here to crush you. So let me tell you what sort of stuff this prodigal son, whom your moral community shuns as if he had the plague, is made of. He can do without any of you—for he is away now.

Bernick. But he said he meant to come back—

Lona. Johan will never come back. He is gone for good, and Dina with him.

Bernick. Never come back?—and Dina with him?

Lona. Yes, to be his wife. That is how these two strike your virtuous community in the face, just as I did once—but never mind that.

Bernick. Gone—and she too—in the "Indian Girl"—

Lona. No; he would not trust so precious a freight to that rascally crew. Johan and Dina are on the "Palm Tree."

Bernick. Ah! Then it is all in vain— (*Goes hurriedly to the door of his room, opens it and calls in.*) Krap, stop the "Indian Girl"—she must not sail to-night!

Krap (from within). The "Indian Girl" is already standing out to sea, Mr. Bernick.

Bernick (shutting the door and speaking faintly). Too late—and all to no purpose—

Lona. What do you mean?

Bernick. Nothing, nothing. Leave me alone!

Lona. Hm!—look here, Karsten. Johan was good enough to say that he entrusted to me the good name and reputation that he once lent to you, and also the good name that you stole from him while he was away. Johan will hold his tongue; and I can act just as I please in the matter. See, I have two letters in my hand.

Bernick. You have got them! And you mean now—this very evening—perhaps when the procession comes—

Lona. I did not come back here to betray you, but to stir your conscience so that you should speak of your own free will. I did not succeed in doing that—so you must remain as you are, with your life founded upon a lie. Look, I am tearing your two letters in pieces. Take the wretched things—there you are. Now there is no evidence against you, Karsten. You are safe now; be happy, too —if you can.

Bernick (much moved). Lona—why did you not do that sooner! Now it is too late; life no longer seems good to me; I cannot live on after to-day.

Lona. What has happened?

Bernick. Do not ask me— But I *must* live on, nevertheless! I *will* live—for Olaf's sake. He shall make amends for everything—expiate everything—

Lona. Karsten—! (HILMAR *comes hurriedly back.*)

Hilmar. I cannot find any one; they are all out—even Betty!

Bernick. What is the matter with you?

Hilmar. I daren't tell you.

Bernick. What is it? You *must* tell me!

Hilmar. Very well—Olaf has run away on board the "Indian Girl."

Bernick (*stumbling back*). Olaf—on board the "Indian Girl"! No, no!

Lona. Yes, he is! Now I understand—I saw him jump out of the window.

Bernick (*calls in through the door of his room in a despairing voice*). Krap, stop the "Indian Girl" at any cost!

Krap. It is impossible, sir. How can you suppose—?

Bernick. We *must* stop her; Olaf is on board!

Krap. What!

Rummel (*coming out of* BERNICK'S *room*). Olaf run away? Impossible!

Sandstad (*following him*). He will be sent back with the pilot, Mr. Bernick.

Hilmar. No, no; he has written to me. (*Shows the letter.*) He says he means to hide among the cargo till they are in the open sea.

Bernick. I shall never see him again!

Rummel. What nonsense!—a good strong ship, newly repaired—

Vigeland (*who has followed the others out of* BERNICK'S *room*). And in your own yard, Mr. Bernick!

Bernick. I shall never see him again, I tell you. I have lost him, Lona; and—I see it now—he never was really mine. (*Listens.*) What is that?

Rummel. Music. The procession must be coming.

Bernick. I cannot take any part in it—I will not.

Rummel. What are you thinking of! That is impossible.

Sandstad. Impossible, Mr. Bernick; think what you have at stake.

Bernick. What does it all matter to me now? What have I to work for now?

Rummel. Can you ask? You have us and the community.

Vigeland. Quite true.

Sandstad. Aud surely, Mr. Bernick, you have not for-gotten that we—(MARTHA *comes in through the farther door to the left. Music is heard in the distance, down the street.*)

Martha. The procession is just coming, but Betty is not in the house. I don't understand where she—

Bernick. Not in the house! There, you see, Lona— no support to me, either in gladness or in sorrow.

Rummel. Draw back the curtains! Come and help me, Mr. Krap—and you, Mr. Sandstad. It is a thousand pities that the family should not be united just now; it is quite contrary to the programme. (*They draw back all the curtains. The whole street is seen to be illuminated. Opposite the house is a large transparency, bearing the words:* "Long live Karsten Bernick, Pillar of our Society"!

Bernick (*shrinking back*). Take all that away! I don't want to see it! Put it out, put it out!

Rummel. Excuse me, Mr. Bernick, but are you not well?

Martha. What is the matter with him, Lona?

Lona. Hush! (*Whispers to her.*)

Bernick. Take away those mocking words, I tell you! Can't you see that all these lights are grinning at us?

Rummel. Well, really, I must confess—

Bernick. Oh, how could you understand—! But I, I—! It is all like candles in a dead-room!

Rummel. Well, let me tell you that you are taking the thing a great deal too seriously.

Sandstad. The boy will enjoy a trip across the Atlantic, and then you will have him back.

Vigeland. Only put your trust in the Almighty, Mr. Bernick.

Rummel. And in the vessel, Bernick; it is not likely to sink, I know.

Krap. Hm—

Rummel. Now if it were one of those floating coffins

that one hears are sent out by men in the bigger countries—

Bernick. I am sure my hair must be turning grey! (MRS. BERNICK *comes in from the garden, with a shawl thrown over her head.*)

Mrs. Bernick. Karsten, Karsten, do you know—?

Bernick. Yes, I know; but you—you, who see nothing that is going on—you, who have no mother's eyes for your son—!

Mrs. Bernick. Listen to me, do!

Bernick. Why did you not look after him? Now I have lost him. Give him back to me, if you can.

Mrs. Bernick. I can! I have got him!

Bernick. You have got him!

The Men. Ah!

Hilmar. Yes, I thought so.

Martha. You have got him back, Karsten!

Lona. Yes—make him you own, now.

Bernick. You have got him! Is that true? Where is he?

Mrs. Bernick. I shall not tell you, till you have forgiven him.

Bernick. Forgiven! But how did you know—?

Mrs. Bernick. Do you not think a mother sees? I was in mortal fear of your getting to know anything about it. Some words he let fall yesterday—and then his room was empty, and his knapsack and clothes missing—

Bernick. Yes, yes?

Mrs. Bernick. I ran, and got hold of Aune; we went out in his boat; the American ship was on the point of sailing. Thank God, we were in time—got on board—searched the hold—found him! Oh, Karsten, you must not punish him!

Bernick. Betty!

Mrs. Bernick. Nor Aune, either!

Bernick. Aune? What do you know about him? Is the "Indian Girl" under sail again?

Mrs. Bernick. No, that is just it.

Bernick. Speak, speak!

Mrs. Bernick. Aune was just as agitated as I was; the search took us some time; it had grown dark, and the pilot made objections; and so Aune took upon himself—in your name—

Bernick. Well?

Mrs. Bernick. To stop the ship's sailing till to-morrow.

Krap. Hm—

Bernick. Oh, how glad I am!

Mrs. Bernick. You are not angry?

Bernick. I cannot tell you how glad I am, Betty!

Rummel. You really take things far too seriously.

Hilmar. Oh yes, as soon as it is a question of a little struggle with the elements—ugh!

Krap (going to the window). The procession is just coming through your garden gate, Mr. Bernick.

Bernick. Yes, they can come now.

Rummel. The whole garden is full of people.

Sandstad. The whole street is crammed.

Rummel. The whole town is afoot, Bernick. It really is a moment that makes one proud.

Vigeland. Let us take it in a humble spirit, Mr. Rummel.

Rummel. All the banners are out! What a procession! Here comes the committee, with Mr. Rörlund at their head.

Bernick. Yes, let them come in!

Rummel. But, Bernick—in your present agitated frame of mind—

Bernick. Well, what?

Rummel. I am quite willing to speak instead of you, if you like.

Bernick. No, thank you; I will speak for myself to-night.

Rummel. But are you sure you know what to say?

Bernick. Yes, make your mind easy, Rummel—I know now what to say. (*The music grows louder. The veran-*

dah door is opened. Rörlund *comes in, at the head of the Committee, escorted by a couple of hired waiters, who carry a covered basket. They are followed by townspeople of all classes, as many as can get into the room. An apparently endless crowd of people, waving banners and flags, are visible in the garden and the street.*)

Rörlund. Mr. Bernick! I see, from the surprise depicted upon your face, that it is as unexpected guests that we are intruding upon your happy family circle and your peaceful fireside, where we find you surrounded by honoured and energetic fellow-citizens and friends. But it is our hearts that have bidden us come to offer you our homage— not for the first time, it is true, but for the first time on such a comprehensive scale. We have on many occasions given you our thanks for the broad moral foundation upon which you have, so to speak, reared the edifice of our community. On this occasion we offer our homage especially to the clearsighted, indefatigable, unselfish—nay, self-sacrificing—citizen who has taken the initiative in an undertaking which, we are assured on all sides, will give a powerful impetus to the temporal prosperity and welfare of our community.

Voices. Bravo, bravo!

Rörlund. You, sir, have for many years been a shining example in our midst. This is not the place for me to speak of your family life, which has been a model to us all; still less to enlarge upon your unblemished personal character. Such topics belong to the stillness of a man's own chamber, not to a festal occasion such as this! I am here to speak of your public life as a citizen, as it lies open to all men's eyes. Well-equipped vessels sail away from your shipyard and carry our flag far and wide over the seas. A numerous and happy band of workmen look up to you as to a father By calling new branches of industry into existence, you have laid the foundation of the welfare of hundreds of families. In a word—you are, in the fullest sense of the term, the mainstay of our community.

Voices. Hear, hear! Bravo!

Rörlund. And, sir, it is just that disinterestedness, which colours all your conduct, that is so beneficial to our community—more so than words can express—and especially at the present moment. You are now on the point of procuring for us what I have no hesitation in calling bluntly by its prosaic name—a railway!

Voices. Bravo, bravo!

Rörlund. But it would seem as though the undertaking were beset by certain difficulties, the outcome of narrow and selfish considerations.

Voices. Hear, hear!

Rörlund. For the fact has come to light that certain individuals, who do not belong to our community, have stolen a march upon the hard-working citizens of this place, and have laid hands on certain sources of profit which by rights should have fallen to the share of our town.

Voices. That's right! Hear, hear!

Rörlund. This regrettable fact has naturally come to your knowledge also, Mr. Bernick. But it has not had the slightest effect in deterring you from proceeding steadily with your project, well knowing that a patriotic man should not solely take local interests into consideration.

Voices. Oh!—No, no!—Yes, yes!

Rörlund. It is to such a man—to the patriot citizen, whose character we all should emulate—that we bring our homage this evening. May your undertaking grow to be a real and lasting source of good fortune to this community! It is true enough that a railway may be the means of our exposing ourselves to the incursion of pernicious influences from without; but it gives us also the means of quickly expelling them from within. For even we, at the present time, cannot boast of being entirely free from the danger of such outside influences; but as we have, on this very evening—if rumour is to be believed—fortunately got rid of certain elements of that nature, sooner than was to be expected—

Voices. Order, order!

Rörlund. I regard the occurrence as a happy omen for our undertaking. My alluding to such a thing at such a moment only emphasises the fact that the house in which we are now standing is one where the claims of morality are esteemed even above ties of family.

Voices. Hear, hear! Bravo!

Bernick (at the same moment). Allow me—

Rörlund. I have only a few more words to say, Mr. Bernick. What you have done for your native place we all know has not been done with any underlying idea of its bringing tangible profit to yourself. But, nevertheless, you must not refuse to accept a slight token of grateful appreciation at the hands of your fellow-citizens—least of all at this important moment when, according to the assurances of practical men, we are standing on the threshold of a new era.

Voices. Bravo! Hear, hear!

(RÖRLUND *signs to the servants, who bring forward the basket. During the following speech, members of the Committee take out and present the various objects mentioned.*)

Rörlund. And so, Mr. Bernick, we have the pleasure of presenting you with this silver coffee-service. Let it grace your board when in the future, as so often in the past, we have the happiness of being assembled under your hospitable roof.

You, too, gentlemen, who have so generously seconded the leader of our community, we ask to accept a small souvenir. This silver goblet is for you, Mr. Rummel. Many a time have you, amidst the clink of glasses, defended the interests of your fellow-citizens in well-chosen words; may you often find similar worthy opportunities to raise and empty this goblet in some patriotic toast! To you, Mr. Sandstad, I present this album containing photographs of your fellow-citizens. Your well-known and conspicuous liberality has put you in the pleasant position of being able to number your friends amongst all classes of society. And to you, Mr. Vigeland, I have to offer this book of Family Devotions, printed on vellum and handsomely bound, to grace your study table. The mellowing influence of time has led you to take an earnest view of life; your zeal in carrying out your daily duties has, for a long period of years, been purified and ennobled by thoughts of higher and holier things. (*Turns to the crowd.*) And now, friends, three cheers for Mr. Bernick and his fellow-workers! Three cheers for the Pillars of our Society!

The whole crowd. Bernick! Pillars of Society! Hurrah—hurrah—hurrah!

Lona. I congratulate you, brother-in-law!

(*An expectant hush follows.*)

Bernick (*speaking seriously and slowly*). Fellow citizens —your spokesman said just now that to-night we are standing on the threshold of a new era. I hope that will prove to be the case. But before that can come to pass, we must lay fast hold of *Truth*—truth which, till to-night, has been altogether and in all circumstances a stranger to this community of ours. (*Astonishment among the audience*). To that end, I must begin by deprecating the praises with which you, Mr. Rörlund, according to custom on such occasions, have overwhelmed me. I do not deserve them; because, until to-day, my actions have by no means been disinterested. Even though I may not always have aimed at pecuniary profit, I at all events recognise now that a craving for power, influence and position has been the moving spirit of most of my actions.

Rummel (*half aloud*). What next!

Bernick. Standing before my fellow citizens, I do not reproach myself for that; because I still think I am entitled to a place in the front rank of our capable men of affairs.

Voices. Yes, yes, yes!

Bernick. But what I charge myself with is that I have so often been weak enough to resort to deceitfulness, because I knew and feared the tendency of the community to espy unclean motives behind everything a prominent man here undertakes. And now I am coming to a point which will illustrate that.

Rummel (*uneasily*). Hm—hm!

Bernick. There have been rumours of extensive purchases of property outside the town. These purchases have been made by me—by me alone, and by no one else. (*Murmurs are heard:* "What does he say?—He?—Bernick?") The properties are, for the time being, in my hands. Naturally I have confided in my fellow-workers, Mr. Rummel, Mr. Vigeland and Mr. Sandstad, and we are all agreed that—

Rummel. It is not true! Prove it—prove it!

Vigeland. We are not all agreed about anything!

Sandstad.—Well, really I must say—!

Bernick. That is quite true—we are not yet agreed upon the matter I was going to mention. But I confidently hope that these three gentlemen will agree with me when I announce to you that I have to-night come to the decision that these properties shall be exploited as a company of which the shares shall be offered for public subscription; any one that wishes can take shares.

Voices. Hurrah! Three cheers for Bernick!

Rummel (*in a low voice, to* BERNICK). This is the basest treachery—!

Sandstad (*also in an undertone*). So you have been fooling us—!

Vigeland. Well, then, devil take—! Good lord, what am I saying? (*Cheers are heard without.*)

Bernick. Silence, gentlemen. I have no right to this homage you offer me; because the decision I have just come to does not represent what was my first intention. My intention was to keep the whole thing for myself; and, even now, I am of opinion that these properties would be worked to best advantage if they remained in one man's hands. But you are at liberty to choose. If you wish it, I am willing to administer them to the best of my abilities.

Voices. Yes, yes, yes!

Bernick. But, first of all, my fellow-townsmen must know me thoroughly. And let each man seek to know himself thoroughly, too; and so let it really come to pass that to-night we begin a new era. The old era—with its affectation, its hypocrisy and its emptiness, its pretence of virtue and its miserable fear of public opinion—shall be for us like a museum, open for purposes of instruction; and to that museum we will present—shall we not, gentlemen?—the coffee service, and the goblet, and the album, and the Family Devotions printed on vellum and handsomely bound.

Rummel. Oh, of course.

Vigeland (*muttering*). If you have taken everything else, then—

Sandstad. By all means.

Bernick. And now for the principal reckoning I have to make with the community. Mr. Rörlund said that certain pernicious elements had left us this evening. I can add what you do not yet know. The man referred to did not go away alone; with him, to become his wife, went—

Lona (*loudly*). Dina Dorf!

Rörlund. What?

Mrs. Bernick. What? (*Great commotion.*)

Rörlund. Fled? Run away—with him! Impossible!

Bernick. To become his wife, Mr. Rörlund. And I will add more. (*In a low voice, to his wife.*) Betty, be strong to bear what is coming. (*Aloud.*) This is what I have to say: hats off to that man, for he has nobly taken another's guilt upon his shoulders. My friends, I want to have done with falsehood; it has very nearly poisoned every fibre of my being. You shall know all. Fifteen years ago, *I* was the guilty man.

Mrs. Bernick (*softly and tremblingly*). Karsten!

Martha (similarly). Ah, Johan—!

Lona. Now at last you have found yourself!

(*Speechless consternation among the audience.*)

Bernick. Yes, friends, I was the guilty one, and he went away. The vile and lying rumours that were spread abroad afterwards, it is beyond human power to refute now; but I have no right to complain of that. For fifteen years I have climbed up the ladder of success by the help of those rumours; whether now they are to cast me down again, or not, each of you must decide in his own mind.

Rörlund. What a thunderbolt! Our leading citizen—! (*In a low voice, to* BETTY.) How sorry I am for you, Mrs. Bernick!

Hilmar. What a confession! Well, I must say—!

Bernick. But come to no decision to-night. I entreat every one to go home—to collect his thoughts—to look into his own heart. When once more you can think calmly, then it will be seen whether I have lost or won by speaking out. Good-bye! I have still much—very much—to repent of; but that concerns my own conscience only. Good-night! Take away all these signs of rejoicing. We must all feel that they are out of place here.

Rörlund. That they certainly are. (*In an undertone to* MRS. BERNICK.) Run away! So then she was completely unworthy of me. (*Louder, to the Committee.*) Yes, gentlemen, after this I think we had better disperse as quietly as possible.

Hilmar. How, after this, any one is to manage to hold the Ideal's banner high— Ugh!

(*Meantime the news has been whispered from mouth to mouth. The crowd gradually disperses from the garden.* RUMMEL, SANDSTAD *and* VIGELAND *go out, arguing eagerly but in a low voice.* HILMAR *slinks away to the right. When silence is restored, there only remain in the room* BERNICK, MRS. BERNICK, MARTHA, LONA *and* KRAP.)

Bernick. Betty, can you forgive me?

Mrs. Bernick (*looking at him with a smile*). Do you know, Karsten, that you have opened out for me the happiest prospect I have had for many a year?

Bernick. How?

Mrs. Bernick. For many years I have felt that once you were mine and that I had lost you. Now I know that you never have been mine yet; but I shall win you.

Bernick (*folding her in his arms*). Oh, Betty, you *have* won me. It was through Lona that I first learned really to know you. But now let Olaf come to me.

Mrs. Bernick. Yes, you shall have him now. Mr. Krap—! (*Talks softly to* KRAP *in the background. He goes out by the garden door. During what follows the illuminations and lights in the houses are gradually extinguished.*)

Bernick (*in a low voice*). Thank you, Lona—you have saved what was best in me—and for me.

Lona. Do you suppose I wanted to do anything else?

Bernick. Yes, was that so—or not? I cannot quite make you out.

Lona. Hm—

Bernick. Then it was not hatred? Not revenge? Why did you come back, then?

Lona. Old friendship does not rust.

Bernick. Lona!

Lona. When Johan told me about the lie, I swore to myself that the hero of my youth should stand free and true.

Bernick. What a wretch I am!—and how little I have deserved it of you!

Lona. Oh, if we women always looked for what we deserve, Karsten—! (AUNE *comes in with* OLAF *from the garden.*)

Bernick (*going to meet them*). Olaf!

Olaf. Father, I promise I will never do it again—

Bernick. Never run away?

Olaf. Yes, yes, I promise you, father.

Bernick. And I promise you, you shall never have reason to. For the future you shall be allowed to grow up, not as the heir to *my* life's work, but as one who has his own life's work before him.

Olaf. And shall I be allowed to be what I like, when I grow up?

Bernick. Yes.

Olaf. Oh, thank you! Then I won't be a pillar of society.

Bernick. No? Why not?

Olaf. No—I think it must be so dull.

Bernick. You shall be yourself, Olaf; the rest may take care of itself.—And you, Aune—

Aune. I know, Mr. Bernick; I am dismissed.

Bernick. We remain together, Aune; and forgive me—

Aune. What? The ship has not sailed to-night.

Bernick. Nor will it sail to-morrow, either. I gave you too short grace. It must be looked to more thoroughly.

Aune. It shall, Mr. Bernick—and with the new machines!

Bernick. By all means—but thoroughly and conscientiously. There are many among us who need thorough and conscientious repairs, Aune. Well, good-night.

Aune. Good-night, sir—and thank you, thank you. (*Goes out.*)

Mrs. Bernick. Now they are all gone.

Bernick. And we are alone. My name is not shining in letters of fire any longer; all the lights in the windows are out.

Lona. Would you wish them lit again?

Bernick. Not for anything in the world. Where have I been! You would be horrified if you knew. I feel now as if I had come back to my right senses, after being poisoned. But I feel this—that I *can* be young and healthy again. Oh, come nearer—come closer round me. Come, Betty!

Come, Olaf, my boy! And you, Martha—it seems to me as if I had never seen you all these years.

Lona. No, I can believe that. Your community is a community of bachelor souls; you do not see women.

Bernick. That is quite true; and for that very reason— this is a bargain, Lona—you must not leave Betty and me.

Mrs. Bernick. No, Lona, you must not.

Lona. No, how could I have the heart to go away and leave you young people who are just setting up housekeeping? Am I not your foster-mother? You and I, Martha, the two old aunts— What are you looking at?

Martha. Look how the sky is clearing, and how light it is over the sea. The "Palm Tree" is going to be lucky.

Lona. It carries its good luck on board.

Bernick. And we—we have a long earnest day of work ahead of us; I most of all. But let it come; only keep close round me, you true, loyal women. I have learnt *this* too, in these last few days; it is you women that are the pillars of society.

Lona. You have learnt a poor sort of wisdom, then, brother-in-law. (*Lays her hand firmly upon his shoulder.*) No, my friend; the spirit of truth and the spirit of freedom—they are the pillars of society.

HEDDA GABLER
(1890)

PLAY IN THREE ACTS

four

DRAMATIS PERSONÆ

GEORGE TESMAN.*

HEDDA TESMAN, *his wife*.

MISS JULIANA TESMAN, *his aunt*.

MRS. ELVSTED.

JUDGE† BRACK.

EILERT LÖVBORG.

BERTA, *searvant at the Tesmans*.

*The scene of the action is Tesman's villa, in the west
end of Christiania.*

---

* Tesman, whose Christian name in the original is "Jörgen,"
is described as "stipendiat i kulturhistorie"—that is to say, the
holder of a scholarship for purposes of research into the History
of Civilisation.
† In the original "Assessor."

ACT I

A spacious, handsome, and tastefully furnished drawing-room, decorated in dark colours. In the back, a wide doorway with curtains drawn back, leading into a smaller room decorated in the same style as the drawing-room. In the right-hand wall of the front room, a folding door leading out to the hall. In the opposite wall, on the left, a glass door, also with curtains drawn back. Through the panes can be seen part of a verandah outside, and trees covered with autumn foliage. An oval table, with a cover on it, and surrounded by chairs, stands well forward. In front, by the wall on the right, a wide stove of dark porcelain, a high-backed arm-chair, a cushioned foot-rest, and two foot-stools. A settee, with a small round table in front of it, fills the upper right-hand corner. In front, on the left, a little way from the wall, a sofa. Further back than the glass door, a piano. On either side of the doorway at the back a whatnot with terra-cotta and majolica ornaments.— Against the back wall of the inner room a sofa, with a table, and one or two chairs. Over the sofa hangs the portrait of a handsome elderly man in a General's uniform. Over the table a hanging lamp, with an opal glass shade.—A number of bouquets are arranged about the drawing-room, in vases and glasses. Others lie upon the tables. The floors in both rooms are covered with thick carpets.—Morning light. The sun shines in through the glass door.

MISS JULIANA TESMAN, *with her bonnet on and carrying a parasol, comes in from the hall, followed by* BERTA, *who carries a bouquet wrapped in paper.* MISS TESMAN *is a comely and pleasant-looking lady of about sixty-five. She is nicely but simply dressed in a grey walking-costume.* BERTA *is a middle-aged woman of plain and rather countrified appearance.*

Miss Tesman (stops close to the door, listens, and says softly). Upon my word, I don't believe they are stirring yet!

Berta (also softly). I told you so, Miss. Remember how late the steamboat got in last night. And then, when they got home!—good Lord, what a lot the young mistress had to unpack before she could get to bed.

Miss Tesman. Well, well—let them have their sleep out. But let us see that they get a good breath of the fresh morning air when they do appear. *(She goes to the glass door and throws it open.)*

Berta (beside the table, at a loss what to do with the bouquet in her hand). I declare there isn't a bit of room left. I think I'll put it down here, Miss. *(She places it on the piano.)*

Miss Tesman. So you've got a new mistress now, my dear Berta. Heaven knows it was a wrench to me to part with you.

Berta (on the point of weeping). And do you think it wasn't hard for me too, Miss? After all the blessed years I've been with you and Miss Rina.*

Miss Tesman. We must make the best of it, Berta. There was nothing else to be done. George can't do without you, you see—he absolutely can't. He has had you to look after him ever since he was a little boy.

Berta. Ah but, Miss Julia, I can't help thinking of Miss Rina lying helpless at home there, poor thing. And with only that new girl too! She'll never learn to take proper care of an invalid.

Miss Tesman. Oh, I shall manage to train her. And of

---

* Pronounce *Reena.*

course, you know, I shall take most of it upon myself. You needn't be uneasy about my poor sister, my dear Berta.

Berta. Well, but there's another thing, Miss. I'm so mortally afraid I shan't be able to suit the young mistress.

Miss Tesman. Oh well—just at first there may be one or two things—

Berta. Most like she'll be terrible grand in her ways.

Miss Tesman. Well, you can't wonder at that—General Gabler's daughter! Think of the sort of life she was accustomed to in her father's time. Don't you remember how we used to see her riding down the road along with the General? In that long black habit—and with feathers in her hat?

Berta. Yes, indeed—I remember well enough—! But good Lord, I should never have dreamt in those days that she and Master George would make a match of it.

Miss Tesman. Nor I.—But, by-the-bye, Berta—while I think of it: in future you mustn't say Master George. You must say Dr. Tesman.

Berta. Yes, the young mistress spoke of that too—last night—the moment they set foot in the house. Is it true then, Miss?

Miss Tesman. Yes, indeed it is. Only think, Berta—some foreign university has made him a doctor—while he has been abroad, you understand. I hadn't heard a word about it, until he told me himself upon the pier.

Berta. Well, well, he's clever enough for anything, he is. But I didn't think he'd have gone in for doctoring people too.

Miss Tesman. No, no, it's not that sort of doctor he is. (*Nods significantly.*) But let me tell you, we may have to call him something still grander before long.

Berta. You don't say so! What can that be, Miss?

Miss Tesman (*smiling*). H'm—wouldn't you like to know! (*With emotion.*) Ah, dear, dear—if my poor brother could only look up from his grave now, and see what his little boy has grown into! (*Looks around.*) But bless me, Berta—why have you done this? Taken the chintz covers off all the furniture?

Berta. The mistress told me to. She can't abide covers on the chairs, she says.

Miss Tesman. Are they going to make this their everyday sitting-room then?

Berta. Yes, that's what I understood—from the mistress. Master George—the doctor—he said nothing.

GEORGE TESMAN *comes from the right into the inner room, humming to himself, and carrying an unstrapped empty portmanteau. He is a middle-sized, young-looking man of thirty-three, rather stout, with a round, open, cheerful face, fair hair and beard. He wears spectacles, and is somewhat carelessly dressed in comfortable indoor clothes.*

Miss Tesman. Good morning, good morning, George.

Tesman (*in the doorway between the rooms*). Aunt Julia! Dear Aunt Julia! (*Goes up to her and shakes hands warmly.*) Come all this way—so early! Eh?

Miss Tesman. Why, of course I had to come and see how you were getting on.

Tesman. In spite of your having had no proper night's rest?

Miss Tesman. Oh, that makes no difference to me.

Tesman. Well, I suppose you got home all right from the pier? Eh?

Miss Tesman. Yes, quite safely, thank goodness. Judge Brack was good enough to see me right to my door.

Tesman. We were so sorry we couldn't give you a seat in the carriage. But you saw what a pile of boxes Hedda had to bring with her.

Miss Tesman. Yes, she had certainly plenty of boxes.

Berta (*to Tesman*). Shall I go in and see if there's anything I can do for the mistress?

Tesman. No, thank you, Berta—you needn't. She said she would ring if she wanted anything.

Berta (*going towards the right*). Very well.

Tesman. But look here—take this portmanteau with you.

Berta (*taking it*). I'll put it in the attic. (*She goes out by the hall door.*)

Tesman. Fancy, Auntie—I had the whole of that portmanteau chock full of copies of documents. You wouldn't believe how much I have picked up from all the archives I have been examining—curious old details that no one has had any idea of——

Miss Tesman. Yes, you don't seem to have wasted your time on your wedding trip, George.

Tesman. No, that I haven't. But do take off your bonnet, Auntie. Look here! Let me untie the strings—eh?

Miss Tesman (*while he does so*). Well, well—this is just as if you were still at home with us.

Tesman (*with the bonnet in his hand, looks at it from all sides*). Why, what a gorgeous bonnet you've been investing in!

Miss Tesman. I bought it on Hedda's account.

Tesman. On Hedda's account? Eh?

Miss Tesman. Yes, so that Hedda needn't be ashamed of me if we happened to go out together.

Tesman (*patting her cheek*). You always think of everything, Aunt Julia. (*Lays the bonnet on a chair beside the table.*) And now, look here—suppose we sit comfortably on the sofa and have a little chat, till Hedda comes. (*They seat themselves. She places her parasol in the corner of the sofa.*)

Miss Tesman (*takes both his hands and looks at him*). What a delight it is to have you again, as large as life, before my very eyes, George! My George—my poor brother's own boy!

Tesman. And it's a delight for me, too, to see you again, Aunt Julia! You, who have been father and mother in one to me.

Miss Tesman. Oh, yes, I know you will always keep a place in your heart for your old aunts.

Tesman. And what about Aunt Rina? No improvement—eh?

Miss Tesman. Oh, no—we can scarcely look for any improvement in her case, poor thing. There she lies, helpless, as she has lain for all these years. But heaven grant I may not lose her yet awhile! For if I did, I don't know what I should make of my life, George—especially now that I haven't you to look after any more.

Tesman (*patting her back*). There, there, there——!

Miss Tesman (*suddenly changing her tone*). And to think that here are you a married man, George!—And that you should be the one to carry off Hedda Gabler—the beautiful Hedda Gabler! Only think of it—she, that was so beset with admirers!

Tesman (*hums a little and smiles complacently*). Yes, I fancy I have several good friends about town who would like to stand in my shoes—eh?

Miss Tesman. And then this fine long wedding-tour you have had! More than five—nearly six months—

Tesman. Well, for me it has been a sort of tour of research as well. I have had to do so much grubbing among old records—and to read no end of books too, Auntie.

Miss Tesman. Oh, yes, I suppose so. (*More confidentially, and lowering her voice a little.*) But listen now, George—have you nothing—nothing special to tell me?

Tesman. As to our journey?

Miss Tesman. Yes.

Tesman. No, I don't know of anything except what I have told you in my letters. I had a doctor's degree conferred on me—but that I told you yesterday.

Miss Tesman. Yes, yes, you did. But what I mean is—haven't you any—any—expectations——?

Tesman. Expectations?

Miss Tesman. Why, you know, George—I'm your old auntie!

Tesman. Why, of course I have expectations.

Miss Tesman. Ah!

Tesman. I have every expectation of being a professor one of these days.

Miss Tesman. Oh, yes, a professor——

Tesman. Indeed, I may say I am certain of it. But my dear Auntie—you know all about that already!

Miss Tesman (*laughing to herself*). Yes, of course I do. You are quite right there. (*Changing the subject.*) But we were talking about your journey. It must have cost a great deal of money, George?

Tesman. Well, you see—my handsome travelling-scholarship went a good way.

Miss Tesman. But I can't understand how you can have made it go far enough for two.

Tesman. No, that's not so easy to understand—eh?

Miss Tesman. And especially travelling with a lady—they tell me that makes it ever so much more expensive.

Tesman. Yes, of course—it makes it a little more expensive. But Hedda had to have this trip, Auntie! She really had to. Nothing else would have done.

Miss Tesman. No, no, I suppose not. A wedding-tour seems to be quite indispensable nowadays.—But tell me now—have you gone thoroughly over the house yet?

Tesman. Yes, you may be sure I have. I have been afoot ever since daylight.

Miss Tesman. And what do you think of it all?

Tesman. I'm delighted! Quite delighted! Only I can't think what we are to do with the two empty rooms between this inner parlour and Hedda's bedroom.

Miss Tesman (*laughing*). Oh, my dear George, I daresay you may find some use for them—in the course of time.

Tesman. Why of course you are quite right, Aunt Julia! You mean as my library increases—eh?

Miss Tesman. Yes, quite so, my dear boy. It was your library I was thinking of.

Tesman. I am specially pleased on Hedda's account. Often and often, before we were engaged, she said that she would never care to live anywhere but in Secretary Falk's villa.*

Miss Tesman. Yes, it was lucky that this very house should come into the market, just after you had started.

Tesman. Yes, Aunt Julia, the luck was on our side, wasn't it—eh?

Miss Tesman. But the expense, my dear George! You will find it very expensive, all this.

Tesman (looks at her, a little cast down). Yes, I suppose I shall, Aunt!

Miss Tesman. Oh, frightfully!

Tesman. How much do you think? In round numbers?—Eh?

Miss Tesman. Oh, I can't even guess until all the accounts come in.

Tesman. Well, fortunately, Judge Brack has secured the most favourable terms for me,—so he said in a letter to Hedda.

Miss Tesman. Yes, don't be uneasy, my dear boy.— Besides, I have given security for the furniture and all the carpets.

Tesman. Security? You? My dear Aunt Julia—what sort of security could you give?

Miss Tesman. I have given a mortgage on our annuity.

Tesman (jumps up). What! On your — and Aunt Rina's annuity!

Miss Tesman. Yes, I knew of no other plan, you see.

Tesman (placing himself before her). Have you gone out of your senses, Auntie! Your annuity—it's all that you and Aunt Rina have to live upon.

---

* In the original, "Statsradinde Falks villa"—showing that it had belonged to the widow of a cabinet minister.

Miss Tesman. Well, well, don't get so excited about it. It's only a matter of form you know—Judge Brack assured me of that. It was he that was kind enough to arrange the whole affair for me. A mere matter of form, he said.

Tesman. Yes, that may be all very well. But nevertheless——

Miss Tesman. You will have your own salary to depend upon now. And, good heavens, even if we did have to pay up a little——! To eke things out a bit at the start——! Why, it would be nothing but a pleasure to us.

Tesman. Oh, Auntie—will you never be tired of making sacrifices for me!

Miss Tesman (*rises and lays her hands on his shoulders*). Have I any other happiness in this world except to smooth your way for you, my dear boy? You, who have had neither father nor mother to depend on. And now we have reached the goal, George! Things have looked black enough for us, sometimes; but, thank heaven, now you have nothing to fear.

Tesman. Yes, it is really marvellous how everything has turned out for the best.

Miss Tesman. And the people who opposed you—who wanted to bar the way for you—now you have them at your feet. They have fallen, George. Your most dangerous rival—his fall was the worst.—And now he has to lie on the bed he has made for himself—poor misguided creature.

Tesman. Have you heard anything of Eilert? Since I went away, I mean.

Miss Tesman. Only that he is said to have published a new book.

Tesman. What! Eilert Lövborg! Recently—eh?

Miss Tesman. Yes, so they say. Heaven knows whether it can be worth anything! Ah, when your new book appears—that will be another story, George! What is it to be about?

Tesman. It will deal with the domestic industries of Brabant during the Middle Ages.

Miss Tesman. Fancy—to be able to write on such a subject as that!

Tesman. However, it may be some time before the book is ready. I have all these collections to arrange first, you see.

Miss Tesman. Yes, collecting and arranging—no one can beat you at that. There you are my poor brother's own son.

Tesman. I am looking forward eagerly to setting to work at it; especially now that I have my own delightful home to work in.

Miss Tesman. And, most of all, now that you have got the wife of your heart, my dear George.

Tesman (*embracing her*). Oh, yes, yes, Aunt Julia. Hedda—she is the best part of it all! (*Looks towards the doorway.*) I believe I hear her coming—eh?

HEDDA *enters from the left through the inner room. She is a woman of nine-and-twenty. Her face and figure show refinement and distinction. Her complexion is pale and opaque. Her steel-grey eyes express a cold, unruffled repose. Her hair is of an agreeable medium brown, but not particularly abundant. She is dressed in a tasteful, somewhat loose-fitting morning gown.*

Miss Tesman (*going to meet* HEDDA). Good morning, my dear Hedda! Good morning, and a hearty welcome.

Hedda (*holds out her hand*). Good morning, dear Miss Tesman! So early a call! That is kind of you.

Miss Tesman (*with some embarrassment*). Well—has the bride slept well in her new home?

Hedda. Oh yes, thanks. Passably.

Tesman (*laughing*). Passably! Come, that's good, Hedda! You were sleeping like a stone when I got up.

Hedda. Fortunately. Of course one has always to ac-custom one's self to new surroundings, Miss Tesman—little by little. (*Looking towards the left.*) Oh—there the ser-vant has gone and opened the verandah door, and let in a whole flood of sunshine.

Miss Tesman (going towards the door). Well, then, we will shut it.

Hedda. No, no, not that! Tesman, please draw the cur-tains. That will give a softer light.

Tesman (at the door). All right—all right. There now, Hedda, now you have both shade and fresh air.

Hedda. Yes, fresh air we certainly must have, with all these stacks of flowers—— But—won't you sit down, Miss Tesman?

Miss Tesman. No, thank you. Now that I have seen that everything is all right here—thank heaven!—I must be getting home again. My sister is lying longing for me, poor thing.

Tesman. Give her my very best love, Auntie; and say I shall look in and see her later in the day.

Miss Tesman. Yes, yes, I'll be sure to tell her. But by-the-bye, George—(*feeling in her dress pocket*)—I had al-most forgotten—I have something for you here.

Tesman. What is it, Auntie? Eh?

Miss Tesman (produces a flat parcel wrapped in news-paper and hands it to him). Look here, my dear boy.

Tesman (opening the parcel). Well, I declare!—Have you really saved them for me, Aunt Julia! Hedda! isn't this touching—es?

Hedda (beside the whatnot on the right). Well, what is it?

Tesman. My old morning-shoes! My slippers.

Hedda. Indeed. I remember you often spoke of them while we were abroad.

Tesman. Yes, I missed them terribly. (*Goes up to her.*) Now you shall see them, Hedda!

Hedda (*going towards the stove*). Thanks, I really don't care about it.

Tesman (*following her*). Only think—ill as she was, Aunt Rina embroidered these for me. Oh you can't think how many associations cling to them.

Hedda (*at the table*). Scarcely for me.

Miss Tesman. Of course not for Hedda, George.

Tesman. Well, but now that she belongs to the family, I thought——

Hedda (*interrupting*). We shall never get on with this servant, Tesman.

Miss Tesman. Not get on with Berta?

Tesman. Why, dear, what puts that in your head? Eh?

Hedda (*pointing*). Look there! She has left her old bonnet lying about on a chair.

Tesman (*in consternation, drops the slippers on the floor.*) Why, Hedda—

Hedda. Just fancy, if any one should come in and see it!

Tesman. But Hedda—that's Aunt Julia's bonnet.

Hedda. Is it!

Miss Tesman (*taking up the bonnet.*) Yes, indeed it's mine. And, what's more, it's not old, Madam Hedda.

Hedda. I really did not look closely at it, Miss Tesman.

Miss Tesman (*trying on the bonnet*). Let me tell you it's the first time I have worn it—the very first time.

Tesman. And a very nice bonnet it is too—quite a beauty!

Miss Tesman. Oh, it's no such great things, George. (*Looks around her.*) My parasol——? Ah, here. (*Takes it.*) For this is mine too—(*mutters*)—not Berta's.

Tesman. A new bonnet and a new parasol! Only think, Hedda!

Hedda. Very handsome indeed.

Tesman. Yes, isn't it? Eh? But Auntie, take a good look at Hedda before you go! See how handsome she is!

Miss Tesman. Oh, my dear boy, there's nothing new in

that. Hedda was always lovely. (*She nods and goes towards the right.*)

Tesman (*following*). Yes, but have you noticed what splendid condition she is in? How she has filled out on the journey?

Hedda (*crossing the room*). Oh, do be quiet—!

Miss Tesman (*who has stopped and turned*). Filled out?

Tesman. Of course you don't notice it so much now that she has that dress on. But I, who can see—

Hedda (*at the glass door, impatiently.*) Oh, you can't see anything.

Tesman. It must be the mountain air in the Tyrol—

Hedda (*curtly, interrupting.*) I am exactly as I was when I started.

Tesman. So you insist; but I'm quite certain you are not. Don't you agree with me, Auntie?

Miss Tesman (*who has been gazing at her with folded hands.*) Hedda is lovely—lovely—lovely. (*Goes up to her, takes her head between both hands, draws it downwards, and kisses her hair.*) God bless and preserve Hedda Tesman—for George's sake.

Hedda (*gently freeing herself*). Oh—! Let me go.

Miss Tesman (*in quiet emotion*). I shall not let a day pass without coming to see you.

Tesman. No you won't, will you, Auntie? Eh?

Miss Tesman. Good-bye—good-bye!

(*She goes out by the hall door.* TESMAN *accompanies her. The door remains half open.* TESMAN *can be heard repeating his message to Aunt Rina and his thanks for the slippers.*

(*In the meantime,* HEDDA *walks about the room, raising her arms and clenching her hands as if in desperation. Then she flings back the curtains from the glass door, and stands there looking out.*

(*Presently* TESMAN *returns and closes the door behind him.*

Tesman (*picks up the slippers from the floor*). What are you looking at, Hedda?

Hedda (*once more calm and mistress of herself*). I am only looking at the leaves. They are so yellow—so withered.

Tesman (*wraps up the slippers and lays them on the table.*) Well you see, we are well into September now.

Hedda (*again restless*). Yes, to think of it!—Already in—in September.

Tesman. Don't you think Aunt Julia's manner was strange, dear? Almost solemn? Can you imagine what was the matter with her? Eh?

Hedda. I scarcely know her, you see. Is she not often like that?

Tesman. No, not as she was today.

Hedda (*leaving the glass door*). Do you think she was annoyed about the bonnet?

Tesman. Oh, scarcely at all. Perhaps a little, just at the moment—

Hedda. But what an idea, to pitch her bonnet about in the drawing-room! No one does that sort of thing.

Tesman. Well you may be sure Aunt Julia won't do it again.

Hedda. In any case, I shall manage to make my peace with her.

Tesman. Yes, my dear, good Hedda, if you only would.

Hedda. When you call this afternoon, you might invite her to spend the evening here.

Tesman. Yes, that I will. And there's one thing more you could do that would delight her heart.

Hedda. What is it?

Tesman. If you could only prevail on yourself to say *du** to her. For my sake, Hedda? Eh?

---

* *Du* = thou; Tesman means, "If you could persuade yourself to *tutoyer* her.'

Hedda. No no, Tesman—you really mustn't ask that of me. I have told you so already. I shall try to call her "Aunt"; and you must be satisfied with that.

Tesman. Well, well. Only I think now that you belong to the family, you—

Hedda. H'm—I can't in the least see why—

(*She goes up towards the middle doorway.*

Tesman (*after a pause*). Is there anything the matter with you, Hedda? Eh?

Hedda. I'm only looking at my old piano. It doesn't go at all well with all the other things.

Tesman. The first time I draw my salary, we'll see about exchanging it.

Hedda. No, no—no exchanging. I don't want to part with it. Suppose we put it there in the inner room, and then get another here in its place. When it's convenient, I mean.

Tesman (*a little taken aback*). Yes—of course we could do that.

Hedda (*takes up the bouquet from the piano*). These flowers were not here last night when we arrived.

Tesman. Aunt Julia must have brought them for you.

Hedda (*examining the bouquet*). A visiting-card. (*Takes it out and reads:*) "Shall return later in the day." Can you guess whose card it is?

Tesman. No. Whose? Eh?

Hedda. The name is "Mrs. Elvsted."

Tesman. Is it really? Sheriff Elvsted's wife? Miss Rysing that was.

Hedda. Exactly. The girl with the irritating hair, that she was always showing off. An old flame of yours I've been told.

Tesman (*laughing*). Oh, that didn't last long; and it was before I knew you, Hedda. But fancy her being in town!

Hedda. It's odd that she should call upon us. I have scarcely seen her since we left school.

Tesman. I haven't seen her either for—heaven knows how long. I wonder how she can endure to live in such an out-of-the-way hole—eh?

Hedda (after a moment's thought says suddenly). Tell me, Tesman—isn't it somewhere near there that he—that—Eilert Lövborg is living?

Tesman. Yes, he is somewhere in that part of the country.

BERTA *enters by the hall door.*

Berta. That lady, ma'am, that brought some flowers a little while ago, is here again. (*Pointing.*) The flowers you have in your hand, ma'am.

Hedda. Ah, is she? Well, please show her in.

BERTA *opens the door for* MRS. ELVSTED, *and goes out herself.*—MRS. ELVSTED *is a woman of fragile figure, with pretty, soft features. Her eyes are light blue, large, round, and somewhat prominent, with a startled, inquiring expression. Her hair is remarkably light, almost flaxen, and unusually abundant and wavy. She is a couple of years younger than* HEDDA. *She wears a dark visiting dress, tasteful, but not quite in the latest fashion.*

Hedda (receives her warmly). How do you do, my dear Mrs. Elvsted? It's delightful to see you again.

Mrs. Elvsted (nervously, struggling for self-control). Yes, it's a very long time since we met.

Tesman (gives her his hand). And we too—eh?

Hedda. Thanks for your lovely flowers—

Mrs. Elvsted. Oh, not at all— I would have come straight here yesterday afternoon; but I heard that you were away—

Tesman. Have you just come to town? Eh?

Mrs. Elvsted. I arrived yesterday, about midday. Oh, I was quite in despair when I heard that you were not at home.

Hedda. In despair! How so?

Tesman. Why, my dear Mrs. Rysing—I mean Mrs. Elvsted—

Hedda. I hope that you are not in any trouble?

Mrs. Elvsted. Yes, I am. And I don't know another living creature here that I can turn to.

Hedda (*laying the bouquet on the table*). Come—let us sit here on the sofa—

Mrs. Elvsted. Oh, I am too restless to sit down.

Hedda. Oh no, you're not. Come here. (*She draws* Mrs. Elvsted *down upon the sofa and sits at her side.*)

Tesman. Well? What is it, Mrs. Elvsted?

Hedda. Has anything particular happened to you at home?

Mrs. Elvsted. Yes—and no. Oh—I am so anxious you should not misunderstand me—

Hedda. Then your best plan is to tell us the whole story, Mrs. Elvsted.

Tesman. I suppose that's what you have come for—eh?

Mrs. Elvsted. Yes, yes—of course it is. Well then, I must tell you—if you don't already know—that Eilert Lövborg is in town, too.

Hedda. Lövborg—!

Tesman. What! Has Eilert Lövborg come back? Fancy that, Hedda!

Hedda. Well, well—I hear it.

Mrs. Elvsted. He has been here a week already. Just fancy—a whole week! In this terrible town, alone! With so many temptations on all sides.

Hedda. But my dear Mrs. Elvsted—how does he concern you so much?

Mrs. Elvsted. (*Looks at her with a startled air, and says rapidly.*) He was the children's tutor.

Hedda. Your children's?

Mrs. Elvsted. My husband's. I have none.

Hedda. Your step-children's, then?

Mrs. Elvsted. Yes.

Tesman (*somewhat hesitatingly*). Then was he—I don't know how to express it—was he—regular enough in his habits to be fit for the post? Eh?

Mrs. Elvsted. For the last two years his conduct has been irreproachable.

Tesman. Has it indeed? Fancy that, Hedda!

Hedda. I hear it.

Mrs. Elvsted. Perfectly irreproachable, I assure you! In every respect. But all the same—now that I know he is here—in this great town—and with a large sum of money in his hands—I can't help being in mortal fear for him.

Tesman. Why did he not remain where he was? With you and your husband? Eh?

Mrs. Elvsted. After his book was published he was too restless and unsettled to remain with us.

Tesman. Yes, by-the-bye, Aunt Julia told me he had published a new book.

Mrs. Elvsted. Yes, a big book, dealing with the march of civilisation—in broad outline, as it were. It came out about a fortnight ago. And since it has sold so well, and been so much read—and made such a sensation——

Tesman. Has it indeed? It must be something he has had lying by since his better days.

Mrs. Elvsted. Long ago, you mean?

Tesman. Yes.

Mrs. Elvsted. No, he has written it all since he has been with us—within the last year.

Tesman. Isn't that good news, Hedda? Think of that.

Mrs. Elvsted. Ah, yes, if only it would last!

Hedda. Have you seen him here in town?

Mrs. Elvsted. No, not yet. I have had the greatest difficulty in finding out his address. But this morning I discovered it at last.

Hedda (*looks searchingly at her*). Do you know, it seems to me a little odd of your husband—h'm——

Mrs. Elvsted (*starting nervously*). Of my husband! What?

Hedda. That he should send you to town on such an errand—that he does not come himself and look after his friend.

Mrs. Elvsted. Oh no, no—my husband has no time. And besides, I—I had some shopping to do.

Hedda (*with a slight smile*). Ah, that is a different matter.

Mrs. Elvsted (*rising quickly and uneasily*). And now I beg and implore you, Mr. Tesman—receive Eilert Lövborg kindly if he comes to you! And that he is sure to do. You see you were such great friends in the old days. And then you are interested in the same studies—the same branch of science—so far as I can understand.

Tesman. We used to be, at any rate.

Mrs. Elvsted. That is why I beg so earnestly that you— you too—will keep a sharp eye upon him. Oh, you will promise me that, Mr. Tesman—won't you?

Tesman. With the greatest of pleasure, Mrs. Rysing——

Hedda. Elvsted.

Tesman. I assure you I shall do all I possibly can for Eilert. You may rely upon me.

Mrs. Elvsted. Oh, how very, very kind of you! (*Presses his hands.*) Thanks, thanks, thanks! (*Frightened.*) You see, my husband is so very fond of him!

Hedda (*rising*). You ought to write to him, Tesman. Perhaps he may not care to come to you of his own accord.

Tesman. Well, perhaps it would be the right thing to do, Hedda? Eh?

Hedda. And the sooner the better. Why not at once?

Mrs. Elvsted (*imploringly*). Oh, if you only would!

Tesman. I'll write this moment. Have you his address, Mrs.—Mrs. Elvsted.

Mrs. Elvsted. Yes. (*Takes a slip of paper from her pocket, and hands it to him.*) Here it is.

Tesman. Good, good. Then I'll go in—— (*Looks about him.*) By-the-bye,—my slippers? Oh, here. (*Takes the packet, and is about to go.*)

Hedda. Be sure you write him a cordial, friendly letter. And a good long one too.

Tesman. Yes, I will.

Mrs. Elvsted. But please, please don't say a word to show that I have suggested it.

Tesman. No, how could you think I would? Eh? (*He goes out to the right, through the inner room.*)

Hedda (*goes up to* Mrs. Elvsted, *smiles, and says in a low voice.*) There! We have killed two birds with one stone.

Mrs. Elvsted. What do you mean?

Hedda. Could you not see that I wanted him to go?

Mrs. Elvsted. Yes, to write the letter——

Hedda. And that I might speak to you alone.

Mrs. Elvsted (*confused*). About the same thing?

Hedda. Precisely.

Mrs. Elvsted (*apprehensively*). But there is nothing more, Mrs. Tesman! Absolutely nothing!

Hedda. Oh, yes, but there is. There is a great deal more—I can see that. Sit here—and we'll have a cosy, confidential chat. (*She forces* Mrs. Elvsted *to sit in the easy-chair beside the stove, and seats herself on one of the footstools.*)

Mrs. Elvsted (*anxiously, looking at her watch*). But, my dear Mrs. Tesman—I was really on the point of going.

Hedda. Oh, you can't be in such a hurry.—Well? Now tell me something about your life at home.

Mrs. Elvsted. Oh, that is just what I care least to speak about.

Hedda. But to me, dear——? Why, weren't we school-fellows?

Mrs. Elvsted. Yes, but you were in the class above me. Oh, how dreadfully afraid of you I was then!

Hedda. Afraid of me?

Mrs. Elvsted. Yes, dreadfully. For when we met on the stairs you used always to pull my hair.

Hedda. Did I, really?

Mrs. Elvsted. Yes, and once you said you would burn it off my head.

Hedda. Oh, that was all nonsense, of course.

Mrs. Elvsted. Yes, but I was so silly in those days.— And since then, too—we have drifted so far—far apart from each other. Our circles have been so entirely different.

Hedda. Well then, we must try to drift together again. Now listen! At school we said *du* to each other; and we called each other by our Christian names——

Mrs. Elvsted. No, I am sure you must be mistaken.

Hedda. No, not at all! I can remember quite distinctly. So now we are going to renew our old friendship. (*Draws the footstool closer to* Mrs. Elvsted.) There now! (*Kisses her cheek.*) You must say *du* to me and call me Hedda.

Mrs. Elvsted (*presses and pats her hands*). Oh, how good and kind you are! I am not used to such kindness.

Hedda. There, there, there! And I shall say *du* to you, as in the old days, and call you my dear Thora.

Mrs. Elvstead. My name is Thea.*

Hedda. Why, of course! I meant Thea. (*Looks at her compassionately.*) So you are not accustomed to goodness and kindness, Thea? Not in your own home?

Mrs. Elvsted. Oh, if I only had a home! But I haven't any; I have never had a home.

Hedda (*looks at her for a moment*). I almost suspected as much.

Mrs. Elvsted (*gazing helplessly before her*). Yes—yes—yes.

---

* Pronounce *Tora* and *Taya.*

Hedda. I don't quite remember—was it not as house-keeper that you first went to Mr. Elvsted's?

Mrs. Elvsted. I really went as governess. But his wife —his late wife—was an invalid,—and rarely left her room. So I had to look after the housekeeping as well.

Hedda. And then—at last—you became mistress of the house.

Mrs. Elvsted (*sadly*). Yes, I did.

Hedda. Let me see—about how long ago was that?

Mrs. Elvsted. My marriage?

Hedda. Yes.

Mrs. Elvsted. Five years ago.

Hedda. To be sure; it must be that.

Mrs. Elvsted. Oh, those five years——! Or at all events the last two or three of them! Oh, if you* could only imagine——

Hedda (*giving her a little slap on the hand*). De? Fie, Thea!

Mrs. Elvsted. Yes, yes, I will try—— Well, if—you could only imagine and understand——

Hedda (*lightly*). Eilert Lövborg has been in your neighbourhood about three years, hasn't he?

Mrs. Elvsted (*looks at her doubtfully*). Eilert Lövborg? Yes—he has.

Hedda. Had you known him before, in town here?

Mrs. Elvsted. Scarcely at all. I mean—I knew him by name of course.

Hedda. But you saw a good deal of him in the country?

Mrs. Elvsted. Yes, he came to us every day. You see, he gave the children lessons; for in the long run I couldn't manage it all myself.

Hedda. No, that's clear.—And your husband——? I suppose he is often away from home?

---

* Mrs. Elvsted here uses the formal pronoun *De,* whereupon Hedda rebukes her. In her next speech Mrs. Elvsted says *du.*

Mrs. Elvsted. Yes. Being sheriff, you know, he has to travel about a good deal in his district.

Hedda (leaning against the arm of the chair). Thea—my poor, sweet Thea—now you must tell me everything —exactly as it stands.

Mrs. Elvsted. Well then, you must question me.

Hedda. What sort of man is your husband, Thea? I mean—you know—in everyday life. Is he kind to you?

Mrs. Elvsted (evasively). I am sure he means well in everything.

Hedda. I should think he must be altogether too old for you. There is at least twenty years' difference between you, is there not?

Mrs. Elvsted (irritably). Yes, that is true, too. Everything about him is repellent to me! We have not a thought in common. We have no single point of sympathy—he and I.

Hedda. But is he not fond of you all the same? In his own way?

Mrs. Elvsted. Oh, I really don't know. I think he regards me simply as a useful property. And then it doesn't cost much to keep me. I am not expensive.

Hedda. That is stupid of you.

Mrs. Elvsted (shakes her head). It cannot be otherwise—not with him. I don't think he really cares for any one but himself—and perhaps a little for the children.

Hedda. And for Eilert Lövborg, Thea.

Mrs. Elvsted (looking at her). For Eilert Lövborg? What puts that into your head?

Hedda. Well, my dear—I should say, when he sends you after him all the way to town—— *(Smiling almost imperceptibly.)* And besides, you said so yourself, to Tesman.

Mrs. Elvsted (with a little nervous twitch). Did I? Yes, I suppose I did. *(Vehemently, but not loudly.)* No—I may just as well make a clean breast of it at once! For it must all come out in any case.

Hedda. Why, my dear Thea——?

Mrs. Elvsted. Well, to make a long story short: My husband did not know that I was coming.

Hedda. What! Your husband didn't know it!

Mrs. Elvsted. No, of course not. For that matter, he was away from home himself—he was travelling. Oh, I could bear it no longer, Hedda! I couldn't indeed—so utterly alone as I should have been in future.

Hedda. Well? And then?

Mrs. Elvsted. So I put together some of my things— what I needed most—as quietly as possible. And then I left the house.

Hedda. Without a word?

Mrs. Elvsted. Yes—and took the train straight to town.

Hedda. Why, my dear, good Thea—to think of you daring to do it!

Mrs. Elvsted (rises and moves about the room). What else could I possibly do?

Hedda. But what do you think your husband will say when you go home again?

Mrs. Elvsted (at the table, looks at her). Back to him?

Hedda. Of course.

Mrs. Elvsted. I shall never go back to him again.

Hedda (rising and going towards her). Then you have left your home—for good and all?

Mrs. Elvsted. Yes. There was nothing else to be done.

Hedda. But then—to take flight so openly.

Mrs. Elvsted. Oh, it's impossible to keep things of that sort secret.

Hedda. But what do you think people will say of you, Thea?

Mrs. Elvsted. They may say what they like, for aught *I* care. (*Seats herself wearily and sadly on the sofa.*) I have done nothing but what I had to do.

Hedda (after a short silence). And what are your plans now? What do you think of doing?

Mrs. Elvsted. I don't know yet. I only know this, that I must live here, where Eilert Lövborg is—if I am to live at all.

Hedda (takes a chair from the table, seats herself beside her, and strokes her hands). My dear Thea—how did this —this friendship—between you and Eilert Lövborg come about?

Mrs. Elvsted. Oh, it grew up gradually. I gained a sort of influence over him.

Hedda. Indeed?

Mrs. Elvsted. He gave up his old habits. Not because I asked him to, for I never dared do that. But of course he saw how repulsive they were to me; and so he dropped them.

Hedda (concealing an invluntary smile of scorn). Then you have reclaimed him—as the saying goes—my little Thea.

Mrs. Elvsted. So he says himself, at any rate. And he, on his side, has made a real human being of me— taught me to think, and to understand so many things.

Hedda. Did he give you lessons too, then?

Mrs. Elvsted. No, not exactly lessons. But he talked to me—talked about such an infinity of things. And then came the lovely, happy time when I began to share in his work—when he allowed me to help him!

Hedda. Oh, he did, did he?

Mrs. Elvsted. Yes! He never wrote anything without my assistance.

Hedda. You were two good comrades, in fact?

Mrs. Elvsted (eagerly). Comrades! Yes, fancy, Hedda —that is the very word he used!—Oh, I ought to feel perfectly happy; and yet I cannot; for I don't know how long it will last.

Hedda. Are you no surer of him than that?

Mrs. Elvsted (*gloomily*). A woman's shadow stands between Eilert Lövborg and me.

Hedda (*looks at her anxiously*). Who can that be?

Mrs. Elvsted. I don't know. Some one he knew in his—in his past. Some one he has never been able wholly to forget.

Hedda. What has he told you—about this?

Mrs. Elvsted. He has only once—quite vaguely—alluded to it.

Hedda. Well! And what did he say?

Mrs. Elvsted. He said that when they parted, she threatened to shoot him with a pistol.

Hedda (*with cold composure*). Oh, nonsense! No one does that sort of thing here.

Mrs. Elvsted. No. And that is why I think it must have been that red-haired singing-woman whom he once—

Hedda. Yes, very likely.

Mrs. Elvsted. For I remember they used to say of her that she carried loaded firearms.

Hedda. Oh—then of course it must have been she.

Mrs. Elvsted (*wringing her hands*). And now just fancy, Hedda—I hear that this singing-woman—that she is in town again! Oh, I don't know what to do——

Hedda (*glancing towards the inner room*). Hush! Here comes Tesman. (*Rises and whispers.*) Thea—all this must remain between you and me.

Mrs. Elvsted (*springing up*). Oh, yes, yes! for heaven's sake——!

GEORGE TESMAN, *with a letter in his hand, comes from the right through the inner room.*

Tesman. There now—the epistle is finished.

Hedda. That's right. And now Mrs. Elvsted is just going. Wait a moment—I'll go with you to the garden gate.

Tesman. Do you think Berta could post the letter, Hedda dear?

Hedda (*takes it*). I will tell her to.

BERTA *enters from the hall.*

Berta. Judge Brack wishes to know if Mrs. Tesman will receive him.

Hedda. Yes, ask Judge Brack to come in. And look here—put this letter in the post.

Berta (taking the letter). Yes, ma'am. *(She opens the door for* JUDGE BRACK *and goes out herself.* BRACK *is a man of forty-five; thick-set, but well-built and elastic in his movements. His face is roundish with an aristocratic profile. His hair is short, still almost black, and carefully dressed. His eyes are lively and sparkling. His eyebrows thick. His moustaches are also thick, with short-cut ends. He wears a well-cut walking-suit, a little too youthful for his age. He uses an eye-glass, which he now and then lets drop.*

Judge Brack (with his hat in his hand, bowing). May one venture to call so early in the day?

Hedda. Of course one may.

Tesman (presses his hand). You are welcome at any time. *(Introducing him.)* Judge Brack—Miss Rysing——

Hedda. Oh——!

Brack (bowing). Ah—delighted——

Hedda (looks at him and laughs). It's nice to have a look at you by daylight, Judge!

Brack. Do you find me—altered?

Hedda. A little younger, I think.

Brack. Thank you so much.

Tesman. But what do you think of Hedda—eh? Doesn't she look flourishing? She has actually——

Hedda. Oh, do leave me alone. You haven't thanked Judge Brack for all the trouble he has taken——

Brack. Oh, nonsense—it was a pleasure to me——

Hedda. Yes, you are a friend indeed. But here stands Thea all impatience to be off—so *au revoir* Judge. I shall be back again presently. *(Mutual salutations.* MRS. ELVSTED *and* HEDDA *go out by the hall door.)*

Brack. Well,—is your wife tolerably satisfied——

Tesman. Yes, we can't thank you sufficiently. Of course she talks of a little re-arrangement here and there; and one or two things are still wanting. We shall have to buy some additional trifles.

Brack. Indeed!

Tesman. But we won't trouble you about these things. Hedda says she herself will look after what is wanting.— Shan't we sit down? Eh?

Brack. Thanks, for a moment. (*Seats himself beside the table.*) There is something I wanted to speak to you about, my dear Tesman.

Tesman. Indeed? Ah, I understand! (*Seating himself.*) I suppose it's the serious part of the frolic that is coming now. Eh?

Brack. Oh, the money question is not so very pressing; though, for that matter, I wish we had gone a little more economically to work.

Tesman. But that would never have done, you know! Think of Hedda, my dear fellow! You, who know her so well——. I couldn't possibly ask her to put up with a shabby style of living!

Brack. No, no—that is just the difficulty.

Tesman. And then—fortunately—it can't be long before I receive my appointment.

Brack. Well, you see—such things are often apt to hang fire for a time.

Tesman. Have you heard anything definite? Eh?

Brack. Nothing exactly definite—— (*Interrupting himself.*) But, by-the-bye—I have one piece of news for you.

Tesman. Well?

Brack. Your old friend, Eilert Lövborg, has returned to town.

Tesman. I know that already.

Brack. Indeed! How did you learn it?

Tesman. From that lady who went out with Hedda.

Brack. Really? What was her name? I didn't quite catch it.

Tesman. Mrs. Elvsted.

Brack. Aha—Sheriff Elvsted's wife? Of course—he has been living up in their regions.

Tesman. And fancy—I'm delighted to hear that he is quite a reformed character!

Brack. So they say.

Tesman. And then he has published a new book—eh?

Brack. Yes, indeed he has.

Tesman. And I hear it has made some sensation!

Brack. Quite an unusual sensation.

Tesman. Fancy—isn't that good news! A man of such extraordinary talents—— I felt so grieved to think that he had gone irretrievably to ruin.

Brack. That was what everybody thought.

Tesman. But I cannot imagine what he will take to now! How in the world will he be able to make his living? Eh?

(*During the last words,* HEDDA *has entered by the hall door.*)

Hedda (*to* BRACK, *laughing with a touch of scorn*). Tesman is for ever worrying about how people are to make their living.

Tesman. Well, you see, dear—we were talking about poor Eilert Lövborg.

Hedda (*glancing at him rapidly*). Oh, indeed? (*Seats herself in the arm-chair beside the stove and asks indifferently:*) What is the matter with him?

Tesman. Well—no doubt he has run through all his property long ago; and he can scarcely write a new book every year—eh? So I really can't see what is to become of him.

Brack. Perhaps I can give you some information on that point.

Tesman. Indeed!

Brack. You must remember that his relations have a good deal of influence.

Tesman. Oh, his relations, unfortunately, have entirely washed their hands of him.

Brack. At one time they called him the hope of the family.

Tesman. At one time, yes! But he has put an end to all that.

Hedda. Who knows? (*With a slight smile.*) I hear they have reclaimed him up at Sheriff Elvsted's——

Brack. And then this book that he has published——

Tesman. Well, well, I hope to goodness they may find something for him to do. I have just written to him. I asked him to come and see us this evening, Hedda dear.

Brack. But, my dear fellow, you are booked for my bachelors' party this evening. You promised on the pier last night.

Hedda. Had you forgotten, Tesman?

Tesman. Yes, I had utterly forgotten.

Brack. But it doesn't matter, for you may be sure he won't come.

Tesman. What makes you think that? Eh?

Brack (*with a little hesitation, rising and resting his hands on the back of his chair*). My dear Tesman—and you too, Mrs. Tesman—I think I ought not to keep you in the dark about something that—that——

Tesman. That concerns Eilert——?

Brack. Both you and him.

Tesman. Well, my dear Judge, out with it.

Brack. You must be prepared to find your appointment deferred longer than you desired or expected.

Tesman (*jumping up uneasily*). Is there some hitch about it? Eh?

Brack. The nomination may perhaps be made conditional on the result of a competition——

Tesman. Competition! Think of that, Hedda!

Hedda (leans farther back in the chair). Aha—aah!

Tesman. But who can my competitor be? Surely not——?

Brack. Yes, precisely—Eilert Lövborg.

Tesman (clasping his hands). No, no—it's quite inconceivable! Quite impossible! Eh?

Brack. H'm—that is what it may come to, all the same.

Tesman. Well but, Judge Brack—it would show the most incredible lack of consideration for me. *(Gesticulates with his arms.)* For—just think—I'm a married man! We have married on the strength of these prospects, Hedda and I; and run deep into debt; and borrowed money from Aunt Julia too. Good heavens, they had as good as promised me the appointment. Eh?

Brack. Well, well, well—no doubt you will get it in the end; only after a contest.

Hedda (immovable in her arm-chair.) Fancy, Tesman, there will be a sort of sporting interest in that.

Tesman. Why, my dearest Hedda, how can you be so indifferent about it.

Hedda (as before). I am not at all indifferent. I am most eager to see who wins.

Brack. In any case, Mrs. Tesman, it is best that you should know how matters stand. I mean—before you set about the little purchases I hear you are threatening.

Hedda. This can make no difference.

Brack. Indeed! Then I have no more to say. Goodbye! *(To* TESMAN.*)* I shall look in on my way back from my afternoon walk, and take you home with me.

Tesman. Oh yes, yes—your news has quite upset me.

Hedda (reclining, holds out her hand). Good-bye, Judge; and be sure you call in the afternoon.

Brack. Many thanks. Good-bye, good-bye!

Tesman (accompanying him to the door). Good-bye, my

dear Judge! You must really excuse me—— (JUDGE BRACK *goes out by the hall door.*)

Tesman (*crosses the room*). Oh, Hedda—one should never rush into adventures. Eh?

Hedda (*looks at him, smiling*). Do you do that?

Tesman. Yes, dear—there is no denying—it was adventurous to go and marry and set up house upon mere expectations.

Hedda. Perhaps you are right there.

Tesman. Well—at all events, we have our delightful home, Hedda! Fancy, the home we both dreamed of— the home we were in love with, I may almost say. Eh?

Hedda (*rising slowly and wearily*). It was part of our compact that we were to go into society—to keep open house.

Tesman. Yes, if you only knew how I had been looking forward to it! Fancy—to see you as hostess—in a select circle! Eh? Well, well, well—for the present we shall have to get on without society, Hedda—only to invite Aunt Julia now and then.—Oh, I intended you to lead such an utterly different life, dear——!

Hedda. Of course I cannot have my man in livery just yet.

Tesman. Oh no, unfortunately. It would be out of the question for us to keep a footman, you know.

Hedda. And the saddle-horse I was to have had——

Tesman (*aghast*). The saddle-horse!

Hedda. ——I suppose I must not think of that now.

Tesman. Good heavens, no!—that's as clear as daylight.

Hedda (*goes up the room*). Well, I shall have one thing at least to kill time with in the meanwhile.

Tesman (*beaming*). Oh, thank heaven for that! What is it, Hedda? Eh?

Hedda (*in the middle doorway, looks at him with covert scorn*). My pistols, George.

Tesman (*in alarm*). Your pistols!

Hedda (*with cold eyes*).   General Gabler's pistols.   (*She goes out through the inner room, to the left.*)

Tesman (*rushes up to the middle doorway and calls after her:*)   No, for heaven's sake, Hedda darling—don't touch those dangerous things!   For my sake, Hedda!   Eh?

ACT II

The room at the TESMANS' *as in the first Act, except that the piano has been removed, and an elegant little writing-table with book-shelves put in its place. A smaller table stands near the sofa on the left. Most of the bouquets have been taken away.* MRS. ELVSTED'S *bouquet is upon the large table in front.—It is afternoon.*

HEDDA, *dressed to receive callers, is alone in the room. She stands by the open glass door, loading a revolver. The fellow to it lies in an open pistol-case on the writing-table.*

Hedda (looks down the garden, and calls:) So you are here again, Judge!

Brack (is heard calling from a distance). As you see, Mrs. Tesman!

Hedda (raises the pistol and points). Now I'll shoot you, Judge Brack!

Brack (calling unseen). No, no, no! Don't stand aiming at me!

Hedda. This is what comes of sneaking in by the back way.* *(She fires.)*

Brack (nearer). Are you out of your senses——!

Hedda. Dear me—did I happen to hit you?

Brack (still outside). I wish you would let these pranks alone!

Hedda. Come in then, Judge.

JUDGE BRACK, *dressed as though for a men's party, enters by the glass door. He carries a light overcoat over his arm.*

---

* "Bagveje" means both "back ways" and "underhand courses."

Brack. What the deuce—haven't you tired of that sport, yet? What are you shooting at?

Hedda. Oh, I am only firing in the air.

Brack (*gently takes the pistol out of her hand*). Allow me, madam! (*Looks at it.*) Ah—I know this pistol well! (*Looks around.*) Where is the case? Ah, here it is. (*Lays the pistol in it, and shuts it.*) Now we won't play at that game any more to-day.

Hedda. Then what in heaven's name would you have me do with myself?

Brack. Have you had no visitors?

Hedda (*closing the glass door*). Not one. I suppose all our set are still out of town.

Brack. And is Tesman not at home either?

Hedda (*at the writing-table, putting the pistol-case in a drawer which she shuts*). No. He rushed off to his aunt's directly after lunch; he didn't expect you so early.

Brack. H'm—how stupid of me not to have thought of that!

Hedda (*turning her head to look at him*). Why stupid?

Brack. Because if I had thought of it I should have come a little—earlier.

Hedda (*crossing the room*). Then you would have found no one to receive you; for I have been in my room changing my dress ever since lunch.

Brack. And is there no sort of little chink that we could hold a parley through?

Hedda. You have forgotten to arrange one.

Brack. That was another piece of stupidity.

Hedda. Well, we must just settle down here—and wait. Tesman is not likely to be back for some time yet.

Brack. Never mind; I shall not be impatient.

HEDDA *seats herself in the corner of the sofa.* BRACK *lays his overcoat over the back of the nearest chair, and sits down, but keeps his hat in his hand. A short silence. They look at each other.*

Hedda. Well?

Brack (*in the same tone*). Well?

Hedda. I spoke first.

Brack (*bending a little forward*). Come, let us have a cosy little chat, Mrs. Hedda.*

Hedda (*leaning further back in the sofa*). Does it not seem like a whole eternity since our last talk? Of course I don't count those few words yesterday evening and this morning.

Brack. You mean since our last confidential talk? Our last *tête-à-tête*?

Hedda. Well, yes—since you put it so.

Brack. Not a day has passed but I have wished that you were home again.

Hedda. And I have done nothing but wish the same thing.

Brack. You? Really, Mrs. Hedda? And I thought you had been enjoying your tour so much!

Hedda. Oh, yes, you may be sure of that!

Brack. But Tesman's letters spoke of nothing but happiness.

Hedda. Oh, Tesman! You see, he thinks nothing so delightful as grubbing in libraries and making copies of old parchments, or whatever you call them.

Brack (*with a spice of malice*). Well, that is his vocation in life—or part of it at any rate.

Hedda. Yes, of course; and no doubt when it's your vocation—— But *I!* Oh, my dear Mr. Brack, how mortally bored I have been.

Brack (*sympathetically*). Do you really say so? In downright earnest?

---

* As this form of address is contrary to English usage, and as the note of familiarity would be lacking in "Mrs. Tesman," Brack may, in stage representation, say "Miss Hedda," thus ignoring her marriage and reverting to the form of address no doubt customary between them of old.

Hedda. Yes, you can surely understand it——! To go for six whole months without meeting a soul that knew anything of our circle, or could talk about the things we are interested in.

Brack. Yes, yes—I too should feel that a deprivation.

Hedda. And then, what I found most intolerable of all——

Brack. Well?

Hedda. ——was being everlastingly in the company of —one and the same person——

Brack (*with a nod of assent*). Morning, noon, and night, yes—at all possible times and seasons.

Hedda. I said "everlastingly."

Brack. Just so. But I should have thought, with our excellent Tesman, one could——

Hedda. Tesman is—a specialist, my dear Judge.

Brack. Undeniably.

Hedda. And specialists are not at all amusing to travel with. Not in the long run at any rate.

Brack. Not even—the specialist one happens to love?

Hedda. Faugh—don't use that sickening word!

Brack (*taken aback*). What do you say, Mrs. Hedda?

Hedda (*half laughing, half irritated*). You should just try it! To hear of nothing but the history of civilisation, morning, noon, and night——

Brack. Everlastingly.

Hedda. Yes, yes, yes! And then all this about the domestic industry of the middle ages——! That's the most disgusting part of it!

Brack (*looks searchingly at her*). But tell me—in that case, how am I to understand your——? H'm——

Hedda. My accepting George Tesman, you mean?

Brack. Well, let us put it so.

Hedda. Good heavens, do you see anything so wonderful in that?

Brack. Yes and no—Mrs. Hedda.

Hedda. I had positively danced myself tired, my dear Judge. My day was done—— (*With a slight shudder.*) Oh no—I won't say that; nor think it either!

Brack. You have assuredly no reason to.

Hedda. Oh, reasons—— (*Watching him closely.*) And George Tesman—after all, you must admit that he is correctness itself.

Brack. His correctness and respectability are beyond all question.

Hedda. And I don't see anything absolutely ridiculous about him.—Do you?

Brack. Ridiculous? N—no—I shouldn't exactly say so——

Hedda. Well—and his powers of research, at all events, are untiring.—I see no reason why he should not one day come to the front, after all.

Brack (*looks at her hesitatingly*). I thought that you, like every one else, expected him to attain the highest distinction.

Hedda (*with an expression of fatigue*). Yes, so I did.— And then, since he was bent, at all hazards, on being allowed to provide for me—I really don't know why I should not have accepted his offer?

Brack. No—if you look at it in that light——

Hedda. It was more than my other adorers were prepared to do for me, my dear Judge.

Brack (*laughing*). Well, I can't answer for all the rest; but as for myself, you know quite well that I have always entertained a—a certain respect for the marriage tie—for marriage as an institution, Mrs. Hedda.

Hedda (*jestingly*). Oh, I assure you I have never cherished any hopes with respect to you.

Brack. All I require is a pleasant and intimate interior, where I can make myself useful in every way, and am free to come and go as—as a trusted friend——

Hedda. Of the master of the house, do you mean?

Brack (bowing). Frankly—of the mistress first of all; but of course of the master, too, in the second place. Such a triangular friendship—if I may call it so—is really a great convenience for all parties, let me tell you.

Hedda. Yes, I have many a time longed for some one to make a third on our travels. Oh—those railway-carriage *tête-à-têtes*——!

Brack. Fortunately your wedding journey is over now.

Hedda (shaking her head). Not by a long—long way. I have only arrived at a station on the line.

Brack. Well, then the passengers jump out and move about a little, Mrs. Hedda.

Hedda. I never jump out.

Brack. Really?

Hedda. No—because there is always some one standing by to——

Brack (laughing). To look at your ankles, do you mean?

Hedda. Precisely.

Brack. Well but, dear me——

Hedda (with a gesture of repulsion). I won't have it. I would rather keep my seat where I happen to be—and continue the *tête-à-tête*.

Brack. But suppose a third person were to jump in and join the couple.

Hedda. Ah—that is quite another matter!

Brack. A trusted, sympathetic friend——

Hedda. ——with a fund of conversation on all sorts of lively topics——

Brack. ——and not the least bit of a specialist!

Hedda (with an audible sigh). Yes, that would be a relief indeed.

Brack (hears the front door open, and glances in that direction). The triangle is completed.

Hedda (half aloud). And on goes the train.

GEORGE TESMAN, *in a grey walking-suit, with a soft felt*

hat, enters from the hall. He has a number of unbound books under his arm and in his pockets.

Tesman (goes up to the table beside the corner settee). Ouf—what a load for a warm day—all these books. (*Lays them on the table.*) I'm positively perspiring, Hedda. Hallo—are you there already, my dear Judge? Eh? Berta didn't tell me.

Brack (rising). I came in through the garden.

Hedda. What books have you got there?

Tesman (stands looking them through). Some new books on my special subjects—quite indispensable to me.

Hedda. Your special subjects?

Brack. Yes, books on his special subjects, Mrs. Tesman. (BRACK *and* HEDDA *exchange a confidential smile.*)

Hedda. Do you need still more books on your special subjects?

Tesman. Yes, my dear Hedda, one can never have too many of them. Of course one must keep up with all that is written and published.

Hedda. Yes, I suppose one must.

Tesman (searching among his books). And look here—I have got hold of Eilert Lövborg's new book too. (*Offering it to her.*) Perhaps you would like to glance through it, Hedda? Eh?

Hedda. No, thank you. Or rather—afterwards perhaps.

Tesman. I looked into it a little on the way home.

Brack. Well, what do you think of it—as a specialist?

Tesman. I think it shows quite remarkable soundness of judgment. He never wrote like that before. (*Putting the books together.*) Now I shall take all these into my study. I'm longing to cut the leaves——! And then I must change my clothes. (*To* BRACK.) I suppose we needn't start just yet? Eh?

Brack. Oh, dear no—there is not the slightest hurry.

Tesman. Well then, I will take my time. (*Is going with his books, but stops in the doorway and turns.*) By·

the-bye, Hedda—Aunt Julia is not coming this evening.

Hedda. Not coming? Is it that affair of the bonnet that keeps her away?

Tesman. Oh, not at all. How could you think such a thing of Aunt Julia? Just fancy——! The fact is, Aunt Rina is very ill.

Hedda. She always is.

Tesman. Yes, but to-day she is much worse than usual, poor dear.

Hedda. Oh, then it's only natural that her sister should remain with her. I must bear my disappointment.

Tesman. And you can't imagine, dear, how delighted Aunt Julia seemed to be—because you had come home looking so flourishing!

Hedda (*half aloud, rising*). Oh, those everlasting aunts!

Tesman. What?

Hedda (*going to the glass door*). Nothing.

Tesman. Oh, all right. (*He goes through the inner room, out to the right.*)

Brack. What bonnet were you talking about?

Hedda. Oh, it was a little episode with Miss Tesman this morning. She had laid down her bonnet on the chair there—(*looks at him and smiles.*)—And I pretended to think it was the servant's.

Brack (*shaking his head*). Now my dear Mrs. Hedda, how could you do such a hing? To that excellent old lady, too!

Hedda (*nervously crossing the room*). Well, you see— these impulses come over me all of a sudden; and I cannot resist them. (*Throws herself down in the easy-chair by the stove.*) Oh, I don't know how to explain it.

Brack (*behind the easy-chair*). You are not really happy —that is at the bottom of it.

Hedda (*looking straight before her*). I know of no reason why I should be—happy. Perhaps you can give me one?

Brack. Well—amongst other things, because you have got exactly the home you had set your heart on.

Hedda (*looks up at him and laughs*). Do you too believe in that legend?

Brack. Is there nothing in it, then?

Hedda. Oh, yes, there is something in it.

Brack. Well?

Hedda. There is this in it, that I made use of Tesman to see me home from evening parties last summer—

Brack. I, unfortuntely, had to go quite a different way.

Hedda. That's true. I know you were going a different way last summer.

Brack (*laughing*). Oh fie, Mrs. Hedda! Well, then—you and Tesman——?

Hedda. Well, we happened to pass here one evening; Tesman, poor fellow, was writhing in the agony of having to find conversation; so I took pity on the learned man——

Brack (*smiles doubtfully*). You took pity? H'm——

Hedda. Yes, I really did. And so—to help him out of his torment—I happened to say, in pure thoughtlessness, that I should like to live in this villa.

Brack. No more than that?

Hedda. Not that evening.

Brack. But afterwards?

Hedda. Yes, my thoughtlessness had consequences, my dear Judge.

Brack. Unfortunately that too often happens, Mrs. Hedda.

Hedda. Thanks! So you see it was this enthusiasm for Secretary's Falk's villa that first constituted a bond of sympathy between George Tesman and me. From that came our engagement and our marriage, and our wedding journey, and all the rest of it. Well, well, my dear Judge—as you make your bed so you must lie, I could almost say.

Brack. This is exquisite! And you really cared not a rap about it all the time?

Hedda. No, heaven knows I didn't.

Brack. But now? Now that we have made it so home-like for you?

Hedda. Uh—the rooms all seem to smell of lavender and dried rose-leaves.—But perhaps it's Aunt Julia that has brought that scent with her.

Brack (laughing). No, I think it must be a legacy from the late Mrs. Secretary Falk.

Hedda. Yes, there is an odour of mortality about it. It reminds me of a bouquet—the day after the ball. *(Clasps her hands behind her head, leans back in her chair and looks at him.)* Oh, my dear Judge—you cannot imagine how horribly I shall bore myself here.

Brack. Why should not you, too, find some sort of vocation in life, Mrs. Hedda?

Hedda. A vocation—that should attract me?

Brack. If possible, of course.

Hedda. Heaven knows what sort of vocation that could be. I often wonder whether—— *(Breaking off.)* But that would never do either.

Brack. Who can tell? Let me hear what it is.

Hedda. Whether I might not get Tesman to go into politics, I mean.

Brack (laughing). Tesman? No, really now, political life is not the thing for him—not at all in his line.

Hedda. No, I daresay not.—But if I could get him into it all the same?

Brack. Why—what satisfaction could you find in that? If he is not fitted for that sort of thing, why should you want to drive him into it?

Hedda. Because I am bored, I tell you! *(After a pause.)* So you think it quite out of the question that Tesman should ever get into the ministry?

Brack. H'm—you see, my dear Mrs. Hedda—to get into the ministry, he would have to be a tolerably rich man.

Hedda (rising impatiently). Yes, there we have it! It

is this genteel poverty I have managed to drop into——!
(*Crosses the room.*) That is what makes life so pitiable!
So utterly ludicrous!—For that's what it is.

Brack. Now *I* should say the fault lay elsewhere.

Hedda. Where, then?

Brack. You have never gone through any really stimulating experience.

Hedda. Anything serious, you mean?

Brack. Yes, you may call it so. But now you may perhaps have one in store.

Hedda (*tossing her head*). Oh, you're thinking of the
annoyances about this wretched professorship! But that
must be Tesman's own affair. I assure you I shall not waste
a thought upon it.

Brack. No, no, I daresay not. But suppose now that
what people call—in elegant language—a solemn responsibility were to come upon you? (*Smiling.*) A new responsibility, Mrs. Hedda?

Hedda (*angrily*). Be quiet! Nothing of that sort will
ever happen!

Brack (*warily*). We will speak of this again a year hence
—at the very outside.

Hedda (*curtly*). I have no turn for anything of the sort,
Judge Brack. No responsibilities for me!

Brack. Are you so unlike the generality of women as to
have no turn for duties which——?

Hedda (*beside the glass door*). Oh, be quiet, I tell you!
—I often think there is only one thing in the world I have
any turn for.

Brack (*drawing near to her*). And what is that, if I
may ask?

Hedda (*stands looking out*). Boring myself to death.
Now you know it. (*Turns, looks towards the inner room,
and laughs.*) Yes, as I thought! Here comes the Professor.

Brack (softly, in a tone of warning). Come, come, come, Mrs. Hedda!

GEORGE TESMAN, *dressed for the party, with his gloves and hat in his hand, enters from the right through the inner room.*

Tesman. Hedda, has no message come from Eilert Lövborg? Eh?

Hedda. No.

Tesman. Then you'll see he'll be here presently.

Brack. Do you really think he will come?

Tesman. Yes, I am almost sure of it. For what you were telling us this morning must have been a mere floating rumour.

Brack. You think so?

Tesman. At any rate, Aunt Julia said she did not believe for a moment that he would ever stand in my way again. Fancy that!

Brack. Well then, that's all right.

Tesman (placing his hat and gloves on a chair on the right.) Yes, but you must really let me wait for him as long as possible.

Brack. We have plenty of time yet. None of my guests will arrive before seven or half-past.

Tesman. Then meanwhile we can keep Hedda company, and see what happens. Eh?

Hedda (placing BRACK's hat and overcoat upon the corner settee.) And at the worst Mr. Lövborg can remain here with me.

Brack (offering to take his things). Oh, allow me, Mrs. Tesman!—What do you mean by "At the worst"?

Hedda. If he won't go with you and Tesman.

Tesman (looks dubiously at her). But, Hedda dear—do you think it would quite do for him to remain with you? Eh? Remember, Aunt Julia can't come.

Hedda. No, but Mrs. Elvsted is coming. We three can have a cup of tea together.

Tesman. Oh, yes, that will be all right.

Brack (smiling). And that would perhaps be the safest plan for him.

Hedda. Why so?

Brack. Well, you know, Mrs. Tesman, how you used to gird at my little bachelor parties. You declared they were adapted only for men of the strictest principles.

Hedda. But no doubt Mr. Lövborg's principles are strict enough now. A converted sinner—— (BERTA *appears at the hall door.*)

Berta. There's a gentleman asking if you are at home, ma'am——

Hedda. Well, show him in.

Tesman (softly). I'm sure it is he! Fancy that!

EILERT LÖVBORG *enters from the hall. He is slim and lean; of the same age as* TESMAN, *but looks older and somewhat worn-out. His hair and beard are of a blackish brown, his face long and pale, but with patches of colour on the cheek-bones. He is dressed in a well-cut black visiting suit, quite new. He has dark gloves and a silk hat. He stops near the door, and makes a rapid bow, seeming somewhat embarrassed.*

Tesman (goes up to him and shakes him warmly by the hand). Well, my dear Eilert—so at last we meet again!

Eilert Lövborg (speaks in a subdued voice). Thanks for your letter, Tesman. (*Approaching* HEDDA.) Will you too shake hands with me, Mrs. Tesman?

Hedda (taking his hand). I am glad to see you, Mr. Lövborg. (*With a motion of her hand.*) I don't know whether you two gentlemen——?

Lövborg (bowing slightly). Judge Brack, I think.

Brack (doing likewise). Oh yes,—in the old days——

Tesman (to LÖVBORG, *with his hands on his shoulders).* And now you must make yourself entirely at home, Eilert! Mustn't he, Hedda?—For I hear you are going to settle in town again? Eh?

Lövborg. Yes, I am.

Tesman. Quite right, quite right. Let me tell you, I have got hold of your new book; but I haven't had time to read it yet.

Lövborg. You may spare yourself the trouble.

Tesman. Why so?

Lövborg. Because there is very little in it.

Tesman. Just fancy—how can you say so?

Brack. But it has been very much praised, I hear.

Lövborg. That was what I wanted; so I put nothing into the book but what every one would agree with.

Brack. Very wise of you.

Tesman. Well but, my dear Eilert——!

Lövborg. For now I mean to win myself a position again —to make a fresh start.

Tesman (*a little embarrassed*). Ah, that is what you wish to do? Eh?

Lövborg (*smiling, lays down his hat, and draws a packet, wrapped in paper, from his coat pocket*). But when this one appears, George Tesman, you will have to read it. For this is the real book—the book I have put my true self into.

Tesman. Indeed? And what is it?

Lövborg. It is the continuation.

Tesman. The continuation? Of what?

Lövborg. Of the book.

Tesman. Of the new book?

Lövborg. Of course.

Tesman. Why, my dear Eilert—does it not come down to our own days?

Lövborg. Yes, it does; and this one deals with the future.

Tesman. With the future! But, good heavens, we know nothing of the future!

Lövborg. No; but there is a thing or two to be said about it all the same. (*Opens the packet.*) Look here——

Tesman. Why, that's not your handwriting.

Lövborg. I dictated it. (*Turning over the pages.*) It falls into two sections. The first deals with the civilising forces of the future. And here is the second—(*running through the pages towards the end*)—forecasting the probable line of development.

Tesman. How odd now! I should never have thought of writing anything of that sort.

Hedda (*at the glass door, drumming on the pane*). H'm —I daresay not.

Lövborg (*replacing the manuscript in its paper and laying the packet on the table*). I brought it, thinking I might read you a little of it this evening.

Tesman. That was very good of you, Eilert. But this evening——? (*Looking at* Brack.) I don't quite see how we can manage it——

Lövborg. Well then, some other time. There is no hurry.

Brack. I must tell you, Mr. Lövborg—there is a little gathering at my house this evening—mainly in honour of Tesman, you know——

Lövborg (*looking for his hat*). Oh—then I won't detain you——

Brack. No, but listen—will you not do me the favour of joining us?

Lövborg (*curtly and decidedly*). No, I can't—thank you very much.

Brack. Oh, nonsense—do! We shall be quite a select little circle. And I assure you we shall have a "lively time," as Mrs. Hed—as Mrs. Tesman says.

Lövborg. I have no doubt of it. But nevertheless——

Brack. And then you might bring your manuscript with you, and read it to Tesman at my house. I could give you a room to yourselves.

Tesman. Yes, think of that, Eilert,—why shouldn't you? Eh?

Hedda (*interposing*). But, Tesman, if Mr. Lövborg would really rather not! I am sure Mr. Lövborg is much more inclined to remain here and have supper with me.

Lövborg (*looking at her*). With you, Mrs. Tesman?

Hedda. And with Mrs. Elvsted.

Lövborg. Ah—— (*Lightly.*) I saw her for a moment this morning.

Hedda. Did you? Well, she is coming this evening. So you see you are almost bound to remain, Mr. Lövborg, or she will have no one to see her home.

Lövborg. That's true. Many thanks, Mrs. Tesman—in that case I will remain.

Hedda. Then I have one or two orders to give the servant—— (*She goes to the hall door and rings.* BERTA *enters.* HEDDA *talks to her in a whisper, and points towards the inner room.* BERTA *nods and goes out again.*

Tesman (*at the same time, to* LÖVBORG). Tell me, Eilert —is it this new subject—the future—that you are going to lecture about?

Lövborg. Yes.

Tesman. They told me at the bookseller's that you are going to deliver a course of lectures this autumn.

Lövborg. That is my intention. I hope you won't take it ill, Tesman.

Tesman. Oh no, not in the least! But——?

Lövborg. I can quite understand that it must be disagreeable to you.

Tesman (*cast down*). Oh, I can't expect you, out of consideration for me, to——

Lövborg. But I shall wait till you have received your appointment.

Tesman. Will you wait? Yes, but——yes, but——are you not going to compete with me? Eh?

Lövborg. No; it is only the moral victory I care for.

Tesman. Why, bless me—then Aunt Julia was right after all! Oh yes——I knew it! Hedda! Just fancy—Eilert Lövborg is not going to stand in our way!

Hedda (*curtly*). Our way? Pray leave me out of the

question. (*She goes up towards the inner room, where* BERTA *is placing a tray with decanters and glasses on the table.* HEDDA *nods approval, and comes forward again.* BERTA *goes out.*)

Tesman (*at the same time*). And you, Judge Brack—what do you say to this? Eh?

Brack. Well, I say that a moral victory—h'm—may be all very fine——

Tesman. Yes, certainly. But all the same——

Hedda (*looking at* TESMAN *with a cold smile.*) You stand there looking as if you were thunderstruck——

Tesman. Yes—so I am—I almost think——

Brack. Don't you see, Mrs. Tesman, a thunderstorm has just passed over?

Hedda (*pointing towards the inner room*). Will you not take a glass of cold punch, gentlemen?

Brack (*looking at his watch*). A stirrup-cup? Yes, it wouldn't come amiss.

Tesman. A capital idea, Hedda! Just the thing! Now that the weight has been taken off my mind——

Hedda. Will you not join them, Mr. Lövborg?

Lövborg (*with a gesture of refusal*). No, thank you. Nothing for me.

Brack. Why, bless me—cold punch is surely not poison.

Lövborg. Perhaps not for every one.

Hedda. I will keep Mr. Lövborg company in the meantime.

Tesman. Yes, yes, Hedda dear, do. (*He and* BRACK *go into the inner room, seat themselves, drink punch, smoke cigarettes, and carry on a lively conversation during what follows.* EILERT LÖVBORG *remains standing beside the stove.* HEDDA *goes to the writing-table.*

Hedda (*raising her voice a little*). Do you care to look at some photographs, Mr. Lövborg? You know Tesman and I made a tour in the Tyrol on our way home? (*She takes up an album, and places it on the table beside the sofa,*

in the further corner of which she seats herself. EILERT
LÖVBORG *approaches, stops, and looks at her. Then he
takes a chair and seats himself to her left, with his back
towards the inner room.*

Hedda (opening the album). Do you see this range of
mountains, Mr. Lövborg? It's the Ortler group. Tesman
has written the name underneath. Here it is: "The Ortler
group near Meran."

*Lövborg (who has never taken his eyes off her, says softly
and slowly:)* Hedda—Gabler!

Hedda (glancing hastily at him). Ah! Hush!

Lövborg (repeats softly). Hedda Gabler!

Hedda (looking at the album). That was my name in
the old days—when we two knew each other.

Lövborg. And I must teach myself never to say Hedda
Gabler again—never, as long as I live.

Hedda (still turning over the pages). Yes, you must.
And I think you ought to practise in time. The sooner the
better, I should say.

Lövborg (in a tone of indignation). Hedda Gabler married? And married to—George Tesman!

Hedda. Yes—so the world goes.

Lövborg. Oh, Hedda, Hedda—how could you* throw
yourself away!

Hedda (looks sharply at him). What? I can't allow
this!

Lövborg. What do you mean? (TESMAN *comes into the
room and goes towards the sofa.*)

*Hedda (hears him coming and says in an indifferent
tone).* And this is a view from the Val d'Ampezzo, Mr.
Lövborg. Just look at these peaks! (*Looks affectionately
up at* TESMAN.) What's the name of these curious peaks,
dear?

Tesman. Let me see. Oh, those are the Dolomites.

---

* He uses the familiar *du.*

Hedda. Yes, that's it!—Those are the Dolomites, Mr. Lövborg.

Tesman. Hedda dear,—I only wanted to ask whether I shouldn't bring you a little punch after all? For yourself at any rate—eh?

Hedda. Yes, do, please; and perhaps a few biscuits.

Tesman. No cigarettes?

Hedda. No.

Tesman. Very well. (*He goes into the inner room and out to the right.* BRACK *sits in the inner room, and keeps an eye from time to time on* HEDDA *and* LÖVBORG.

Lövborg (*softly, as before*). Answer me, Hedda—how could you go and do this?

Hedda (*apparently absorbed in the album*). If you continue to say *du* to me I won't talk to you.

Lövborg. May I not say *du* when we are alone?

Hedda. No. You may think it; but you mustn't say it.

Lövborg. Ah, I understand. It is an offence against George Tesman, whom you*—love.

Hedda (*glances at him and smiles.*) Love? What an idea!

Lövborg. You don't love him then!

Hedda. But I won't hear of any sort of unfaithfulness! Remember that.

Lövborg. Hedda—answer me one thing—

Hedda. Hush! (TESMAN *enters with a small tray from the inner room.*)

Tesman. Here you are! Isn't this tempting? (*He puts the tray on the table.*)

Hedda. Why do you bring it yourself?

Tesman (*filling the glasses*). Because I think it's such fun to wait upon you, Hedda.

Hedda. But you have poured out two glasses. Mr. Lövborg said he wouldn't have any—

---

* From this point onward Lövborg uses the formal *De.*

Tesman. No, but Mrs. Elvsted will soon be here, won't she?

Hedda. Yes, by-the-bye—Mrs. Elvsted—

Tesman. Had you forgotten her? Eh?

Hedda. We were so absorbed in these photographs. (*Shows him a picture.*) Do you remember this little village?

Tesman. Oh, it's that one just below the Brenner Pass. It was there we passed the night—

Hedda. —and met that lively party of tourists.

Tesman. Yes, that was the place. Fancy—if we could only have had you with us, Eilert! Eh? (*He returns to the inner room and sits beside* BRACK.)

Lövborg. Answer me this one thing, Hedda—

Hedda. Well?

Lövborg. Was there no love in your friendship for me either? Not a spark—not a tinge of love in it?

Hedda. I wonder if there was? To me it seems as though we were two good comrades—two thoroughly intimate friends. (*Smilingly.*) You especially were frankness itself.

Lövborg. It was you that made me so.

Hedda. As I look back upon it all, I think there was really something beautiful, something fascinating—something daring—in—in that secret intimacy—that comradeship which no living creature so much as dreamed of.

Lövborg. Yes, yes, Hedda! Was there not?—When I used to come to your father's in the afternoon—and the General sat over at the window reading his papers—with his back towards us—

Hedda. And we two on the corner sofa—

Lövborg. Always with the same illustrated paper before us—

Hedda. For want of an album, yes.

Lövborg. Yes, Hedda, and when I made my confessions to you—told you about myself, things that at that time no one else knew! There I would sit and tell you of my esca-

pades—my days and nights of devilment. Oh, Hedda—
what was the power in you that forced me to confess these
things?

Hedda. Do you think it was any power in me?

Lövborg. How else can I explain it? And all those—
those roundabout questions you used to put to me—

Hedda. Which you understood so particularly well—

Lövborg. How could you sit and question me like that?
Question me quite frankly—

Hedda. In roundabout terms, please observe.

Lövborg. Yes, but frankly nevertheless. Cross-question
me about—all that sort of thing?

Hedda. And how could you answer, Mr. Lövborg?

Lövborg. Yes, that is just what I can't understand—in
looking back upon it. But tell me now, Hedda—was there
not love at the bottom of our friendship? On your side, did
you not feel as though you might purge my stains away—if
I made you my confessor? Was it not so?

Hedda. No, not quite.

Lövborg. What was your motive, then?

Hedda. Do you think it quite incomprehensible that a
young girl—when it can be done—without any one knowing—

Lövborg. Well?

Hedda. —should be glad to have a peep, now and then,
into a world which—

Lövborg. Which—?

Hedda. —which she is forbidden to know anything
about?

Lövborg. So that was it?

Hedda. Partly. Partly—I almost think.

Lövborg. Comradeship in the thirst for life. But why
should not that, at any rate, have continued?

Hedda. The fault was yours.

Lövborg. It was you that broke with me.

Hedda. Yes, when our friendship threatened to develop

into something more serious. Shame upon you, Eilert Lövborg! How could you think of wronging your—your frank
comrade?

Lövborg (*clenching his hands*). Oh, why did you not
carry out your threat? Why did you not shoot me down?

Hedda. Because I have such a dread of scandal.

Lövborg. Yes, Hedda, you are a coward at heart.

Hedda. A terrible coward. (*Changing her tone.*) But it
was a lucky thing for you. And now you have found ample
consolation at the Elvsteds'.

Lövborg. I know what Thea has confided to you.

Hedda. And perhaps you have confided to her some
thing about us?

Lövborg. Not a word. She is too stupid to understand
anything of that sort.

Hedda. Stupid?

Lövborg. She is stupid about matters of that sort.

Hedda. And I am cowardly. (*Bends over towards him,
without looking him in the face, and says more softly:*) But
now I will confide something to you.

Lövborg (*eagerly*). Well?

Hedda. The fact that I dared not shoot you down—

Lövborg. Yes!

Hedda. —that was not my most arrant cowardice—that
evening.

Lövborg (*looks at her a moment, understands, and
whispers passionately*). Oh, Hedda! Hedda Gabler! Now
I begin to see a hidden reason beneath our comradeship!
You* and I——! After all, then, it was your craving for
life—

Hedda (*softly, with a sharp glance*). Take care! Believe
nothing of the sort!

(*Twilight has begun to fall. The hall door is opened from
without by* BERTA.)

---

* In this speech he once more says *du*. Hedda addresses him
throughout as *De*.

Hedda. (*Closes the album with a bang and calls smilingly:*) Ah, at last! My darling Thea,—come along!

Mrs. Elvsted *enters from the hall. She is in evening dress. The door is closed behind her.*

Hedda. (*on the sofa, stretches out her arms towards her.*) My sweet Thea—you can't think how I have been longing for you!

(Mrs. Elvsted, *in passing, exchanges slight salutations with the gentlemen in the inner room, then goes up to the table and gives* Hedda *her hand.* Eilert Lövborg *has risen. He and* Mrs. Elvsted *greet each other with a silent nod.*)

Mrs. Elvsted. Ought I to go in and talk to your husband for a moment?

Hedda. Oh, not at all. Leave those two alone. They will soon be going.

Mrs. Elvsted. Are they going out?

Hedda. Yes, to a supper-party.

Mrs. Elvsted (*quickly, to* Lövborg.) Not you?

Lövborg. No.

Hedda. Mr. Lövborg remains with us.

Mrs. Elvsted (*Takes a chair and is about to seat herself at his side.*) Oh, how nice it is here!

Hedda. No, thank you, my little Thea! Not there! You'll be good enough to come over here to me. I will sit between you.

Mrs. Elvsted. Yes, just as you please.

(*She goes round the table and seats herself on the sofa on* Hedda's *right.* Lövborg *re-seats himself on his chair.*

Lövborg (*after a short pause, to* Hedda.) Is not she lovely to look at?

Hedda (*lightly stroking her hair.*) Only to look at?

Lövborg. Yes. For we two—she and I—we are two real comrades. We have absolute faith in each other; so we can sit and talk with perfect frankness——

Hedda. Not round about, Mr. Lövborg?

Lövborg. Well——

Mrs. Elvsted (softly clinging close to HEDDA). Oh, how happy I am, Hedda; For, only think, he says I have inspired him too.

Hedda. (*Looks at her with a smile.*) Ah! Does he say that, dear?

Lövborg. And then she is so brave, Mrs. Tesman!

Mrs. Elvsted. Good heavens—am I brave?

Lövborg. Exceedingly—where your comrade is concerned.

Hedda. Ah yes—courage! If one only had that!

Lövborg. What then? What do you mean?

Hedda. Then life would perhaps be liveable, after all. (*With a sudden change of tone.*) But now, my dearest Thea, you really must have a glass of cold punch.

Mrs. Elvsted. No, thanks—I never take anything of that kind.

Hedda. Well then, you, Mr. Lövborg.

Lövborg. Nor I, thank you.

Mrs. Elvsted. No, he doesn't either.

Hedda. (*Looks fixedly at him.*) But if I say you shall?

Lövborg. It would be no use.

Hedda (*laughing*). Then I, poor creature, have no sort of power over you?

Lövborg. Not in that respect.

Hedda. But seriously, I think you ought to—for your own sake.

Mrs. Elvsted. Why, Hedda——!

Lövborg. How so?

Hedda. Or rather on account of other people.

Lövborg. Indeed?

Hedda. Otherwise people might be apt to suspect that —in your heart of hearts—you did not feel quite secure— quite confident in yourself.

Mrs. Elvsted (*softly*). Oh please, Hedda—.

Lövborg. People may suspect what they like—for the present.

Mrs. Elvsted (*joyfully*). Yes, let them!

Hedda. I saw it plainly in Judge Brack's face a moment ago.

Lövborg. What did you see?

Hedda. His contemptuous smile, when you dared not go with them into the inner room.

Lövborg. Dared not? Of course I preferred to stop here and talk to you.

Mrs. Elvsted. What could be more natural, Hedda?

Hedda. But the Judge could not guess that. And I saw, too, the way he smiled and glanced at Tesman when you dared not accept his invitation to this wretched little supper-party of his.

Lövborg. Dared not! Do you say I dared not?

Hedda. *I* don't say so. But that was how Judge Brack understood it.

Lövborg. Well, let him.

Hedda. Then you are not going with them?

Lövborg. I will stay here with you and Thea.

Mrs. Elvsted. Yes, Hedda—how can you doubt that?

Hedda (*smiles and nods approvingly to* Lövborg). Firm as a rock! Faithful to your principles, now and for ever! Ah, that is how a man should be! (*Turns to* Mrs. Elvsted *and caresses her.*) Well now, what did I tell you, when you came to us this morning in such a state of distraction—

Lövborg (*surprised.*) Distraction!

Mrs. Elvsted (*terrified.*) Hedda—oh Hedda——!

Hedda. You can see for yourself; You haven't the slightest reason to be in such mortal terror——(*Interrupting herself.*) There! Now we can all three enjoy ourselves!

Lövborg (*who has given a start.*) Ah—what is all this, Mrs. Tesman?

Mrs. Elvsted. Oh my God, Hedda! What are you saying? What are you doing?

Hedda. Don't get excited! That horrid Judge Brack is sitting watching you.

Lövborg. So she was in mortal terror! On my account!

Mrs. Elvsted (softly and piteously.) Oh, Hedda—now you have ruined everything!

Lövborg. (Looks fixedly at her for a moment. His face is distorted.) So that was my comrade's frank confidence in me?

Mrs. Elvsted (imploringly.) Oh, my dearest friend— only let me tell you—

Lövborg. (Takes one of the glasses of punch, raises it to his lips, and says in a low, husky voice.) Your health, Thea!

(He empties the glass, puts it down, and takes the second.)

Mrs. Elvsted (softly). Oh, Hedda, Hedda—how could you do this?

Hedda. I do it? I? Are you crazy?

Lövborg. Here's to your health too, Mrs. Tesman. Thanks for the truth. Hurrah for the truth!

(He empties the glass and is about to re-fill it.)

Hedda. (Lays her hand on his arm.) Come, come—no more for the present. Remember you are going out to supper.

Mrs. Elvsted. No, no, no!

Hedda. Hush! They are sitting watching you.

Lövborg (putting down the glass.) Now, Thea—tell me the truth—

Mrs. Elvsted. Yes.

Lövborg. Did your husband know that you had come after me?

Mrs. Elvsted (wringing her hands.) Oh, Hedda—do you hear what he is asking?

Lövborg. Was it arranged between you and him that you were to come to town and look after me? Perhaps it was the Sheriff himself that urged you to come? Aha, my dear —no doubt he wanted my help in his office! Or was it at the card-table that he missed me?

Mrs. Elvsted (*softly, in agony*). Oh, Lövborg, Lövborg—!

Lövborg. (*Seizes a glass and is on the point of filling it.*) Here's a glass for the old Sheriff too!

Hedda. (*preventing him.*) No more just now. Remember you have to read your manuscript to Tesman.

Lövborg (*calmly, putting down the glass*). It was stupid of me all this, Thea—to take it in this way, I mean. Don't be angry with me, my dear, dear comrade. You shall see— both you and the others—that if I was fallen once—now I have risen again! Thanks to you, Thea.

Mrs. Elvsted (*radiant with joy*). Oh, heaven be praised—!

(BRACK *has in the meantime looked at his watch. He and* TESMAN *rise and come into the drawing-room.*)

Brack. (*Takes his hat and overcoat.*) Well, Mrs. Tesman, our time has come.

Hedda. I suppose it has.

Lövborg (*rising*). Mine too, Judge Brack.

Mrs. Elvsted (*softly and imploringly*). Oh, Lövborg, don't do it!

Hedda (*pinching her arm*). They can hear you!

Mrs. Elvsted (*with a suppressed shriek*). Ow!

Lövborg (*to* BRACK). You were good enough to invite me.

Brack. Well, are you coming after all?

Lövborg. Yes, many thanks.

Brack. I'm delighted—

Lövborg (*to* TESMAN, *putting the parcel of MS. in his pocket*). I should like to show you one or two things before I send it to the printers.

Tesman. Fancy—that will be delightful. But, Hedda dear, how is Mrs. Elvsted to get home? Eh?

Hedda. Oh, that can be managed somehow.

Lövborg (*looking towards the ladies*). Mrs. Elvsted? Of

course, I'll come again and fetch her. (*Approaching.*) At ten or thereabouts, Mrs. Tesman? Will that do?

Hedda. Certainly. That will do capitally.

Tesman. Well, then, that's all right. But you must not expect me so early, Hedda.

Hedda.—Oh, you may stop as long—as long as ever you please.

Mrs. Elvsted (*trying to conceal her anxiety*). Well then, Mr. Lövborg—I shall remain here until you come.

Lövborg (*with his hat in his hand*). Pray do, Mrs. Elvsted.

Brack. And now off goes the excursion train, gentlemen! I hope we shall have a lively time, as a certain fair lady puts it.

Hedda. Ah, if only the fair lady could be present unseen—!

Brack. Why unseen?

Hedda. In order to hear a little of your liveliness at first hand, Judge Brack.

Brack (*laughing*). I should not advise the fair lady to try it.

Tesman (*also laughing*). Come, you're a nice one Hedda! Fancy that!

Brack. Well, good-bye, good-bye, ladies.

Lövborg (*bowing*). About ten o'clock, then.

(BRACK, LÖVBORG, *and* TESMAN *go out by the hall door. At the same time,* BERTA *enters from the inner room with a lighted lamp, which she places on the dining-room table; she goes out by the way she came.*)

Mrs. Elvsted (*who has risen and is wandering restlessly about the room*). Hedda—Hedda—what will come of all this?

Hedda. At ten o'clock—he will be here. I can see him already—with vine-leaves in his hair—flushed and fearless—

Mrs. Elvsted. Oh, I hope he may.

Hedda. And then, you see—then he will have regained

control over himself. Then he will be a free man for all his days.

Mrs. Elvsted. Oh God!—if he would only come as you see him now!

Hedda. He will come as I see him—so, and not otherwise! (*Rises and approaches* THEA.) You may doubt him as long as you please; *I* believe in him. And now we will try—

Mrs. Elvsted. You have some hidden motive in this, Hedda!

Hedda. Yes, I have. I want for once in my life to have power to mould a human destiny.

Mrs. Elvsted. Have you not the power?

Hedda. I have not—and have never had it.

Mrs. Elvsted. Not your husband's?

Hedda. Do you think that is worth the trouble? Oh, if you could only understand how poor I am. And fate has made you so rich! (*Clasps her passionately in her arms.*) I think I must burn your hair off, after all.

Mrs. Elvsted. Let me go! Let me go! I am afraid of you, Hedda!

Berta (*in the middle doorway*). Tea is laid in the diningroom, ma'am.

Hedda. Very well. We are coming.

Mrs. Elvsted. No, no, no! I would rather go home alone! At once!

Hedda. Nonsense! First you shall have a cup of tea, you little stupid. And then—at ten o'clock—Eilert Lövborg will be here—with vine-leaves in his hair.

(*She drags* MRS. ELVSTED *almost by force towards the middle doorway.*)

ACT III

The room at the TESMANS'. *The curtains are drawn over the middle doorway, and also over the glass door. The lamp, half turned down, and with a shade over it, is burning on the table. In the stove, the door of which stands open, there has been a fire, which is now nearly burnt out.*

MRS. ELVSTED, *wrapped in a large shawl, and with her feet upon a foot-rest, sits close to the stove, sunk back in the arm-chair.* HEDDA, *fully dressed, lies sleeping upon the sofa, with a sofa-blanket over her.*

Mrs. Elvsted (after a pause, suddenly sits up in her chair, and listens eagerly. Then she sinks back again wearily, moaning to herself). `Not yet!—Oh God—oh God—not yet!

BERTA *slips cautiously in by the hall door. She has a letter in her hand.*

Mrs. Elvsted. (Turns and whispers eagerly.) Well—has any one come?

Berta (softly). Yes, a girl has brought this letter.

Mrs. Elvsted (quickly, holding out her hand). A letter! Give it to me!

Berta. No, it's for Dr. Tesman, ma'am.

Mrs. Elvsted. Oh, indeed.

Berta. It was Miss Tesman's servant that brought it. I'll lay it here on the table.

Mrs. Elvsted. Yes, do.

Berta (laying down the letter). I think I had better put out the lamp. It's smoking.

Mrs. Elvsted. Yes, put it out. It must soon be daylight now.

Berta (*putting out the lamp*). It is daylight already, ma'am.

Mrs. Elvsted. Yes, broad day! And no one come back yet—!

Berta. Lord bless you, ma'am—I guessed how it would be.

Mrs. Elvsted. You guessed?

Berta. Yes, when I saw that a certain person had come back to town—and that he went off with them. For we've heard enough about that gentleman before now.

Mrs. Elvsted. Don't speak so loud. You will waken Mrs. Tesman.

Berta (*looks towards the sofa and sighs*). No, no—let her sleep, poor thing. Shan't I put some wood on the fire?

Mrs. Elvsted. Thanks, not for me.

Berta. Oh, very well. (*She goes softly out by the hall door.*)

Hedda (*is awakened by the shutting of the door, and looks up*). What's that—?

Mrs. Elvsted. It was only the servant—

Hedda (*looking about her*). Oh, we're here—! Yes, now I remember. (*Sits erect upon the sofa, stretches herself, and rubs her eyes.*) What o'clock is it, Thea?

Mrs. Elvsted. (*Looks at her watch.*) It's past seven.

Hedda. When did Tesman come home?

Mrs. Elvsted. He has not come.

Hedda. Not come home yet?

Mrs. Elvsted (*rising*). No one has come.

Hedda. Think of our watching and waiting here till four in the morning—

Mrs. Elvsted (*wringing her hands*). And how I watched and waited for him!

Hedda. (*Yawns, and says with her hand before her*

mouth.) Well well—we might have spared ourselves the trouble.

Mrs. Elvsted. Did you get a little sleep?

Hedda. Oh yes; I believe I have slept pretty well. Have you not?

Mrs. Elvsted. Not for a moment. I couldn't, Hedda!—not to save my life.

Hedda. (*Rises and goes towards her.*) There there there! There's nothing to be so alarmed about. I understand quite well what has happened.

Mrs. Elvsted. Well, what do you think? Won't you tell me?

Hedda. Why, of course it has been a very late affair at Judge Brack's—

Mrs. Elvsted. Yes, yes, that is clear enough. But all the same—

Hedda. And then, you see, Tesman hasn't cared to come home and ring us up in the middle of the night. (*Laughing.*) Perhaps he wasn't inclined to show himself either—immediately after a jollification.

Mrs. Elvsted. But in that case—where can he have gone?

Hedda. Of course he has gone to his aunts' and slept there. They have his old room ready for him.

Mrs. Elvsted. No, he can't be with them; for a letter has just come for him from Miss Tesman. There it lies.

Hedda. Indeed? (*Looks at the address.*) Why yes, it's addressed in Aunt Julia's own hand. Well then, he has remained at Judge Brack's. And as for Eilert Lövborg—he is sitting, with vine leaves in his hair, reading his manuscript.

Mrs. Elvsted. Oh Hedda, you are just saying things you don't believe a bit.

Hedda. You really are a little blockhead, Thea.

Mrs. Elvsted. Oh yes, I suppose I am.

Hedda. And how mortally tired you look.

Mrs. Elvsted. Yes, I am mortally tired.

Hedda. Well then, you must do as I tell you. You must go into my room and lie down for a little while.

Mrs. Elvsted. Oh no, no—I shouldn't be able to sleep.

Hedda. I am sure you would.

Mrs. Elvsted. Well, but your husband is certain to come soon now; and then I want to know at once—

Hedda. I shall take care to let you know when he comes.

Mrs. Elvsted. Do you promise me, Hedda?

Hedda. Yes, rely upon me. Just you go in and have a sleep in the meantime.

Mrs. Elvsted. Thanks; then I'll try to. (*She goes off through the inner room.*)

(HEDDA *goes up to the glass door and draws back the curtains. The broad daylight streams into the room. Then she takes a little hand-glass from the writing-table looks at herself in it, and arranges her hair. Next she goes to the hall door and presses the bell-button.*)

BERTA *presently appears at the hall door.*

Berta. Did you want anything, ma'am?

Hedda. Yes; you must put some more wood in the stove. I am shivering.

Berta. Bless me—I'll make up the fire at once. (*She rakes the embers together and lays a piece of wood upon them; then stops and listens.*) That was a ring at the front door, ma'am.

Hedda. Then go to the door. I will look after the fire.

Berta. It'll soon burn up. (*She goes out by the hall door.*)

(HEDDA *kneels on the foot-rest and lays some more pieces of wood in the stove.*)

After a short pause, GEORGE TESMAN *enters from the hall. He looks tired and rather serious. He steals on tiptoe towards the middle doorway and is about to slip through the curtains.*

Hedda. (*At the stove, without looking up.*) Good morning.

Tesman. (*Turns.*) Hedda! (*Approaching her.*) Good heavens—are you up so early? Eh?

Hedda. Yes, I am up very early this morning.

Tesman. And I never doubted you were still sound asleep! Fancy that, Hedda!

Hedda. Don't speak so loud. Mrs. Elvsted is resting in my room.

Tesman. Has Mrs. Elvsted been here all night?

Hedda. Yes, since no one came to fetch her.

Tesman. Ah, to be sure.

Hedda. (*Closes the door of the stove and rises.*) Well, did you enjoy yourselves at Judge Brack's?

Tesman. Have you been anxious about me? Eh?

Hedda. No, I should never think of being anxious. But I asked if you had enjoyed yourself.

Tesman. Oh yes,—for once in a way. Especially the beginning of the evening; for then Eilert read me part of his book. We arrived more than an hour too early—fancy that! And Brack had all sorts of arrangements to make—so Eilert read to me.

Hedda (*seating herself by the table on the right*). Well? Tell me, then—

Tesman (*sitting on a footstool near the stove.*) Oh Hedda, you can't conceive what a book that is going to be! I believe it is one of the most remarkable things that have ever been written. Fancy that!

Hedda. Yes, yes; I don't care about that——

Tesman. I must make a confession to you, Hedda. When he had finished reading—a horrid feeling came over me.

Hedda. A horrid feeling?

Tesman. I felt jealous of Eilert for having had it in him to write such a book. Only think, Hedda!

Hedda. Yes, yes, I am thinking!

Tesman. And then how pitiful to think that he—with all his gifts—should be irreclaimable, after all.

Hedda. I suppose you mean that he has more courage than the rest?

Tesman. No, not at all—I mean that he is incapable of taking his pleasures in moderation.

Hedda. And what came of it all—in the end?

Tesman. Well, to tell the truth, I think it might best be described as an orgie, Hedda.

Hedda. Had he vine-leaves in his hair?

Tesman. Vine-leaves? No, I saw nothing of the sort. But he made a long, rambling speech in honour of the woman who had inspired him in his work—that was the phrase he used.

Hedda. Did he name her?

Tesman. No, he didn't; but I can't help thinking he meant Mrs. Elvsted. You may be sure he did.

Hedda. Well—where did you part from him?

Tesman. On the way to town. We broke up—the last of us at any rate—all together; and Brack came with us to get a breath of fresh air. And then, you see, we agreed to take Eilert home; for he had had far more than was good for him.

Hedda. I daresay.

Tesman. But now comes the strange part of it, Hedda; or, I should rather say, the melancholy part of it. I declare I am almost ashamed—on Eilert's account—to tell you—

Hedda. Oh, go on—

Tesman. Well, as we were getting near town, you see, I happened to drop a little behind the others. Only for a minute or two—fancy that!

Hedda. Yes, yes, yes, but——?

Tesman. And then, as I hurried after them—what do you think I found by the wayside? Eh?

Hedda. Oh, how should I know!

Tesman. You mustn't speak of it to a soul, Hedda! Do

you hear! Promise me, for Eilert's sake. (*Draws a parcel, wrapped in paper, from his coat pocket.*) Fancy, dear—I found this.

Hedda. Is not that the parcel he had with him yesterday?

Tesman. Yes, it is the whole of his precious, irreplaceable manuscript! And he had gone and lost it, and knew nothing about it. Only fancy, Hedda! So deplorably—

Hedda. But why did you not give him back the parcel at once?

Tesman. I didn't dare to—in the state he was then in—

Hedda. Did you not tell any of the others that you had found it?

Tesman. Oh, far from it! You can surely understand that, for Eilert's sake, I wouldn't do that.

Hedda. So no one knows that Eilert Lövborg's manuscript is in your possession?

Tesman. No. And no one must know it.

Hedda. Then what did you say to him afterwards?

Tesman. I didn't talk to him again at all; for when we got in among the streets, he and two or three of the others gave us the slip and disappeared. Fancy that!

Hedda. Indeed! They must have taken him home then.

Tesman. Yes, so it would appear. And Brack, too, left us.

Hedda. And what have you been doing with yourself since?

Tesman. Well, I and some of the others went home with one of the party, a jolly fellow, and took our morning coffee with him; or perhaps I should rather call it our night coffee —eh? But now, when I have rested a little, and given Eilert, poor fellow, time to have his sleep out, I must take this back to him.

Hedda. (*Holds out her hand for the packet.*) No—don't give it to him! Not in such a hurry, I mean. Let me read it first.

Tesman. No, my dearest Hedda, I mustn't, I really mustn't.

Hedda. You must not?

Tesman. No—for you can imagine what a state of despair he will be in when he awakens and misses the manuscript. He has no copy of it, you must know! He told me so.

Hedda (*looking searchingly at him*). Can such a thing not be reproduced? Written over again?

Tesman. No, I don't think that would be possible. For the inspiration, you see—

Hedda. Yes, yes—I suppose it depends on that. (*Lightly.*) But, by-the-bye—here is a letter for you.

Tesman. Fancy——!

Hedda (*handing it to him*). It came early this morning.

Tesman. It's from Aunt Julia! What can it be? (*He lays the packet on the other footstool, opens the letter, runs his eye through it, and jumps up.*) Oh, Hedda—she says that poor Aunt Rina is dying!

Hedda. Well, we were prepared for that.

Tesman. And that if I want to see her again, I must make haste. I'll run in to them at once.

Hedda (*suppressing a smile.*) Will you run?

Tesman. Oh, dearest Hedda—if you could only make up your mind to come with me! Just think!

Hedda. (*Rises and says wearily, repelling the idea.*) No, no, don't ask me. I will not look upon sickness and death. I loathe all sorts of ugliness.

Tesman. Well, well, then—! (*Bustling around.*) My hat— My overcoat—? Oh, in the hall— I do hope I mayn't come too late, Hedda! Eh?

Hedda. Oh, if you run—

(BERTA *appears at the hall door.*)

Berta. Judge Brack is at the door, and wishes to know if he may come in.

Tesman. At this time! No, I can't possibly see him.

Hedda. But I can. (*To* BERTA.) Ask Judge Brack to come in. (BERTA *goes out.*)

Hedda (*quickly, whispering.*) The parcel, Tesman! (*She snatches it up from the stool.*)

Tesman. Yes, give it to me!

Hedda. No, no, I will keep it till you come back.

(*She goes to the writing-table and places it in the book-case.* TESMAN *stands in a flurry of haste, and cannot get his gloves on.*)

JUDGE BRACK *enters from the hall.*

Hedda (*nodding to him*). You are an early bird, I must say.

Brack. Yes, don't you think so? (*To* TESMAN.) Are you on the move, too?

Tesman. Yes, I must rush off to my aunts'. Fancy— the invalid one is lying at death's door, poor creature.

Brack. Dear me, is she indeed? Then on no account let me detain you. At such a critical moment—

Tesman. Yes, I must really rush— Good-bye! Good-bye! (*He hastens out by the hall door.*)

Hedda (*approaching*). You seem to have made a particularly lively night of it at your rooms, Judge Brack.

Brack. I assure you I have not had my clothes off, Mrs. Hedda.

Hedda. Not you, either?

Brack. No, as you may see. But what has Tesman been telling you of the night's adventures?

Hedda. Oh, some tiresome story. Only that they went and had coffee somewhere or other.

Brack. I have heard about that coffee-party already. Eilert Lövborg was not with them, I fancy?

Hedda. No, they had taken him home before that.

Brack. Tesman too?

Hedda. No, but some of the others, he said.

Brack (*smiling*). George Tesman is really an ingenuous creature, Mrs. Hedda.

Hedda. Yes, heaven knows he is. Then is there some-thing behind all this?

Brack. Yes, perhaps there may be.

Hedda. Well then, sit down, my dear Judge, and tell your story in comfort.

(*She seats herself to the left of the table.* BRACK *sits near her, at the long side of the table.*)

Hedda. Now then?

Brack. I had special reasons for keeping track of my guests—or rather of some of my guests—last night.

Hedda. Of Eilert Lövborg among the rest, perhaps?

Brack. Frankly, yes.

Hedda. Now you make me really curious—

Brack. Do you know where he and one or two of the others finished the night, Mrs. Hedda?

Hedda. If it is not quite unmentionable, tell me.

Brack. Oh no, it's not at all unmentionable. Well, they put in an appearance at a particularly animated soirée.

Hedda. Of the lively kind?

Brack. Of the very liveliest—

Hedda. Tell me more of this, Judge Brack—

Brack. Lövborg, as well as the others, had been invited in advance. I knew all about it. But he had declined the invitation; for now, as you know, he has become a new man.

Hedda. Up at the Elvsteds', yes. But he went after all, then?

Brack. Well, you see, Mrs. Hedda—unhappily the spirit moved him at my rooms last evening—

Hedda. Yes, I hear he found inspiration.

Brack. Pretty violent inspiration. Well, I fancy that altered his purpose; for we men folk are unfortunately not always so firm in our principles as we ought to be.

Hedda. Oh, I am sure you are an exception, Judge Brack. But as to Lövborg—?

Brack. To make a long story short—he landed at last in Mademoiselle Diana's rooms.

Hedda. Mademoiselle Diana's?

Brack. It was Mademoiselle Diana that was giving the soirée, to a select circle of her admirers and her lady friends.

Hedda. Is she a red-haired woman?

Brack. Precisely.

Hedda. A sort of a—singer?

Brack. Oh yes—in her leisure moments. And moreover a mighty huntress—of men—Mrs. Hedda. You have no doubt heard of her. Eilert Lövborg was one of her most enthusiastic protectors—in the days of his glory.

Hedda. And how did all this end?

Brack. Far from amicably, it appears. After a most tender meeting, they seem to have come to blows—

Hedda. Lövborg and she?

Brack. Yes. He accused her or her friends of having robbed him. He declared that his pocket-book had disappeared—and other things as well. In short, he seems to have made a furious disturbance.

Hedda. And what came of it all?

Brack. It came to a general scrimmage, in which the ladies as well as the gentlemen took part. Fortunately the police at last appeared on the scene.

Hedda. The police too?

Brack. Yes. I fancy it will prove a costly frolic for Eilert Lövborg, crazy being that he is.

Hedda. How so?

Brack. He seems to have made a violent resistance—to have hit one of the constables on the head and torn the coat off his back. So they had to march him off to the police-station with the rest.

Hedda. How have you learnt all this?

Brack. From the police themselves.

Hedda (*gazing straight before her*). So that is what happened. Then he had no vine-leaves in his hair.

Brack. Vine-leaves, Mrs. Hedda?

Hedda (*changing her tone*). But tell me now, Judge—

what is your real reason for tracking out Eilert Lövborg's movements so carefully?

Brack. In the first place, it could not be entirely indifferent to me if it should appear in the police-court that he came straight from my house.

Hedda. Will the matter come into court then?

Brack. Of course. However, I should scarcely have troubled so much about that. But I thought that, as a friend of the family, it was my duty to supply you and Tesman with a full account of his nocturnal exploits.

Hedda. Why so, Judge Brack?

Brack. Why, because I have a shrewd suspicion that he intends to use you as a sort of blind.

Hedda. Oh, how can you think such a thing!

Brack. Good heavens, Mrs. Hedda—we have eyes in our head. Mark my words! This Mrs. Elvsted will be in no hurry to leave town again.

Hedda. Well, even if there should be anything between them, I suppose there are plenty of other places where they could meet.

Brack. Not a single home. Henceforth, as before, every respectable house will be closed against Eilert Lövborg.

Hedda. And so ought mine to be, you mean?

Brack. Yes. I confess it would be more than painful to me if this personage were to be made free of your house. How superfluous, how intrusive, he would be, if he were to force his way into—

Hedda. —into the triangle?

Brack. Precisely. It would simply mean that I should find myself homeless.

Hedda. (*Looks at him with a smile.*) So you want to be the one cock in the basket*—that is your aim.

Brack (*nods slowly and lowers his voice.*) Yes, that

---

* "Eneste hane i kurven"—a proverbial saying.

is my aim. And for that I will fight—with every weapon I can command.

Hedda (*her smile vanishing*). I see you are a dangerous person—when it comes to the point.

Brack. Do you think so?

Hedda. I am beginning to think so. And I am exceedingly glad to think—that you have no sort of hold over me.

Brack (*laughing equivocally*). Well, well, Mrs. Hedda—perhaps you are right there. If I had, who knows what I might be capable of?

Hedda. Come, come now, Judge Brack! That sounds almost like a threat.

Brack (*rising*). Oh, not at all! The triangle, you know, ought, if possible, to be spontaneously constructed.

Hedda. There I agree with you.

Brack. Well, now I have said all I had to say; and I had better be getting back to town. Good-bye, Mrs. Hedda. (*He goes towards the glass door.*)

Hedda (*rising*). Are you going through the garden?

Brack. Yes, it's a short cut for me.

Hedda. And then it is a back way, too.

Brack. Quite so. I have no objection to back ways. They may be piquant enough at times.

Hedda. When there is ball practice going on, you mean?

Brack (*in the doorway, laughing to her*). Oh, people don't shoot their tame poultry, I fancy.

Hedda (*also laughing*). Oh no, when there is only one cock in the basket—

(*They exchange laughing nods of farewell. He goes. She closes the door behind him.*)

(*HEDDA, who has become quite serious, stands for a moment looking out. Presently she goes and peeps through the curtain over the middle doorway. Then she goes to the writing-table, takes LÖVBORG's packet out of the bookcase, and is on the point of looking through its contents. BERTA is heard speaking loudly in the hall.*

HEDDA *turns and listens. Then she hastily locks up the packet in the drawer, and lays the key on the inkstand.*
EILERT LÖVBORG, *with his greatcoat on and his hat in his hand, tears open the hall door. He looks somewhat confused and irritated.*

Lövborg (looking towards the hall). And I tell you I must and will come in! There!

(*He closes the door, turns, sees* HEDDA, *at once regains his self-control, and bows.*)

Hedda (at the writing-table). Well, Mr. Lövborg, this is rather a late hour to call for Thea.

Lövborg. You mean rather an early hour to call on you. Pray pardon me.

Hedda. How do you know that she is still here?

Lövborg. They told me at her lodgings that she had been out all night.

Hedda (going to the oval table). Did you notice anything about the people of the house when they said that?

Lövborg. (Looks inquiringly at her). Notice anything about them?

Hedda. I mean, did they seem to think it odd?

Lövborg (suddenly understanding). Oh yes, of course! I am dragging her down with me! However, I didn't notice anything.—I suppose Tesman is not up yet?

Hedda. No—I think not—

Lövborg. When did he come home?

Hedda. Very late.

Lövborg. Did he tell you anything?

Hedda. Yes, I gathered that you had had an exceedingly jolly evening at Judge Brack's.

Lövborg. Nothing more?

Hedda. I don't think so. However, I was so dreadfully sleepy—

MRS. ELVSTED *enters through the curtains of the middle doorway.*)

Mrs. Elvsted (*going towards him*). Ah, Lövborg! At last——!

Lövborg. Yes, at last. And too late!

Mrs. Elvsted. (*Looks anxiously at him*). What is too late?

Lövborg. Everything is too late now. It is all over with me.

Mrs. Elvsted. Oh no, no—don't say that!

Lövborg. You will say the same when you hear—

Mrs. Elvsted. I won't hear anything!

Hedda. Perhaps you would prefer to talk to her alone! If so, I will leave you.

Lövborg. No, stay—you too. I beg you to stay.

Mrs. Elvsted. Yes, but I won't hear anything, I tell you.

Lövborg. It is not last night's adventures that I want to talk about.

Mrs. Elvsted. What is it then—?

Lövborg. I want to say that now our ways must part.

Mrs. Elvsted. Part!

Hedda (*involuntarily*). I knew it!

Lövborg. You can be of no more service to me, Thea.

Mrs. Elvsted. How can you stand there and say that! No more service to you! Am I not to help you now, as before? Are we not to go on working together?

Lövborg. Henceforward I shall do no work.

Mrs. Elvsted (*despairingly*). Then what am I to do with my life?

Lövborg. You must try to live your life as if you had never known me.

Mrs. Elvsted. But you know I cannot do that!

Lövborg. Try if you cannot, Thea. You must go home again—

Mrs. Elvsted (*in vehement protest*). Never in this world! Where you are, there will I be also! I will not let myself be driven away like this! I will remain here! I will be with you when the book appears.

Hedda (*half aloud, in suspense*). Ah yes—the book!

Lövborg. (*Looks at her.*) My book and Thea's; for that is what it is.

Mrs. Elvsted. Yes, I feel that it is. And that is why I have a right to be with you when it appears! I will see with my own eyes how respect and honour pour in upon you afresh. And the happiness—the happiness—oh, I must share it with you!

Lövborg. Thea—our book will never appear.

Hedda. Ah!

Mrs. Elvsted. Never appear!

Lövborg. Can never appear.

Mrs. Elvsted (*in agonised foreboding*). Lövborg—what have you done with the manuscript?

Hedda. (*Looks anxiously at him*). Yes, the manuscript—?

Mrs. Elvsted. Where is it?

Lövborg. Oh Thea—don't ask me about it!

Mrs. Elvsted. Yes, yes, I will know. I demand to be told at once.

Lövborg. The manuscript— Well then—I have torn the manuscript into a thousand pieces.

Mrs. Elvsted. (*Shrieks*). Oh no, no—!

Hedda (*involuntarily*). But that's not—

Lövborg. (*Looks at her*). Not true, you think?

Hedda (*collecting herself*). Oh well, of course—since you say so. But it sounded so improbable—

Lövborg. It is true, all the same.

Mrs. Elvsted (*wringing her hands*). Oh God—oh God, Hedda—torn his own work to pieces!

Lövborg. I have torn my own life to pieces. So why should I not tear my life-work too—?

Mrs. Elvsted. And you did this last night?

Lövborg. Yes, I tell you! Tore it into a thousand pieces and scattered them on the fiord—far out. There there is cool sea-water at any rate—let them drift upon it—drift with the current and the wind. And then presently they will sink—deeper and deeper—as I shall, Thea.

Mrs. Elvsted. Do you know, Lövborg, that what you have done with the book—I shall think of it to my dying day as though you had killed a little child.

Lövborg. Yes, you are right. It is a sort of child-murder.

Mrs. Elvsted. How could you, then—! Did not the child belong to me too?

Hedda (*almost inaudibly*). Ah, the child—

Mrs. Elvsted (*breathing heavily*). It is all over then. Well, well, now I will go, Hedda.

Hedda. But you are not going away from town?

Mrs. Elvsted. Oh, I don't know what I shall do. I see nothing but darkness before me. (*She goes out by the hall door.*)

Hedda. (*Stands waiting for a moment*). So you are not going to see her home, Mr. Lövborg?

Lövborg. I? Through the streets? Would you have people see her walking with me?

Hedda. Of course I don't know what else may have happened last night. But is it so utterly irretrievable?

Lövborg. It will not end with last night—I know that perfectly well. And the thing is that now I have no taste for that sort of life either. I won't begin it anew. She has broken my courage and my power of braving life out.

Hedda (*looking straight before her*). So that pretty little fool has had her fingers in a man's destiny. (*Looks at him.*) But all the same, how could you treat her so heartlessly.

Lövborg. Oh, don't say that it was heartless!

Hedda. To go and destroy what has filled her whole soul for months and years! You do not call that heartless!

Lövborg. To you I can tell the truth, Hedda.

Hedda. The truth?

Lövborg. First promise me—give me your word—that what I now confide to you Thea shall never know.

Hedda. I give you my word.

Lövborg. Good. Then let me tell you that what I said just now was untrue.

Hedda. About the manuscript?

Lövborg. Yes. I have not torn it to pieces—nor thrown it into the fiord.

Hedda. No, n— But—where is it then?

Lövborg. I have destroyed it none the less—utterly destroyed it, Hedda!

Hedda. I don't understand.

Lövborg. Thea said that what I had done seemed to her like a child-murder.

Hedda. Yes, so she said.

Lövborg. But to kill this child—that is not the worst thing a father can do to it.

Hedda. Not the worst?

Lövborg. No. I wanted to spare Thea from hearing the worst?

Hedda. Then what is the worst?

Lövborg. Suppose now, Hedda, that a man—in the small hours of the morning—came home to his child's mother after a night of riot and debauchery, and said: "Listen—I have been here and there—in this place and in that. And I have taken our child with me—to this place and to that. And I have lost the child—utterly lost it. The devil knows into what hands it may have fallen—who may have had their clutches on it."

Hedda. Well—but when all is said and done, you know —this was only a book—

Lövborg. Thea's pure soul was in that book.

Hedda. Yes, so I understand.

Lövborg. And you can understand, too, that for her and me together no future is possible.

Hedda. What path do you mean to take then?

Lövborg. None. I will only try to make an end of it all —the sooner the better.

Hedda (*a step nearer him*). Eilert Lövborg—listen to me.—Will you not try to—to do it beautifully?

Lövborg. Beautifully? (*Smiling*). With vine-leaves in my hair, as you used to dream in the old days—?

Hedda. No, no. I have lost my faith in the vine-leaves. But beautifully nevertheless! For once in a way!—Good-bye! You must go now—and do not come here any more.

Lövborg. Good-bye, Mrs. Tesman. And give George Tesman my love. (*He is on the point of going.*)

Hedda. No, wait! I must give you a memento to take with you.

(*She goes to the writing-table and opens the drawer and the pistol-case; then returns to* LÖVBORG *with one of the pistols.*)

Lövborg (*looks at her*). This? Is this the memento?

Hedda (*nodding slowly*). Do you recognise it? It was aimed at you once.

Lövborg. You should have used it then.

Hedda. Take it—and do you use it now.

Lövborg (*puts the pistol in his breast pocket*). Thanks!

Hedda. And beautifully, Eilert Lövborg. Promise me that!

Lövborg. Good-bye, Hedda Gabler. (*He goes out by the hall door.*)

(HEDDA *listens for a moment at the door. Then she goes up to the writing-table, takes out the packet of manuscript, peeps under the cover, draws a few of the sheets half out, and looks at them. Next she goes over and seats herself in the arm-chair beside the stove, with the packet in her lap. Presently she opens the stove door, and then the packet.*)

Hedda (*throws one of the quires into the fire and whispers to herself*). Now I am burning your child, Thea!—Burning it, curly-locks! (*Throwing one or two more quires into the stove.*) Your child and Eilert Lövborg's. (*Throws the rest in.*) I am burning—I am burning your child.

ACT IV

The same rooms at the TESMANS'. *It is evening. The drawing-room is in darkness. The back room is lighted by the hanging lamp over the table. The curtains over the glass door are drawn close.*

HEDDA, *dressed in black, walks to and fro in the dark room. Then she goes into the back room and disappears for a moment to the left. She is heard to strike a few chords on the piano. Presently she comes in sight again, and returns to the drawing-room.*

BERTA *enters from the right, through the inner room, with a lighted lamp, which she places on the table in front of the corner settee in the drawing-room. Her eyes are red with weeping, and she has black ribbons in her cap. She goes quietly and circumspectly out to the right.*

HEDDA *goes up to the glass door, lifts the curtain a little aside, and looks out into the darkness.*

Shortly afterwards, MISS TESMAN, *in mourning, with a bonnet and veil on, comes in from the hall.* HEDDA *goes towards her and holds out her hand.*

Miss Tesman. Yes, Hedda, here I am, in mourning and forlorn; for now my poor sister has at last found peace.

Hedda. I have heard the news already, as you see. Tesman sent me a card.

Miss Tesman. Yes, he promised me he would. But nevertheless I thought that to Hedda—here in the house of life—I ought myself to bring the tidings of death.

Hedda. That was very kind of you.

288

Miss Tesman. Ah, Rina ought not to have left us just now. This is not the time for Hedda's house to be a house of mourning.

Hedda (*changing the subject*). She died quite peacefully, did she not, Miss Tesman?

Miss Tesman. Oh, her end was so calm, so beautiful. And then she had the unspeakable happiness of seeing George once more—and bidding him good-bye.—Has he come home yet?

Hedda. No. He wrote that he might be detained. But won't you sit down?

Miss Tesman. No thank you, my dear, dear Hedda. I should like to, but I have so much to do. I must prepare my dear one for her rest as well as I can. She shall go to her grave looking her best.

Hedda. Can I not help you in any way?

Miss Tesman. Oh, you must not think of it! Hedda Tesman must have no hand in such mournful work. Nor let her thoughts dwell on it either—not at this time.

Hedda. One is not always mistress of one's thoughts——

Miss Tesman (*continuing*). Ah yes, it is the way of the world. At home we shall be sewing a shroud; and here there will soon be sewing too, I suppose—but of another sort, thank God!

GEORGE TESMAN *enters by the hall door.*

Hedda. Ah, you have come at last!

Tesman. You here, Aunt Julia? With Hedda? Fancy that!

Miss Tesman. I was just going, my dear boy. Well, have you done all you promised?

Tesman. No; I'm really afraid I have forgotten half of it. I must come to you again to-morrow. To-day my brain is all in a whirl. I can't keep my thoughts together.

Miss Tesman. Why, my dear George, you mustn't take it in this way.

Tesman. Mustn't——? How do you mean?

Miss Tesman. Even in your sorrow you must rejoice, as I do—rejoice that she is at rest.

Tesman. Oh yes, yes—you are thinking of Aunt Rina.

Hedda. You will feel lonely now, Miss Tesman.

Miss Tesman. Just at first, yes. But that will not last very long, I hope. I daresay I shall soon find an occupant for poor Rina's little room.

Tesman. Indeed? Who do you think will take it? Eh?

Miss Tesman. Oh, there's always some poor invalid or other in want of nursing, unfortunately.

Hedda. Would you really take such a burden upon you again?

Miss Tesman. A burden! Heaven forgive you, child— it has been no burden to me.

Hedda. But suppose you had a total stranger on your hands——

Miss Tesman. Oh, one soon makes friends with sick folk; and it's such an absolute necessity for me to have some one to live for. Well, heaven be praised, there may soon be something in this house, too, to keep an old aunt busy.

Hedda. Oh, don't trouble about anything here.

Tesman. Yes, just fancy what a nice time we three might have together, if——?

Hedda. If——?

Tesman (uneasily). Oh, nothing. It will all come right. Let us hope so—eh?

Miss Tesman. Well, well, I daresay you two want to talk to each other. (*Smiling.*) And perhaps Hedda may have something to tell you too, George. Good-bye! I must go home to Rina. (*Turning at the door.*) How strange it is to think that now Rina is with me and with my poor brother as well!

Tesman. Yes, fancy that, Aunt Julia! Eh? (Miss Tesman *goes out by the hall door.*)

Hedda (follows Tesman *coldly and searchingly with her*

eyes). I almost believe your Aunt Rina's death affects you more than it does your Aunt Julia.

Tesman. Oh, it's not that alone. It's Eilert I am so terribly uneasy about.

Hedda (*quickly*). Is there anything new about him?

Tesman. I looked in at his rooms this afternoon, intending to tell him the manuscript was in safe keeping.

Hedda. Well, did you not find him?

Tesman. No. He wasn't at home. But afterwards I met Mrs. Elvsted, and she told me that he had been here early this morning.

Hedda. Yes, directly after you had gone.

Tesman. And he said that he had torn his manuscript to pieces—eh?

Hedda. Yes, so he declared.

Tesman. Why, good heavens, he must have been completely out of his mind! And I suppose you thought it best not to give it back to him, Hedda?

Hedda. No, he did not get it.

Tesman. But of course you told him that we had it?

Hedda. No. (*Quickly.*) Did you tell Mrs. Elvsted?

Tesman. No; I thought I had better not. But you ought to have told him. Fancy, if, in desperation, he should go and do himself some injury! Let me have the manuscript, Hedda! I will take it to him at once. Where is it?

Hedda (*cold and immovable, leaning on the arm-chair*). I have not got it.

Tesman. Have not got it? What in the world do you mean?

Hedda. I have burnt it—every line of it.

Tesman (*with a violent movement of terror*). Burnt! Burnt Eilert's manuscript!

Hedda. Don't scream so. The servant might hear you.

Tesman. Burnt! Why, good God——! No, no, no! It's impossible!

Hedda. It is so, nevertheless.

Tesman. Do you know what you have done, Hedda? It's unlawful appropriation of lost property. Fancy that! Just ask Judge Brack, and he'll tell you what it is.

Hedda. I advise you not to speak of it—either to Judge Brack, or to any one else.

Tesman. But how could you do anything so unheard-of? What put it into your head? What possessed you? Answer me that—eh?

Hedda (*suppressing an almost imperceptible smile*). I did it for your sake, George.

Tesman. For my sake!

Hedda. This morning, when you told me about what he had read to you——

Tesman. Yes, yes—what then?

Hedda. You acknowledged that you envied him his work.

Tesman. Oh, of course I didn't mean that literally.

Hedda. No matter—I could not bear the idea that any one should throw you into the shade.

Tesman (*in an outburst of mingled doubt and joy*). Hedda! Oh, is this true? But—but—I never knew you to show your love like that before. Fancy that!

Hedda. Well, I may as well tell you that—just at this time—— (*Impatiently, breaking off.*) No, no; you can ask Aunt Julia. She will tell you, fast enough.

Tesman. Oh, I almost think I understand you, Hedda! (*Clasps his hands together.*) Great heavens! do you really mean it! Eh?

Hedda. Don't shout so. The servant might hear.

Tesman (*laughing in irrepressible glee.*) The servant! Why, how absurd you are, Hedda. It's only my old Berta! Why, I'll tell Berta myself.

Hedda (*clenching her hands together in desperation*). Oh, it is killing me,—it is killing me, all this!

Tesman. What is, Hedda? Eh?

Hedda (*coldly, controlling herself*). All this—absurdity —George.

HEDDA GABLER   293

Tesman. Absurdity! Do you see anything absurd in my being overjoyed at the news! But after all—perhaps I had better not say anything to Berta.

Hedda. Oh—why not that too?

Tesman. No, no, not yet! But I must certainly tell Aunt Julia. And then that you have begun to call me George too! Fancy that! Oh, Aunt Julia will be so happy —so happy!

Hedda. When she hears that I have burnt Eilert Löv-borg's manuscript—for your sake?

Tesman. No, by-the-bye—that affair of the manuscript —of course nobody must know about that. But that you love me so much,* Hedda—Aunt Julia must really share my joy in that! I wonder, now, whether this sort of thing is usual in young wives? Eh?

Hedda. I think you had better ask Aunt Julia that question too.

Tesman. I will indeed, some time or other. (*Looks uneasy and downcast again.*) And yet the manuscript— the manuscript! Good God! it is terrible to think what will become of poor Eilert now.

MRS. ELVSTED, *dressed as in the first Act, with hat and cloak, enters by the hall door.*

Mrs. Elvsted (*greets them hurriedly, and says in evident agitation*). Oh, dear Hedda, forgive my coming again.

Hedda. What is the matter with you, Thea?

Tesman. Something about Eilert Lövborg again—eh?

Mrs. Elvsted. Yes! I am dreadfully afraid some misfortune has happened to him.

Hedda (*seizes her arm*). Ah,—do you think so?

Tesman. Why, good Lord—what makes you think that, Mrs. Elvsted?

Mrs. Elvsted. I heard them talking of him at my board-

---

* Literally, "That you burn for me"

ing-house—just as I came in. Oh, the most incredible rumours are afloat about him to-day.

Tesman. Yes, fancy, so I heard too! And I can bear witness that he went straight home to bed last night. Fancy that!

Hedda. Well, what did they say at the boarding-house?

Mrs. Elvsted. Oh, I couldn't make out anything clearly. Either they knew nothing definite, or else—— They stopped talking when they saw me; and I did not dare to ask.

Tesman (*moving about uneasily*). We must hope—we must hope that you misunderstood them, Mrs. Elvsted.

Mrs. Elvsted. No, no; I am sure it was of him they were talking. And I heard something about the hospital or——

Tesman. The hospital?

Hedda. No—surely that cannot be!

Mrs. Elvsted. Oh, I was in such mortal terror! I went to his lodgings and asked for him there.

Hedda. You could make up your mind to that, Thea!

Mrs. Elvsted. What else could I do? I really could bear the suspense no longer.

Tesman. But you didn't find him either—eh?

Mrs. Elvsted. No. And the people knew nothing about him. He hadn't been home since yesterday afternoon, they said.

Tesman. Yesterday! Fancy, how could they say that?

Mrs. Elvsted. Oh, I am sure something terrible must have happened to him.

Tesman. Hedda dear—how would it be if I were to go and make inquiries——?

Hedda. No, no—don't you mix yourself up in this affair.

JUDGE BRACK, *with his hat in his hand, enters by the hall door, which* BERTA *opens, and closes behind him. He looks grave and bows in silence.*

Tesman. Oh, is that you, my dear Judge? Eh?

Brack. Yes. It was imperative I should see you this evening.

Tesman. I can see you have heard the news about Aunt Rina?

Brack. Yes, that among other things.

Tesman. Isn't it sad—eh?

Brack. Well, my dear Tesman, that depends on how you look at it.

Tesman (looks doubtfully at him). Has anything else happened?

Brack. Yes.

Hedda (in suspense). Anything sad, Judge Brack?

Brack. That, too, depends on how you look at it, Mrs. Tesman.

Mrs. Elvsted (unable to restrain her anxiety). Oh! it is something about Eilert Lövborg!

Brack (with a glance at her). What makes you think that, Madam? Perhaps you have already heard something——?

Mrs. Elvsted (in confusion). No, nothing at all, but——

Tesman. Oh, for heaven's sake, tell us!

Brack (shrugging his shoulders). Well, I regret to say Eilert Lövborg has been taken to the hospital. He is lying at the point of death.

Mrs. Elvsted (shrieks). Oh God! Oh God——!

Tesman. To the hospital! And at the point of death.

Hedda (involuntarily). So soon then——

Mrs. Elvsted (wailing). And we parted in anger, Hedda!

Hedda (whispers). Thea—Thea—be careful!

Mrs. Elvsted (not heeding her). I must go to him! I must see him alive!

Brack. It is useless, Madam. No one will be admitted.

Mrs. Elvsted. Oh, at least tell me what has happened to him? What is it?

Tesman. You don't mean to say that he has himself—— Eh?

Hedda. Yes, I am sure he has.

Tesman. Hedda, how can you——?

Brack (keeping his eyes fixed upon her). Unfortunately you have guessed quite correctly, Mrs. Tesman.

Mrs. Elvsted. Oh, how horrible!

Tesman. Himself, then! Fancy that!

Hedda. Shot himself!

Brack. Rightly guessed again, Mrs. Tesman.

Mrs. Elvsted (with an effort at self-control). When did it happen, Mr. Brack?

Brack. This afternoon—between three and four.

Tesman. But, good Lord, where did he do it? Eh?

Brack (with some hesitation). Where? Well—I suppose at his lodgings.

Mrs. Elvsted. No, that cannot be; for I was there between six and seven.

Brack. Well, then, somewhere else. I don't know exactly. I only know that he was found——. He had shot himself—in the breast.

Mrs. Elvsted. Oh, how terrible! That he should die like that!

Hedda (to Brack). Was it in the breast?

Brack. Yes—as I told you.

Hedda. Not in the temple?

Brack. In the breast, Mrs. Tesman.

Hedda. Well, well—the breast is a good place, too.

Brack. How do you mean, Mrs. Tesman?

Hedda (evasively). Oh, nothing—nothing.

Tesman. And the wound is dangerous, you say—eh?

Brack. Absolutely mortal. The end has probably come by this time.

Mrs. Elvsted. Yes, yes, I feel it. The end! The end! Oh, Hedda——!

Tesman. But tell me, how have you learnt all this?

Brack (curtly). Through one of the police. A man I had some business with.

Hedda (in a clear voice). At last a deed worth doing!

Tesman (terrified). Good heavens, Hedda! what are you saying?

Hedda. I say there is beauty in this.

Brack. H'm, Mrs. Tesman——

Tesman. Beauty! Fancy that!

Mrs. Elvsted. Oh, Hedda, how can you talk of beauty in such an act!

Hedda. Eilert Lövborg has himself made up his account with life. He has had the courage to do—the one right thing.

Mrs. Elvsted. No, you must never think that was how it happened! It must have been in delirium that he did it.

Tesman. In despair!

Hedda. That he did not. I am certain of that.

Mrs. Elvsted. Yes, yes! In delirium! Just as when he tore up our manuscript.

Brack (starting). The manuscript? Has he torn that up?

Mrs. Elvsted. Yes, last night.

Tesman (whispers softly). Oh, Hedda, we shall never get over this.

Brack. H'm, very extraordinary.

Tesman (moving about the room). To think of Eilert going out of the world in this way! And not leaving behind him the book that would have immortalised his name——

Mrs. Elvsted. Oh, if only it could be put together again!

Tesman. Yes, if it only could! I don't know what I would not give——

Mrs. Elvsted. Perhaps it can, Mr. Tesman.

Tesman. What do you mean?

Mrs. Elvsted (searches in the pocket of her dress). Look here. I have kept all the loose notes he used to dictate from.

Hedda (a step forward). Ah——!

Tesman. You have kept them, Mrs. Elvsted! Eh?

Mrs. Elvsted. Yes, I have them here. I put them in my pocket when I left home. Here they still are——

Tesman. Oh, do let me see them!

Mrs. Elvsted (hands him a bundle of papers). But they are in such disorder—all mixed up.

Tesman. Fancy, if we could make something out of them, after all! Perhaps if we two put our heads together——

Mrs. Elvsted. Oh, yes, at least let us try——

Tesman. We will manage it! We must! I will dedicate my life to this task.

Hedda. You, George? Your life?

Tesman. Yes, or rather all the time I can spare. My own collections must wait in the meantime. Hedda—you understand, eh? I owe this to Eilert's memory.

Hedda. Perhaps.

Tesman. And so, my dear Mrs. Elvsted, we will give our whole minds to it. There is no use in brooding over what can't be undone—eh? We must try to control our grief as much as possible, and——

Mrs. Elvsted. Yes, yes, Mr. Tesman, I will do the best I can.

Tesman. Well then, come here. I can't rest until we have looked through the notes. Where shall we sit? Here? No, in there, in the back room. Excuse me, my dear Judge. Come with me, Mrs. Elvsted.

Mrs. Elvsted. Oh, if only it were possible! (TESMAN *and* MRS. ELVSTED *go into the back room. She takes off her hat and cloak. They both sit at the table under the hanging lamp, and are soon deep in an eager examination of the papers.* HEDDA *crosses to the stove and sits in the arm-chair. Presently* BRACK *goes up to her.*)

Hedda (in a low voice). Oh, what a sense of freedom it gives one, this act of Eilert Lövborg's.

Brack. Freedom, Mrs. Hedda? Well, of course, it is a release for him——

Hedda. I mean for me. It gives me a sense of freedom to know that a deed of deliberate courage is still possible in this world,—a deed of spontaneous beauty.

Brack (*smiling*). H'm—my dear Mrs. Hedda——

Hedda. Oh, I know what you are going to say. For
you are a kind of specialist too, like—you know!

Brack (*looking hard at her*). Eilert Lövborg was more
to you than perhaps you are willing to admit to yourself.
Am I wrong?

Hedda. I don't answer such questions. I only know
that Eilert Lövborg has had the courage to live his life
after his own fashion. And then—the last great act, with
its beauty! Ah! that he should have the will and the
strength to turn away from the banquet of life—so early.

Brack. I am sorry, Mrs. Hedda,—but I fear I must
dispel an amiable illusion.

Hedda. Illusion?

Brack. Which could not have lasted long in any case.

Hedda. What do you mean?

Brack. Eilert Lövborg did not shoot himself—voluntarily.

Hedda. Not voluntarily?

Brack. No. The thing did not happen exactly as I
told it.

Hedda (*in suspense*). Have you concealed something?
What is it?

Brack. For poor Mrs. Elvsted's sake I idealised the facts
a little.

Hedda. What are the facts?

Brack. First, that he is already dead.

Hedda. At the hospital?

Brack. Yes—without regaining consciousness.

Hedda. What more have you concealed?

Brack. This—the event did not happen at his lodgings.

Hedda. Oh, that can make no difference.

Brack. Perhaps it may. For I must tell you—Eilert

Lövborg was found shot in—in Mademoiselle Diana's boudoir.

Hedda (makes a motion as if to rise, but sinks back again). That is impossible, Judge Brack! He cannot have been there again to-day.

Brack. He was there this afternoon. He went there, he said, to demand the return of something which they had taken from him. Talked wildly about a lost child——

Hedda. Ah—so that was why——

Brack. I thought probably he meant his manuscript; but now I hear he destroyed that himself. So I suppose it must have been his pocket-book.

Hedda. Yes, no doubt. And there—there he was found?

Brack. Yes, there. With a pistol in his breast-pocket, discharged. The ball had lodged in a vital part.

Hedda. In the breast—yes.

Brack. No—in the bowels.

Hedda (looks up at him with an expression of loathing). That too! Oh, what curse is it that makes everything I touch turn ludicrous and mean?

Brack. There is one point more, Mrs. Hedda—another disagreeable feature in the affair.

Hedda. And what is that?

Brack. The pistol he carried——

Hedda (breathless). Well? What of it?

Brack. He must have stolen it.

Hedda (leaps up). Stolen it! That is not true! He did not steal it!

Brack. No other explanation is possible. He must have stolen it—— Hush!

TESMAN *and* MRS. ELVSTED *have risen from the table in the back room, and come into the drawing room.*

Tesman (with the papers in both his hands). Hedda dear, it is almost impossible to see under that lamp. Think of that!

Hedda. Yes, I am thinking.

Tesman. Would you mind our sitting at your writing-table—eh?

Hedda. If you like. (*Quickly.*) No, wait! Let me clear it first!

Tesman. Oh, you needn't trouble, Hedda. There is plenty of room.

Hedda. No, no, let me clear it, I say! I will take these things in and put them on the piano. There! (*She has drawn out an object, covered with sheet music, from under the bookcase, places several other pieces of music upon it, and carries the whole into the inner room, to the left.* TESMAN *lays the scraps of paper on the writing-table, and moves the lamp there from the corner table. He and* MRS. ELVSTED *sit down and proceed with their work.* HEDDA *returns.*)

Hedda (*behind* MRS. ELVSTED'S *chair, gently ruffling her hair*). Well, my sweet Thea,—how goes it with Eilert Lövborg's monument?

Mrs. Elvsted (*looks dispiritedly up at her*). Oh, it will be terribly hard to put in order.

Tesman. We must manage it. I am determined. And arranging other people's papers is just the work for me. (HEDDA *goes over to the stove, and seats herself on one of the footstools.* BRACK *stands over her, leaning on the arm-chair.*)

Hedda (*whispers*). What did you say about the pistol?

Brack (*softly*). That he must have stolen it.

Hedda. Why stolen it?

Brack. Because every other explanation ought to be impossible, Mrs. Hedda.

Hedda. Indeed?

Brack (*glances at her*). Of course Eilert Lövborg was here this morning. Was he not?

Hedda. Yes.

Brack. Were you alone with him?

Hedda. Part of the time.

Brack. Did you not leave the room whilst he was here?

Hedda. No.

Brack. Try to recollect. Were you not out of the room a moment?

Hedda. Yes, perhaps just a moment—out in the hall.

Brack. And where was your pistol-case during that time?

Hedda. I had it locked up in——

Brack. Well, Mrs. Hedda?

Hedda. The case stood there on the writing-table.

Brack. Have you looked since, to see whether both the pistols are there?

Hedda. No.

Brack. Well, you need not. I saw the pistol found in Lövborg's pocket, and I knew it at once as the one I had seen yesterday—and before, too.

Hedda. Have you it with you?

Brack. No; the police have it.

Hedda. What will the police do with it?

Brack. Search till they find the owner.

Hedda. Do you think they will succeed?

Brack (*bends over her and whispers*). No, Hedda Gabler—not so long as I say nothing.

Hedda (*looks frightened at him*). And if you do not say nothing,—what then?

Brack (*shrugs his shoulders*). There is always the possibility that the pistol was stolen.

Hedda (*firmly*). Death rather than that.

Brack (*smiling*). People say such things—but they don't do them.

Hedda (*without replying*). And supposing the pistol was not stolen, and the owner is discovered? What then?

Brack. Well, Hedda—then comes the scandal.

Hedda. The scandal!

Brack. Yes, the scandal—of which you are mortally afraid. You will, of course, be brought before the court—both you and Mademoiselle Diana. She will have to ex-

plain how the thing happened—whether it was an accidental
shot or murder. Did the pistol go off as he was trying to
take it out of his pocket, to threaten her with? Or did
she tear the pistol out of his hand, shoot him, and push
it back into his pocket? That would be quite like her;
for she is an able-bodied young person, this same Mademoiselle Diana.

Hedda. But *I* have nothing to do with all this repulsive
business.

Brack. No. But you will have to answer the question:
Why did you give Eilert Lövborg the pistol? And what
conclusions will people draw from the fact that you did
give it to him?

Hedda (*lets her head sink*). That is true. I did not
think of that.

Brack. Well, fortunately, there is no danger, so long as
[ ] say nothing.

Hedda (*looks up at him*). So I am in your power, Judge
[Brac]k. You have me at your beck and call, from this time
[forwar]d.

Bra[c]k (*whispers softly*). Dearest Hedda—believe me—
[I wil]l not abuse my advantage.

[He]dda. I am in your power none the less. Subject to
[your] will and your demands. A slave, a slave then! (*Rises
[impe]tuously.*) No, I cannot endure the thought of that!
[Nev]er!

Brack (*looks half-mockingly at her*). People generally
[get] used to the inevitable.

Hedda (*returns his look*). Yes, perhaps. (*She crosses
[to] the writing-table. Suppressing an involuntary smile,
[sh]e imitates* TESMAN'S *intonations.*) Well? Are you get-
[t]ing on, George? Eh?

Tesman. Heaven knows, dear. In any case it will be
[t]he work of months.

Hedda (*as before*). Fancy that! (*Passes her hands
[so]ftly through* MRS. ELVSTED'S *hair.*) Doesn't it seem

strange to you, Thea?   Here are you sitting with Tesman—
just as you used to sit with Eilert Lövborg?

Mrs. Elvsted. Ah, if I could only inspire your husband
in the same way.

Hedda. Oh, that will come too—in time.

Tesman. Yes, do you know, Hedda—I really think I
begin to feel something of the sort. But won't you go
and sit with Brack again?

Hedda. Is there nothing I can do to help you two?

Tesman. No, nothing in the world. (*Turning his head.*)
I trust to you to keep Hedda company, my dear Brack.

Brack (*with a glance at* HEDDA). With the very greatest of pleasure.

Hedda. Thanks. But I am tired this evening. I will
go in and lie down a little on the sofa.

Tesman. Yes, do dear—eh? (HEDDA *goes into the back
room and draws the curtains. A short pause. Suddenl*
she is heard playing a wild dance on the piano.)

Mrs. Elvsted (*starts from her chair*). Oh—what is

Tesman (*runs to the doorway*). Why, my dearest
—don't play dance music to-night! Just think o
Rina! And of Eilert too!

Hedda (*puts her head out between the curtains*). A
Aunt Julia. And of all the rest of them.—After th
will be quiet. (*Closes the curtains again.*)

Tesman (*at the writing-table*). It's not good for he
see us at this distressing work. I'll tell you what, I
Elvsted,—you shall take the empty room at Aunt Jul
and then I will come over in the evenings, and we can
and work there—eh?

Hedda (*in the inner room*). I hear what you are sa
ing, Tesman. But how am *I* to get through the evenin
out here?

Tesman (*turning over the papers*). Oh, I daresay Jud
Brack will be so kind as to look in now and then, ev
though I am out.

Brack (*in the arm-chair, calls out gaily*). Every blessed evening, with all the pleasure in life, Mrs. Tesman! We shall get on capitally together, we two!

Hedda (*speaking loud and clear*). Yes, don't you flatter yourself we will, Judge Brack? Now that you are the one cock in the basket—— (*A shot is heard within.* TESMAN, MRS. ELVSTED, *and* BRACK *leap to their feet.*)

Tesman. Oh, now she is playing with those pistols again. (*He throws back the curtains and runs in, followed by* MRS. ELVSTED. HEDDA *lies stretched on the sofa, lifeless. Confusion and cries.* BERTA *enters in alarm from the right.*)

Tesman (*shrieks to* BRACK). Shot herself! Shot herself in the temple! Fancy that!

Brack (*half-fainting in the arm-chair*). Good God!— people don't do such things.

that?
Hedda
Aunt

nd of
is, I

to
Mrs.
's,
sit

s

e
n

DATE DUE